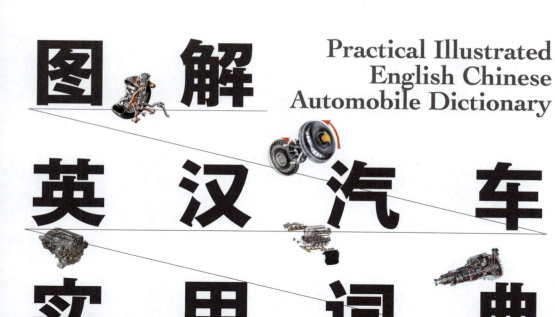

图解英汉汽车实用词典

Practical Illustrated English Chinese Automobile Dictionary

第2版

张金柱 主编

彩色版

化学工业出版社
·北京·

内容简介

本词典采用图解和英汉对照的方式系统地介绍了汽车的结构与原理。全书内容由六部分组成，包括汽车的总体结构、汽车发动机、汽车的底盘、汽车车身、汽车电器和新能源汽车。

本书内容系统全面，彩色插图直观精美，语言简明，可作为学习汽车英语和汽车专业知识的参考书、工具书，适合汽车专业的师生、汽车技术人员、汽车维修人员以及汽车爱好者使用。

图书在版编目（CIP）数据

图解英汉汽车实用词典/张金柱主编．—2版．—北京：化学工业出版社，2022.3
ISBN 978-7-122-40443-5

Ⅰ.①图… Ⅱ.①张… Ⅲ.①汽车工程-图解词典-英、汉 Ⅳ.①U46-61

中国版本图书馆CIP数据核字（2021）第280975号

责任编辑：周　红　　　　　　　　　　　　　装帧设计：尹琳琳
责任校对：李　爽

出版发行：化学工业出版社（北京市东城区青年湖南街13号　邮政编码100011）
印　　刷：三河市航远印刷有限公司
装　　订：三河市宇新装订厂
710mm×1000mm　1/16　印张19½　字数403千字　2022年9月北京第2版第1次印刷

购书咨询：010-64518888　　　　　　　　　　售后服务：010-64518899
网　　址：http://www.cip.com.cn
凡购买本书，如有缺损质量问题，本社销售中心负责调换。

定　　价：129.00元　　　　　　　　　　　　　　　　　版权所有　违者必究

前言
PREFACE

《图解英汉汽车实用词典》(第1版)自2014年出版以来,汽车技术,特别是新能源汽车技术快速发展。2020年11月2日,国务院办公厅正式发布《新能源汽车产业发展规划(2021—2035年)》,到2025年,新能源汽车新车销售量达到汽车新车销售总量的20%左右。到2035年,纯电动汽车成为新销售车辆的主流,公共领域用车全面电动化,燃料电池汽车实现商业化应用,高度自动驾驶汽车实现规模化应用,有效提高节能减排水平和社会运行效率的提升。为帮助读者了解和掌握新能源汽车技术,本次修订大幅度增加了新能源汽车内容,主要包括新能源汽车类型,新能源汽车电机与电池、典型纯电动汽车、混合动力汽车、燃料电池汽车、燃气汽车的结构与原理等。此外,还新增了部分新技术、新结构,如智能汽车技术等。也删减部分老旧内容,如发动机化油器等。

第2版保留了原书的结构与框架,删除了英文索引和中文索引。

本书全面而系统地介绍汽车总体及其各总成部件的结构和工作原理,主要内容由六部分组成:第1部分主要介绍汽车的总体结构;第2部分描述汽车发动机,包括曲柄连杆机构、配气机构、燃料供给系统、冷却系统、润滑系统和汽油机电子控制燃油喷射系统等;第3部分详细介绍汽车的底盘,包括离合器、手动变速器、自动变速器、悬架系统、转向系统和制动系统等;第4部分介绍汽车车身;第5部分介绍汽车电器,包括启动系统、充电系统、点火系统、空调系统和智能汽车等;第6部分介绍新能源汽车分类、新能源汽车电机、新能源汽车电池、纯电动汽车、混合动力电动汽车、燃料电池汽车、天然气汽车、液化石油气汽车等。

本版由张金柱任主编,韩玉敏担任副主编。编写成员及分工为:黑龙江工程学院韩玉敏(第1部分第1章至第3章,第2部分第1章至第7章)、哈尔滨技

师学院李鹏（第2部分第8章至第13章）、北油电控燃油喷射系统（天津）有限公司张凯丰（第2部分第14章至第18章）、龙岩学院王悦新（第3部分第1章至第7章）、黑龙江工程学院王强（第3部分第8章至第14章）、哈尔滨电站设备成套设计研究所有限公司李晗宇（第4部分第1章至第3章）、哈尔滨工业大学秦兆慧（第5部分第1章至第5章）、黑龙江工程学院崔江宁（第5部分第6章至第8章，第6部分第6章）、黑龙江工程学院张金柱（第6部分第1章至第5章）、黑龙江工程学院孙远涛（第6部分第7章、第8章）。

  本书在编写过程中查阅了大量书籍、文献和资料，引用了其中一些技术资料和图表，在此谨向书籍、文献和资料的作者表示衷心的感谢。

  由于编者水平有限，在编写过程中难免存在疏漏之处，恳请专家学者和广大读者给予批评指正。

编　者

目录 CONTENTS

PART 1 汽车概述 Automobile overview

- Chapter 1　Types of automobile 汽车分类　/2
- Chapter 2　Main systems of an automobile 汽车组成　/3
  - 2.1　Engine 发动机　/6
  - 2.2　Chassis 底盘　/7
  - 2.3　Automotive body 车身　/8
  - 2.4　Automotive electric system 汽车电器　/9
- Chapter 3　Automobile parameters 汽车参数　/10

PART 2 发动机 Engine

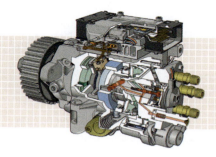

- Chapter 1　Engine introduction 发动机概述　/12
- Chapter 2　Engine classification 发动机类型　/15
  - 2.1　Gasoline engine 汽油发动机　/15
  - 2.2　Diesel engine 柴油发动机　/16

2.3　Rotary engine 转子发动机　/16

Chapter 3　The overall structure of the engine 发动机总体构造　/17

3.1　Crank and connecting rod mechanism 曲柄连杆机构　/17
3.2　Valve train 配气机构　/18
3.3　Cooling system 冷却系统　/18
3.4　Fuel supply system 燃料供给系统　/19
3.5　Lubrication system 润滑系统　/20
3.6　Ignition system 点火系统　/20
3.7　Starting and charging system 启动系统和充电系统　/21

Chapter 4　The arrangement of cylinders 气缸排列形式　/22

4.1　In-line engine 直列发动机　/22
4.2　V-type engine V形发动机　/23
4.3　W-type engine W形发动机　/23
4.4　Horizontal opposed engine 水平对置发动机　/24

Chapter 5　Engine principle 发动机工作原理　/25

5.1　Four stroke gasoline engine operation 四冲程汽油发动机工作原理　/25
5.2　Four stroke diesel engine operation 四冲程柴油发动机工作原理　/26
5.3　Two stroke gasoline engine operation 二冲程汽油发动机工作原理　/27
5.4　Rotary engine operation 转子发动机工作原理　/28

Chapter 6　Engine terms 发动机术语　/28

6.1　Top dead center and bottom dead center 上止点与下止点　/28
6.2　Combustion chamber volume 燃烧室容积　/29
6.3　Compression ratio 压缩比　/29

Chapter 7　Block group 机体组　/30

7.1　Overview 概述　/30
7.2　Cylinder head 气缸盖　/31
7.3　Cylinder block 气缸体　/31
7.4　Cylinder gasket 气缸垫　/32

Chapter 8　Piston and connecting rod assembly 活塞连杆组件　/33

    8.1　Overview 概述　/33

    8.2　Piston 活塞　/34

    8.3　Connecting rod 连杆　/34

Chapter 9　Crankshaft and flywheel assembly 曲轴飞轮组　/35

    9.1　Overview 概述　/35

    9.2　Crankshaft function 曲轴的功用　/36

    9.3　Crankshaft mounting position 曲轴的安装位置　/37

    9.4　Crankshaft bearing cap 曲轴轴承盖　/37

    9.5　How a crankshaft works 曲轴工作原理　/38

    9.6　Balance shafts 平衡轴　/39

    9.7　Engine flywheel 发动机飞轮　/39

Chapter 10　Valve train 配气机构　/40

    10.1　Overview 概述　/40

    10.2　Valve train components 配气机构组成　/41

    10.3　Types of valve train 配气机构类型　/42

    10.4　Valve timing 气门正时　/43

    10.5　Valve train components 配气机构部件　/44

Chapter 11　Variable valve timing and variable valve lift 可变气门正时与可变气门升程　/49

    11.1　Overview 概述　/49

    11.2　Toyota variable valve timing intelligence（VVT-i）丰田智能可变气门正时系统　/50

    11.3　Honda variable valve timing and lift electronic control（VTEC）本田智能可变气门正时和升程电子控制　/51

    11.4　Audi valve lift system（AVS）奥迪气门升程系统　/52

    11.5　BMW Valvetronic variable valve lift system 宝马 Valvetronic 可变气门升程系统　/53

- Chapter 12　Fuel supply system 燃料供给系统　/54

　　12.1　Overview 概述　/54

　　12.2　Gasoline engine fuel supply system 汽油机燃料供给系统　/55

- Chapter 13　Gasoline engine electronic fuel injection（EFI）system 汽油机电子控制燃油喷射系统　/56

　　13.1　Overview 概述　/56

　　13.2　Electronic fuel injection system components 电子燃油喷射系统组成　/57

　　13.3　Electronic fuel injection system construction 电子燃油喷射系统结构　/58

　　13.4　EFI main components EFI主要部件　/59

　　13.5　Gasoline direct-injection（GDI）system 汽油缸内直喷系统　/63

- Chapter 14　Diesel engine fuel supply system 柴油机燃料供给系统　/65

　　14.1　Overview 概述　/65

　　14.2　Fuel injection pump 高压油泵　/66

　　14.3　Diesel electronic control high pressure common rail system 柴油机电控高压共轨系统　/69

　　14.4　High pressure common rail system principle 高压共轨系统原理　/70

- Chapter 15　Exhaust system 排气系统　/71

　　15.1　Overview 概述　/71

　　15.2　Exhaust manifold 排气歧管　/72

　　15.3　Exhaust gas recirculation（EGR）废气再循环　/72

　　15.4　Evaporative emission control system 汽油蒸发控制系统　/75

　　15.5　Three way catalytic converter 三元催化转换器　/77

- Chapter 16　Charger 增压器　/78

　　16.1　Turbocharger 涡轮增压器　/78

　　16.2　Supercharger 机械增压器　/81

　　16.3　Twin turbocharger type engine 双增压发动机　/83

目录 CONTENTS

● Chapter 17　Engine lubrication system 发动机润滑系统　/84

　17.1　Overview 概述　/84
　17.2　Engine lubrication system operation 发动机润滑系统工作原理　/85
　17.3　Lubricating oil passage 发动机润滑油路　/86
　17.4　Oil pump 机油泵　/87
　17.5　Dry sump system 干式油底壳　/87

● Chapter 18　Engine cooling system 发动机冷却系统　/88

　18.1　Overview 概述　/88
　18.2　Cooling system operation 冷却系统工作原理　/89
　18.3　Thermostat 节温器　/90
　18.4　Radiator 散热器　/90
　18.5　Radiator cap 散热器盖　/91

PART 3　底盘 Chassis

● Chapter 1　Chassis introduction 底盘概述　/93

　1.1　Drive line 传动系统　/94
　1.2　Running gear 行驶系统　/95
　1.3　Steering system 转向系统　/95
　1.4　Braking system 制动系统　/96

● Chapter 2　Drive train 传动系统　/96

　2.1　Overview 概述　/96
　2.2　Clutch 离合器　/97

  2.3 Transmission 变速器 /97
  2.4 Propeller shaft and universal joints 传动轴和万向节 /99
  2.5 Final reduction 主减速器 /99
  2.6 Differential and half shaft 差速器与半轴 /100

● Chapter 3 Clutch 离合器 /101

  3.1 Overview 概述 /101
  3.2 Clutch components 离合器组成 /102
  3.3 Clutch operation 离合器原理 /103
  3.4 Clutch control system 离合器操纵机构 /104

● Chapter 4 Manual transmission 手动变速器 /105

  4.1 Overview 概述 /105
  4.2 Transmission principle 变速器原理 /106
  4.3 Manual transmission operation 手动变速器原理 /106
  4.4 5 speed manual transmission 5挡手动变速器 /107
  4.5 Synchronizer 同步器 /109

● Chapter 5 Automatic transmission 自动变速器 /111

  5.1 Overview 概述 /111
  5.2 Hydraulic torque converter 液力变矩器 /112
  5.3 Planetary gear drive 行星齿轮传动 /113
  5.4 AT shift mechanism 自动变速器换挡执行机构 /114
  5.5 Automatic transmission shift control 自动变速器换挡控制 /116

● Chapter 6 Continuously variable transmission 无级变速器 /119

  6.1 Overview 概述 /119
  6.2 CVT operation CVT原理 /120
  6.3 CVT pulley control mechanism CVT滑轮控制机构 /121

● Chapter 7 Dual clutch transmission 双离合器变速器 /122

  7.1 Dual clutch transmission principle 双离合器变速器原理 /122

目录 CONTENTS

7.2　Volkswagen DSG transmission 大众DSG变速器　/124

Chapter 8　Four wheel drive 四轮驱动　/127

8.1　Overview 概述　/127

8.2　Part time four wheel drive 分时四驱　/128

8.3　Real time four wheel drive 适时四驱　/128

8.4　Full time four wheel drive 全时四驱　/129

8.5　Transfer case 分动器　/129

Chapter 9　Propeller shaft 传动轴　/131

9.1　Overview 概述　/131

9.2　Universal joint 万向节　/132

Chapter 10　Differential 差速器　/133

10.1　Overview 概述　/133

10.2　Differential operation 差速器原理　/133

10.3　Limited slip differential 限滑差速器　/134

Chapter 11　Suspension system 悬架系统　/135

11.1　Overview 概述　/135

11.2　Suspension classification 悬架的类型　/136

11.3　Macpherson suspension 麦弗逊式悬架　/137

11.4　Double wishbone suspension 双叉臂式悬架　/138

11.5　Torsion beam axle type suspension 扭转梁式悬架　/138

11.6　Stabilizer bar 稳定杆　/139

11.7　Multi-link suspension 多连杆悬架　/139

11.8　Air suspension 空气悬架　/140

11.9　Shock absorber 减振器　/141

Chapter 12　Tire 轮胎　/142

12.1　Overview 概述　/142

12.2　Wheel alignment 车轮定位　/143

- Chapter 13　Steering system 转向系统　/146

　　13.1　Overview 概述　/146

　　13.2　Rack and pinion steering system 齿轮齿条式转向系统　/147

　　13.3　Recirculating ball type steering system 循环球式转向系统　/150

　　13.4　Steering system components 转向系统部件　/152

　　13.5　Hydraulic power assisted steering（PAS）system 液压助力转向系统　/153

　　13.6　Electric power steering（EPS）system 电动助力转向系统　/155

- Chapter 14　Brake system 制动系统　/156

　　14.1　Overview 概述　/156

　　14.2　Brake system configuration 制动系统的结构　/157

　　14.3　Hydraulic braking system 液压制动系统　/160

　　14.4　Drum brake 鼓式制动器　/161

　　14.5　Disc brake 盘式制动器　/162

　　14.6　Brake booster 制动助力器　/164

　　14.7　Anti-locked braking system（ABS）防抱死制动系统　/165

　　14.8　Electronic stability control system 电子稳定性控制系统　/167

　　14.9　Traction control system 牵引力控制系统　/168

PART 4　车身　Automotive body

- Chapter 1　Overview 概述　/170

- Chapter 2　Frame 车架　/172

　　2.1　Overview 概述　/172

　　2.2　Types of automotive body 车身分类　/172

● Chapter 3　Automotive safety system 汽车安全系统　/174

PART 5　Automobile electrical system 汽车电器

● Chapter 1　Electrical system introduction 汽车电器概述　/176

● Chapter 2　Starting system 启动系统　/177

　　2.1　Overview 概述　/177
　　2.2　Starter components and operation 起动机部件与工作原理　/178
　　2.3　Starter construction 起动机结构　/179

● Chapter 3　Charging system 充电系统　/182

　　3.1　Overview 概述　/182
　　3.2　Generator 发电机　/182
　　3.3　Storage battery 蓄电池　/184

● Chapter 4　Ignition system 点火系统　/186

　　4.1　Overview 概述　/186
　　4.2　Conventional mechanical contact type ignition system operation 传统机械触点式
　　　　点火系统工作原理　/187
　　4.3　Electronic ignition system 电子点火系统　/188
　　4.4　Spark plug 火花塞　/189

- Chapter 5　Instruments 仪表　/190

- Chapter 6　Air conditioning system 空调系统　/191

　　6.1　Overview 概述　/191

　　6.2　Air conditioning system components 空调系统组成　/192

　　6.3　Air conditioning system operation 空调系统原理　/193

　　6.4　Compressor 压缩机　/194

- Chapter 7　Air bag 安全气囊　/195

- Chapter 8　Intelligent vehicle 智能汽车　/196

　　8.1　Intelligent vehicle 智能汽车　/196

　　8.2　Advanced driver assistance system 先进驾驶辅助系统　/197

　　8.3　Adaptive cruise control 自适应巡航控制　/198

PART 6　New energy vehicle 新能源汽车

- Chapter 1　New energy vehicle classification 新能源汽车分类　/203

　　1.1　Electric vehicle 电动汽车　/203

　　1.2　Gas vehicle 燃气汽车　/206

　　1.3　Methanol and alcohol-powered vehicle 醇类汽车　/210

　　1.4　Biodiesel vehicle 生物柴油汽车　/211

- Chapter 2　New energy vehicle motor 新能源汽车电机　/212

　　2.1　DC motor 直流电机　/212

　　2.2　AC asynchronous motor 交流异步电机　/213

2.3　Permanent magnet synchronous motor 永磁同步电机　/215

2.4　Switched reluctance motor 开关磁阻电机　/216

2.5　Hub motor 轮毂电机　/217

2.6　Motor cooling system 电机冷却系统　/218

Chapter 3　New energy vehicle battery 新能源汽车电池　/218

3.1　Lithium ion battery 锂离子电池　/219

3.2　Ni-MH battery 镍氢电池　/220

3.3　Fuel cells 燃料电池　/222

3.4　Supercapacitor 超级电容器　/223

3.5　Flywheel battery 飞轮电池　/224

Chapter 4　Battery electric vehicle 纯电动汽车　/226

4.1　Overview 概述　/226

4.2　Tesla Model S electric vehicle 特斯拉 Model S 电动汽车　/228

4.3　Tesla Model 3 electric vehicle 特斯拉 Model 3 电动汽车　/230

4.4　Audi electric vehicle e-tron 奥迪电动汽车 e-tron　/235

Chapter 5　Hybrid electric vehicle 混合动力电动汽车　/242

5.1　Overview 概述　/242

5.2　Toyota hybrid system 丰田混合动力系统　/244

Chapter 6　Fuel cell electric vehicle 燃料电池汽车　/261

6.1　Overview 概述　/261

6.2　Toyota Mirai fuel cell vehicle 丰田 Mirai 燃料电池汽车　/262

Chapter 7　Natural gas vehicle 天然气汽车　/270

7.1　Overview 概述　/270

7.2　Audi A4 Avant g-tron 奥迪 A4 Avant g-tron 天然气汽车　/271

● Chapter 8　LPG vehicle 液化石油气汽车　/280

　　8.1　Overview 概述　/280

　　8.2　Volkswagen GOLF LPG vehicle 大众高尔夫液化石油气汽车　/282

PART 1

Automobile overview 汽车概述

- Chapter 1　Types of automobile 汽车分类
- Chapter 2　Main systems of an automobile 汽车组成
- Chapter 3　Automobile parameters 汽车参数

PART 1　Automobile overview
汽车概述

Chapter 1
Types of automobile 汽车分类

　　汽车按照功能性可划分为：房车、旅行轿车、轿跑车、跑车、敞篷车等车型（图1-1-1）。

图1-1-1　Types of automobiles 汽车类型

1. hatchback 掀背车（两厢车）
2. sports car 运动车
3. four door sedan 四门轿车
4. limousine 豪华轿车
5. convertible 敞篷车
6. hardtop 硬顶车
7. van 厢式货车
8. pick-up truck 轻型货车（皮卡车）

Chapter 2
Main systems of an automobile 汽车组成

汽车的总体构造基本上由四部分组成：发动机、底盘、车身、电器（图1-2-1）。

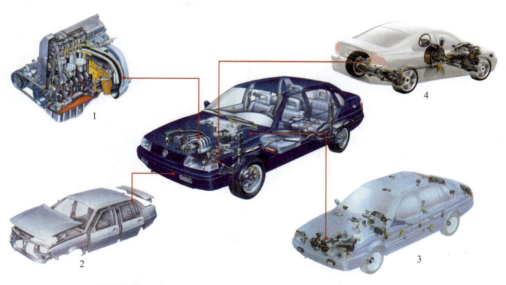

图1-2-1　Overall structure of the automobile 汽车总体结构

1. automotive engine（in-line four cylinder EFI type）汽车发动机（直列四缸电喷型）
2. automotive body（three box four door type）汽车车身（三厢四门式）
3. automotive electrical system 汽车电器
4. automotive chassis 汽车底盘

PART 1　Automobile overview
汽车概述

汽车结构视图如图1-2-2所示。

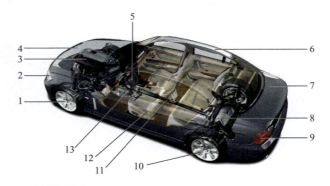

图1-2-2　Automotive structural view 汽车结构视图

1. front wheel 前轮
2. front headlight 前大灯
3. engine 发动机
4. engine hood 发动机罩
5. steering system 转向系统
6. body 车身
7. truck 行李厢
8. driving axle 驱动桥
9. rear steering light 后转向灯
10. rear wheel 后轮
11. propeller shaft 传动轴
12. seats 座椅
13. transmission 变速器

汽车底视图如图1-2-3所示。

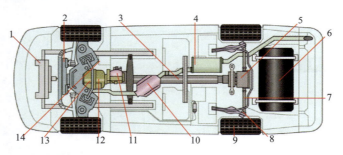

图1-2-3　Automotive viewed from below 汽车底视图

1. radiator 散热器
2. power steering 动力转向
3. line shaft 传动轴
4. exhaust system 排气系统
5. differential 差速器
6. gas tank 汽油箱
7. rear axle 后桥
8. shock absorber 减振器
9. tire 轮胎
10. catalytic converter 催化转换器
11. transmission 变速器
12. crankcase 曲轴箱
13. oil pan 油底壳
14. master cylinder 主缸

汽车总成拆分如图1-2-4所示。

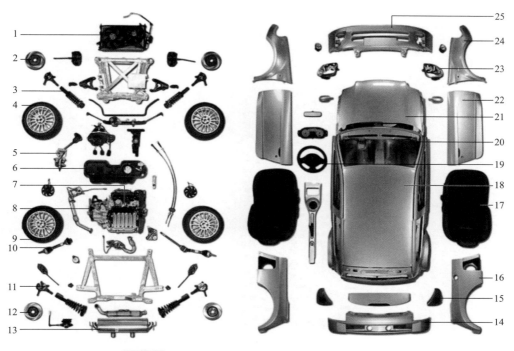

图1-2-4　An automobile disassembled 拆分的汽车

1. radiator fan 散热风扇
2. brake disc 制动盘
3. front suspension 前悬架
4. wheel 车轮
5. steering system 转向系统
6. air conditioning 空调
7. engine 发动机
8. transmission 变速器
9. wheel 车轮
10. half shaft 半轴
11. rear suspension 后悬架
12. brake plate 制动盘
13. exhaust silencer 排气消声器
14. rear mudguard 后挡泥板
15. tail light 尾灯
16. rear fender 后翼子板
17. seat 座椅
18. body 车身
19. steering gear 转向器
20. front window glass 前窗玻璃
21. engine hood 发动机罩
22. door 车门
23. front headlight 前大灯
24. front fender 前翼子板
25. front mudguard 前挡泥板

PART 1 Automobile overview
汽车概述

2.1 Engine 发动机

发动机是汽车的动力装置,其作用是使进入其中的燃料经过燃烧而变成热能,并转化为动能,通过底盘的传动系统驱动汽车行驶(图1-2-5)。

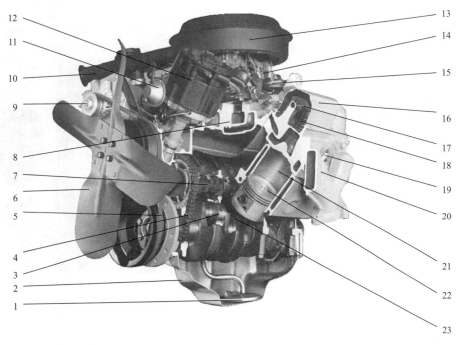

图1-2-5 Overall structure of the engine 汽车发动机结构

1. oil pickup 机油集滤器
2. pan 机油盘
3. crankshaft 曲轴
4. timing chain 正时链
5. fan belt 风扇皮带
6. fan 风扇
7. camshaft 凸轮轴
8. intake manifold 进气歧管
9. alternator 交流发电机
10. air cleaner snorkel 空气滤清器进气管
11. vacuum advance unit 真空提前装置
12. distributor 分电器
13. air cleaner 空气滤清器
14. carburetor 化油器
15. exhaust gas recirculation (EGR) valve 废气再循环阀
16. rocker arm cover 摇臂室盖
17. rocker arm 摇臂
18. valve spring 气门弹簧
19. spark plug 火花塞
20. exhaust manifold 排气歧管
21. cylinder 气缸
22. piston 活塞
23. connecting rod 连杆

2.2 Chassis 底盘

底盘的作用是支撑车身，接受发动机产生的动力，并保证汽车能够正常行驶（图1-2-6）。底盘本身又可分为传动系统、行驶系统、转向系统和制动系统四部分。

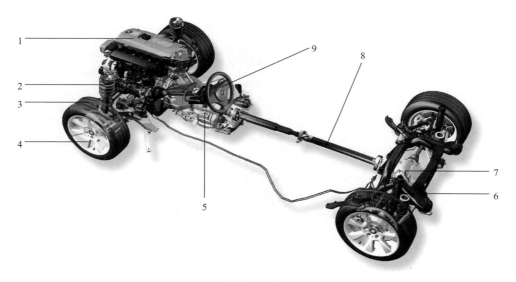

图1-2-6　Chassis 底盘

1. engine assembly 发动机总成
2. front suspension 前悬架
3. wheel 车轮
4. rim 轮辋
5. transmission assembly 变速器总成
6. rear axle 后桥
7. driving axle 驱动桥
8. propeller shaft 传动轴
9. steering system 转向系统

PART 1 Automobile overview 汽车概述

2.3 Automotive body 车身

车身指的是车辆用来载人装货的部分，也指车辆整体。汽车车身结构主要包括：车身壳体、车门、车窗、车前钣制件、车身内外装饰件和车身附件、座椅以及通风、暖气、冷气、空气调节装置等（图1-2-7）。在货车和专用汽车上还包括车厢和其他装备。

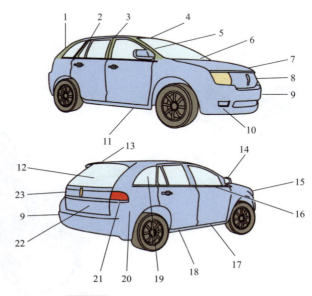

图1-2-7　Automotive body 汽车车身

1. D pillar D 柱
2. C pillar C 柱
3. B pillar B 柱
4. windshield header 挡风玻璃槽
5. A pillar A 柱
6. cowl 前围板
7. hood panel 发动机罩板
8. one piece grill 整体式护栅
9. soft color-keyed bumper 车身同色的保险杠
10. side marker and turning lamp 侧示廓和转向灯
11. rocker panel 门下围板
12. backlight with rear wiper 后灯及后雨刷
13. rear air deflector with integrated stop lamp 后导流板及连同一体的停车灯
14. rear view mirror integrated with A pillar and side glass 与 A 柱一体式的后视镜和侧玻璃
15. front fender 前翼子板
16. belt line 腰线
17. front door 前门
18. rear door 后门
19. DLO（daylight opening）窗玻璃透光部分
20. quarter panel 后侧围板
21. tail lamp with stop and turn function 有停车和转向功能的尾灯
22. lift gate 举升门
23. running tail lamp 日间行车尾灯

2.4 Automotive electric system 汽车电器

电气设备包括电源、发动机启动系统以及汽车照明等用电设备,在强制点火的发动机中还包括发动机的点火系统(图1-2-8)。

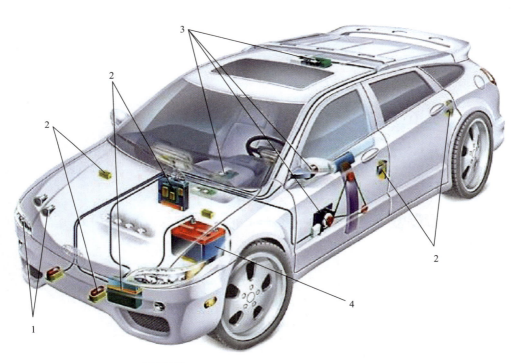

图1-2-8 Automotive electric system 汽车电器

1. lighting components 灯光部件
2. electrical components 电气部件
3. motor components 电机部件
4. energy storage 储能件(电池)

PART 1 Automobile overview 汽车概述

Chapter 3
Automobile parameters 汽车参数

在买车时要了解一款车的空间，当然要看车的总长、轴距等参数。现在各汽车厂商对于车身规格的标注，基本上都统一了，如车身总长、轴距、轮距、前悬、后悬等（图1-3-1和图1-3-2）。

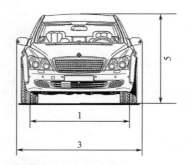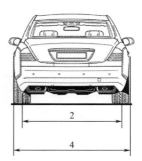

图1-3-1 Overall parameters of the automobile 汽车总体参数（1）

1. front thread 前轮距
2. rear thread 后轮距
3. width（with rear mirror）车宽（含后视镜）
4. width 车宽
5. height 车高

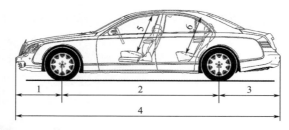

图1-3-2 Overall parameters of the automobile 汽车总体参数（2）

1. front suspension 前悬
2. wheelbase 轴距
3. rear suspension 后悬
4. total length 车身总长
5. front row height 前排高
6. rear row height 后排高

PART 2

Engine 发动机

- Chapter 1 Engine introduction 发动机概述
- Chapter 2 Engine classification 发动机类型
- Chapter 3 The overall structure of the engine 发动机总体构造
- Chapter 4 The arrangement of cylinders 气缸排列形式
- Chapter 5 Engine principle 发动机工作原理
- Chapter 6 Engine terms 发动机术语
- Chapter 7 Block group 机体组
- Chapter 8 Piston and connecting rod assembly 活塞连杆组件
- Chapter 9 Crankshaft and flywheel assembly 曲轴飞轮组
- Chapter 10 Valve train 配气机构
- Chapter 11 Variable valve timing and variable valve lift 可变气门正时与可变气门升程
- Chapter 12 Fuel supply system 燃料供给系统
- Chapter 13 Gasoline engine electronic fuel injection (EFI) system 汽油机电子控制燃油喷射系统
- Chapter 14 Diesel engine fuel supply system 柴油机燃料供给系统
- Chapter 15 Exhaust system 排气系统
- Chapter 16 Charger 增压器
- Chapter 17 Engine lubrication system 发动机润滑系统
- Chapter 18 Engine cooling system 发动机冷却系统

PART2 Engine 发动机

Chapter 1
Engine introduction 发动机概述

  汽车的动力源泉就是发动机，而发动机的动力则来源于气缸内部，发动机气缸就是一个把燃料的内能转化为动能的场所。可以简单理解为，燃料在气缸内燃烧，产生巨大压力推动活塞上下运动，通过连杆把力传给曲轴，最终转化为旋转运动，再通过变速器和传动轴，把动力传递到驱动车轮上，从而推动汽车前进。发动机结构见图2-1-1。

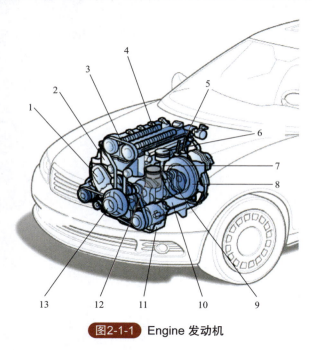

图2-1-1　Engine 发动机

1. oil pump 机油泵
2. cylinder head 气缸盖
3. timing belt 正时皮带
4. camshaft 凸轮轴
5. engine valve 发动机气门
6. piston 活塞
7. connecting rod 连杆
8. flex plate 柔性盘
9. crankshaft 曲轴
10. crankcase 曲轴箱
11. oil pan 机油盘
12. engine cylinder 发动机气缸
13. crankshaft pulley 曲轴带轮

单缸发动机结构见图2-1-2。

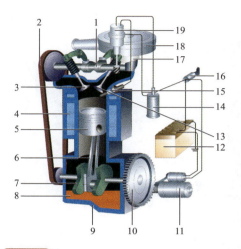

图2-1-2　Single cylinder engine 单缸发动机

1. camshaft 凸轮轴
2. timing belt (or timing sprocket) 正时皮带（或正时链条）
3. exhaust valve 排气门
4. coolant 冷却液（水）
5. piston 活塞
6. connecting rod 连杆
7. crankshaft 曲轴
8. lubrication oil 润滑油
9. oil pan 油底壳
10. flywheel and starter ring gear 飞轮与起动机齿圈
11. starter 起动机
12. storage battery 蓄电池
13. intake valve 进气门
14. ignition coil 点火线圈
15. spark plug 火花塞
16. ignition switch 点火开关
17. carburetor 化油器
18. air cleaner 空气滤清器
19. distributor 分电器

剖视的发动机见图2-1-3。

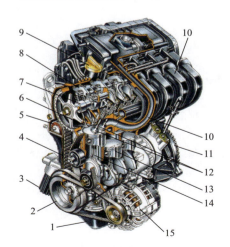

图2-1-3　Engine cutaway view 发动机剖视图

1. oil pan 油底壳
2. crankshaft pulley 曲轴带轮
3. oil filter 机油滤清器
4. timing belt 正时带
5. tension pulley 张紧轮
6. exhaust valve 排气门
7. camshaft 凸轮轴
8. valve rocker arm 气门摇臂
9. oil filler 机油加注口
10. intake manifold 进气歧管
11. flywheel 飞轮
12. intake valve 进气门
13. piston 活塞
14. connecting rod 连杆
15. alternator 交流发电机

PART2 Engine 发动机

分解的发动机见图2-1-4。

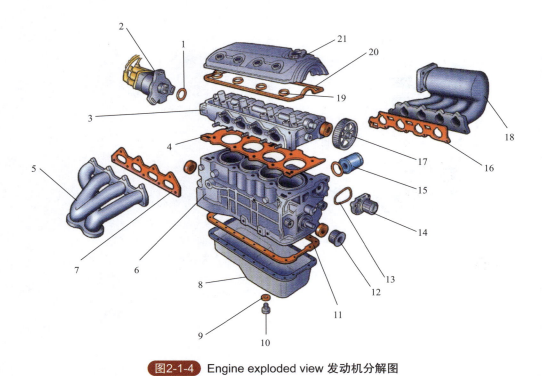

图2-1-4　Engine exploded view 发动机分解图

1. distributor O-ring 分电器O形圈
2. distributor 分电器
3. cylinder head 气缸盖
4. head gasket 气缸盖垫
5. exhaust manifold 排气歧管
6. engine block 发动机缸体
7. exhaust manifold gasket 排气歧管垫
8. oil pan 油底壳，机油盘
9. drain bolt crush washer 放油螺栓衬垫
10. oil pan drain bolt 油底放油螺栓
11. oil pan gasket 油底壳垫
12. timing belt drive pulley 正时皮带驱动轮
13. water pump gasket 水泵垫
14. water pump 水泵
15. oil filter 机油滤清器
16. intake manifold gasket 进气歧管垫
17. camshaft pulley 凸轮轴带轮
18. intake manifold 进气歧管
19. rubber grommets 橡胶垫圈
20. cylinder head cover gasket 气缸盖罩垫
21. cylinder head cover 气缸盖罩

Chapter 2

Engine classification 发动机类型

2.1 Gasoline engine 汽油发动机

　　汽油发动机是以汽油作为燃料的发动机（图2-2-1）。由于汽油黏性小，蒸发快，可以用汽油喷射系统将汽油喷入气缸，经过压缩达到一定的温度和压力后，用火花塞点燃，使气体膨胀做功。

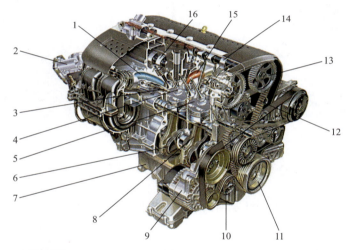

图2-2-1　Gasoline engine cutaway view 汽油发动机剖视图

1. intake manifold 进气歧管
2. throttle valve 节气门
3. spark plug 火花塞
4. intake valve 进气门
5. piston 活塞
6. crankshaft 曲轴
7. oil pan 油底壳
8. connecting rod 连杆
9. alternator 交流发电机
10. pivot shaft 张紧轮
11. crankshaft belt wheel 曲轴带轮
12. timing chain 正时链条
13. exhaust camshaft sprocket wheel 排气凸轮轴链轮
14. exhaust camshaft 排气凸轮轴
15. exhaust manifold 排气歧管
16. intake camshaft 进气凸轮轴

PART2 Engine 发动机

2.2 Diesel engine 柴油发动机

柴油发动机是通过燃烧柴油来获取能量释放的发动机（图2-2-2），它是由德国发明家鲁道夫·狄塞尔（Rudolf Diesel）于1892年发明的，为了纪念这位发明家，柴油就是用他的姓Diesel来表示，而柴油发动机也称为狄塞尔发动机。柴油机是直接将柴油喷入已充满压缩空气的气缸，压缩自燃点火。

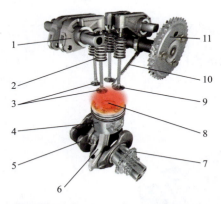

图2-2-2 Diesel engine configuration
柴油发动机构造

1. valve rocker arm 气门摇臂
2. valve spring 气门弹簧
3. exhaust valve 排气门
4. piston 活塞
5. crankshaft 曲轴
6. connecting rod 连杆
7. crankshaft sprocket 曲轴链轮
8. combustion chamber 燃烧室
9. intake valve 进气门
10. injector 喷油器
11. camshaft sprocket 凸轮轴链轮

2.3 Rotary engine 转子发动机

转子发动机又称为米勒循环发动机，由德国人菲加士·汪克尔发明（Felix Wankel）。转子发动机直接将可燃气的燃烧膨胀力转化为驱动转矩。转子发动机的活塞是一个扁平三角形，气缸是一个扁盒子，活塞偏心地安装在空腔内。汽油燃烧产生的膨胀力作用在转子的侧面上，从而将三角形转子的三个面之一推向偏心轴的中心，在向心力和切向力的作用下，活塞在气缸内做行星旋转运动（图2-2-3）。

图2-2-3 Rotary engine configuration
转子发动机构造

1. intake pipe 进气管
2. exhaust pipe 排气管
3. cylinder block 气缸体
4. cooling water jacket 冷却水套
5. central shaft 中心轴
6. rotor 转子

Chapter 3

The overall structure of the engine 发动机总体构造

　　汽油机由以下两大机构和五大系统组成，即由曲柄连杆机构、配气机构和燃料供给系统、润滑系统、冷却系统、点火系统和启动系统组成；柴油机由以下两大机构和四大系统组成，即由曲柄连杆机构、配气机构、燃料供给系统、润滑系统、冷却系统和启动系统组成，柴油机是压燃的，不需要点火系统。

3.1 Crank and connecting rod mechanism 曲柄连杆机构

　　曲柄连杆机构是发动机实现工作循环，完成能量转换的主要运动零件，它由机体组、活塞连杆组和曲轴飞轮组等组成（图2-3-1）。

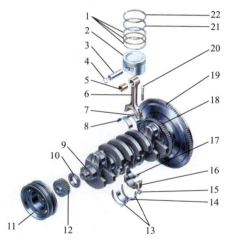

图2-3-1　Crank and connecting rod mechanism 曲柄连杆机构

1. oil ring 油环
2. piston 活塞
3. piston pin 活塞销
4. clip 卡环
5. connecting rod small end bearing insert 连杆小头轴瓦
6. connecting rod 连杆
7. connecting rod big end bearing insert 连杆大头轴瓦
8. upper main bearing insert 主轴承上轴瓦
9. crankshaft 曲轴
10. crankshaft sprocket 曲轴链轮
11. crankshaft pulley 曲轴带轮
12. crankshaft timing belt pulley 曲轴正时齿带轮
13. thrust plate 止推片
14. lower main bearing insert 主轴承下瓦轴
15. connecting rod big end nut 连杆螺母
16. connecting rod big end cap 连杆盖
17. connecting rod big end lower bearing insert 连杆大头下轴瓦
18. speed sensor pulse wheel 转速传感器脉冲轮
19. flywheel 飞轮
20. connecting rod bolt 连杆螺栓
21. second compression ring 第二道气环
22. first compression ring 第一道气环

· 17 ·

3.2 Valve train 配气机构

配气机构的功用是根据发动机的工作顺序和工作过程，定时开启和关闭进气门和排气门，使可燃混合气或空气进入气缸，并使废气从气缸内排出，实现换气过程（图2-3-2）。

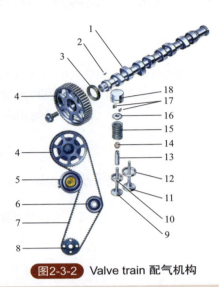

图2-3-2　Valve train 配气机构

1. camshaft 凸轮轴
2. woodruff key 半圆键
3. camshaft oil seal 凸轮轴油封
4. camshaft timing cog belt pulley 凸轮轴正时齿形带轮
5. tension pulley 张紧轮
6. water pump cog belt wheel 水泵齿形带轮
7. timing cog belt 正时齿形带
8. crankshaft timing cog belt pulley 曲轴正时齿形带轮
9. exhuast valve 排气门
10. exhuast valve seat 排气门座
11. intake valve 进气门
12. intake valve seat 进气门座
13. valve guide 气门导管
14. valve oil seal 气门油封
15. valve spring 气门弹簧
16. upper valve spring seat 上气门弹簧座
17. valve keeper 气门锁块
18. tappet body 挺柱体

3.3 Cooling system 冷却系统

冷却系统的功用是将受热零件吸收的部分热量及时散发出去，保证发动机在最适宜的温度状态下工作（图2-3-3）。

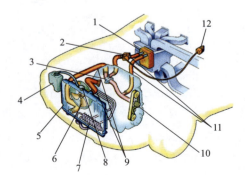

图2-3-3　Cooling system 冷却系统

1. heater core 暖风芯
2. heater valve 暖风阀
3. thermostat housing 节温器壳体
4. coolant reservoir 冷却液储液罐
5. radiator 散热器
6. radiator fan 散热器风扇
7. transmission cooler 变速器冷却器
8. radiator cap 散热器盖
9. radiator hoses 散热器软管
10. water pump 水泵
11. heater hoses 暖风软管
12. temperature control dial 温度调节钮

3.4 Fuel supply system 燃料供给系统

汽油机燃料供给系统的功用是根据发动机的要求，配制出一定数量和浓度的混合气，供入气缸，并将燃烧后的废气从气缸内排出到大气中去；柴油机燃料供给系统的功用是把柴油和空气分别供入气缸，在燃烧室内形成混合气并燃烧，最后将燃烧后的废气排出（图2-3-4）。

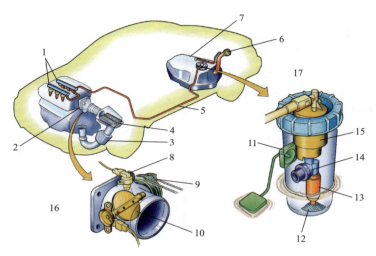

图2-3-4 Fuel supply system 燃料供给系统

1. fuel rail 燃油轨
2. throttle body 节气门体
3. resonator 谐振腔
4. air cleaner 空气滤清器
5. fuel feed line 输油管
6. fuel fill cap 加油盖
7. fuel tank 油箱
8. map sensor 气压传感器
9. throttle valve position sensor 节气门位置传感器
10. butterfly valve 蝶形阀
11. fuel gauge sending unit 燃油表传感器
12. suction filter 进油过滤器
13. fuel pump 燃油泵
14. fuel pressure regulator 油压调节器
15. fuel filter 燃油过滤器
16. throttle body 节气门体
17. fuel tank unit 油箱组件

PART2 Engine 发动机

3.5 Lubrication system 润滑系统

　　润滑系统的功用是向做相对运动的零件表面输送定量的清洁润滑油，减小摩擦阻力，减轻机件的磨损，并对零件表面进行清洗和冷却（图2-3-5）。

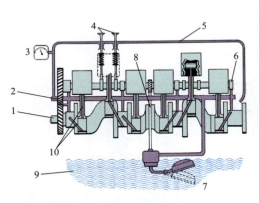

1. crankshaft 曲轴
2. main oil line 主油管路
3. oil gauge 机油表
4. valves 气门
5. oil return 回油管
6. camshaft 凸轮轴
7. floating oil intake and screen 浮动式进油口和滤网
8. drive shaft（powers pump）驱动轴（驱动机油泵）
9. oil pan 油底壳
10. passages（supply oil through crankshaft and connecting rod）油道（向曲轴和连杆供应机油）

图2-3-5　Lubrication system 润滑系统

3.6 Ignition system 点火系统

　　在汽油机中，气缸内的可燃混合气是靠电火花点燃的，为此在汽油机的气缸盖上装有火花塞，火花塞头部伸入燃烧室内。能够按时在火花塞电极间产生电火花的全部设备称为点火系统，点火系统通常由蓄电池、发电机、分电器、点火线圈和火花塞等组成（图2-3-6）。

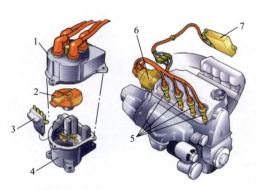

1. cap（分电器）盖
2. rotor 转子
3. ignition control module 点火控制模块
4. housing 壳体
5. spark plugs 火花塞
6. distributor 分电器
7. engine control module 发动机控制模块（ECM）

图2-3-6　Ignition system 点火系统

3.7 Starting and charging system 启动系统和充电系统

启动系统由蓄电池、点火开关、启动继电器、起动机等组成。启动系统的功用是通过起动机将蓄电池的电能转换成机械能，启动发动机运转（图2-3-7）。

充电系统由发电机、调节器、蓄电池以及充电指示灯等组成，是汽车用电设备的电源。

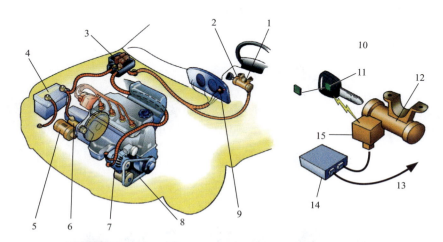

图2-3-7 Starting and charging system 启动系统和充电系统

1. ignition switch 点火开关
2. lock cylinder 锁柱
3. under-hood fuse box 发动机室保险丝盒
4. battery 电池
5. starter 起动机
6. starter solenoid 启动器电磁线圈
7. alternator 交流发电机
8. alternator belt 交流发电机皮带
9. charging system light 充电系统指示灯
10. immobilizer system 发动机切断防盗系统
11. ignition key transponder 点火钥匙发射器（遥控器）
12. key cylinder 钥匙锁柱
13. to the fuel system 到燃油系统
14. ECM/PCM 发动机控制模块/功率控制模块
15. immobilizer control unit-receiver 发动机切断控制单元接收机

PART2 Engine 发动机

Chapter 4
The arrangement of cylinders 气缸排列形式

气缸排列形式是指多气缸内燃机各个气缸排布的形式,也就是一台发动机上气缸所排出的队列形式。目前主流发动机气缸排列形式有直列和V形排列,其他非主流的气缸排列方式还包括W形排列、水平对置发动机和转子发动机等。

4.1 In-line engine 直列发动机

这种布局的发动机的所有气缸均是按同一角度并排成一个平面,并且只使用了一个气缸盖,同时其缸体和曲轴的结构也要相对简单,好比气缸们站成了一列纵队(图2-4-1)。

图2-4-1 In-line 6 cylinders engine 直列6缸发动机

4.2 V-type engine V形发动机

所谓V形发动机，简单地说就是将所有气缸分成两组，把相邻气缸以一定夹角布置一起，使两组气缸形成一个夹角的平面，从侧面看气缸呈V字形（通常的夹角为60°），故称V形发动机（图2-4-2）。

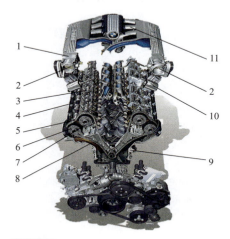

1. throttle body 节气门体
2. throttle valve 节气门
3. intake camshaft 进气凸轮轴
4. exhaust camshaft 排气凸轮轴
5. timing chain 正时链条
6. exhaust camshaft sprocket 排气凸轮轴链轮
7. intake camshaft chain 进气凸轮轴链条
8. timing chain guide 正时链条导板
9. cylinder 气缸体
10. variable throttle servo motor 可变气门伺服电动机
11. intake manifold 进气歧管

图2-4-2 V12 type engine V12型发动机

4.3 W-type engine W形发动机

将V形发动机两侧的气缸再进行小角度的错开，就是W形发动机了（图2-4-3）。W形发动机相对于V形发动机，优点是曲轴可更短一些，重量也可轻些，但是宽度也相应增大，发动机舱也会被塞得更满。缺点是W形发动机结构上被分割成两个部分，结构更为复杂，在运行时会产生很大的振动，所以只有在少数的车上应用。

图2-4-3 W-type engine cylinder arrangement W形发动机气缸布置形式

PART2 Engine 发动机

W12型发动机结构如图2-4-4所示。

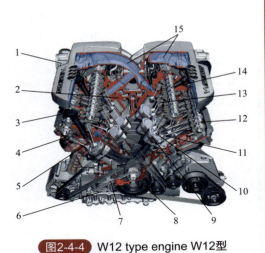

图2-4-4 W12 type engine W12型发动机结构

1. throttle valve 节气门
2. cylinder 气缸体
3. high-voltage ignition cable 高压点火线
4. valve rocker arm 气门摇臂
5. spark plug 火花塞
6. oil pump sprocket 机油泵链轮
7. oil pump chain 机油泵链条
8. crankshaft pulley 曲轴带轮
9. piston 活塞
10. intake valve 进气门
11. exhaust valve 排气门
12. exhaust camshaft 排气凸轮轴
13. valve spring 气门弹簧
14. intake camshaft 进气凸轮轴
15. intake manifold 进气歧管

4.4 Horizontal opposed engine 水平对置发动机

在上面介绍气缸V形排列发动机的时候已经提过，V形布局形成的夹角通常为60°，而水平对置发动机的气缸夹角为180°（图2-4-5），但是水平对置发动机的制造成本和工艺难度相当高，所以目前世界上只有保时捷和斯巴鲁两个厂商在使用。

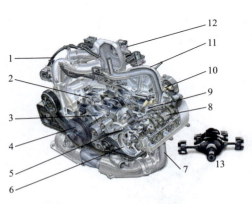

图2-4-5 Horizontal opposed engine 水平对置发动机

1. high-voltage ignition cable 高压点火线
2. piston 活塞
3. crankshaft 曲轴
4. crankshaft pulley 曲轴带轮
5. timing belt 正时皮带
6. camshaft pulley 凸轮轴带轮
7. exhaust manifold 排气歧管
8. intake camshaft 进气门凸轮轴
9. intake valve 进气门
10. injector 喷油器
11. intake manifold 进气歧管
12. throttle valve 节气门
13. horizontal opposed configuration 水平对置结构

Chapter 5
Engine principle 发动机工作原理

5.1 Four stroke gasoline engine operation 四冲程汽油发动机工作原理

发动机之所以能源源不断地提供动力，得益于气缸内的进气、压缩、做功、排气这四个行程有条不紊地循环运行（图2-5-1）。

进气行程，活塞从气缸内上止点移动至下止点时，进气门打开，排气门关闭，新鲜的空气和汽油混合气被吸入气缸内。

压缩行程，进排气门关闭，活塞从下止点移动至上止点，将混合气体压缩至气缸顶部，以提高混合气的温度，为做功行程做准备。

做功行程，火花塞将压缩的气体点燃，混合气体在气缸内发生"爆炸"产生巨大压力，将活塞从上止点推至下止点，通过连杆推动曲轴旋转。

排气行程，活塞从下止点移至上止点，此时进气门关闭，排气门打开，将燃烧后的废气通过排气歧管排出气缸外。

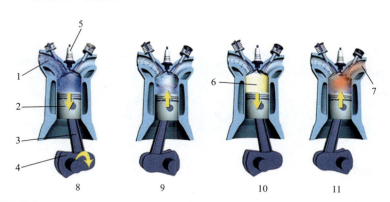

图2-5-1 Four stroke gasoline engine operation 四冲程汽油发动机工作原理

1. intake 进气
2. piston 活塞
3. connecting rod 连杆
4. crankshaft 曲轴
5. spark plug 火花塞
6. combustion chamber 燃烧室
7. exhaust 排气
8. intake stroke 进气行程
9. compression stroke 压缩行程
10. power stroke 做功行程
11. exhaust stroke 排气行程

PART2 Engine 发动机

汽油在气缸内燃烧如图2-5-2所示。

1. exhaust passage 排气道
2. exhaust valve 排气门
3. piston 活塞
4. piston ring 活塞环
5. combustion chamber 燃烧室
6. intake valve 进气门
7. intake passage 进气道

图2-5-2 Gasoline combustion in the cylinder 汽油在气缸内燃烧

5.2 Four stroke diesel engine operation 四冲程柴油发动机工作原理

四冲程柴油机和汽油机一样，每个工作循环也是由进气行程、压缩行程、做功行程和排气行程组成（图2-5-3）。由于柴油机以柴油作燃料，与汽油相比，柴油自燃温度低、黏度大、不易蒸发，因而柴油机采用压缩终点自燃着火。

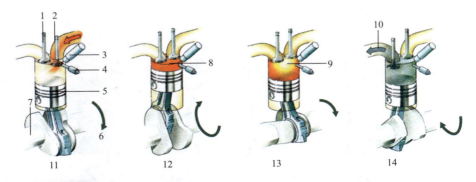

图2-5-3 Four stroke diesel engine operation 四冲程柴油发动机工作原理

1. exhaust valve 排气门
2. inlet valve 进气门
3. injector 喷油器
4. glow plug 预热塞
5. piston 活塞
6. direction of rotation 旋转方向
7. crankshaft 曲轴
8. compressed air 压缩的空气
9. fuel jet 喷油
10. to exhaust 到排气
11. induction stroke 进气冲程
12. compression stroke 压缩冲程
13. injection stroke（working stroke）喷油冲程（做功冲程）
14. exhaust stroke 排气冲程

5.3 Two stroke gasoline engine operation 二冲程汽油发动机工作原理

发动机气缸体上有三个孔，即进气孔、排气孔和换气孔，这三个孔分别在一定时刻由活塞关闭（图2-5-4）。其工作循环包含的两个行程如下。

第一冲程：活塞自下止点向上移动，三个气孔同时被关闭后，进入气缸的混合气被压缩；在进气孔露出时，可燃混合气流入曲轴箱。

第二冲程：活塞压缩到上止点附近时，火花塞点燃可燃混合气，燃气膨胀推动活塞下移做功。这时进气孔关闭，密闭在曲轴箱内的可燃混合气被压缩；当活塞接近下止点时排气孔开启，废气冲出；随后换气孔开启，受预压的可燃混合气冲入气缸，驱除废气，进行换气行程。

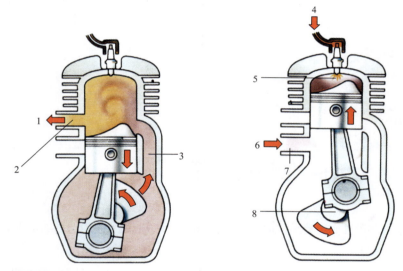

图2-5-4 Two stroke gasoline engine operation 二冲程汽油发动机工作原理

1. exhaust gases 排气
2. exhaust port 排气口
3. transfer port 过渡（换气）口
4. current 电流
5. spark 火花
6. petrol-air mixture 汽油-空气混合气
7. inlet port 进气口
8. crankshaft 曲轴

PART2 Engine 发动机

5.4 Rotary engine operation 转子发动机工作原理

壳体的内部空间（或旋轮线室）总是被分成三个工作室（图2-5-5）。在转子的运动过程中，三个工作室的容积不停地变动，在摆线形缸体内相继完成进气、压缩、燃烧和排气四个行程。每个行程都是在摆线形缸体中的不同位置进行。

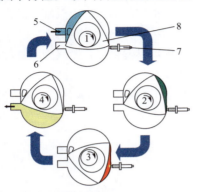

图2-5-5 Rotary engine operation
转子发动机工作原理图

1. intake stroke 进气行程
2. compression stroke 压缩行程
3. power stroke 做功行程
4. exhaust stroke 排气行程
5. intake valve 进气门
6. exhaust valve 排气门
7. spark plug 火花塞
8. rotor 转子

Chapter 6
Engine terms 发动机术语

6.1 Top dead center and bottom dead center 上止点与下止点（图2-6-1）

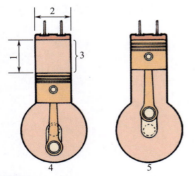

图2-6-1 Top dead center and bottom dead center 上止点与下止点

1. stroke 冲程，上、下止点间的距离称为活塞行程
2. bore 缸径
3. piston displacement 活塞排量，活塞从上止点移动到下止点所通过的空间容积称为活塞（气缸）排量，或工作容积；发动机所有气缸排量之和称为发动机排量，通常用升（L）来表示
4. bottom dead center 下止点，活塞顶离曲轴回转中心最近处为下止点
5. top dead center 上止点，活塞顶离曲轴回转中心最远处为上止点

6.2 Combustion chamber volume 燃烧室容积（图2-6-2）

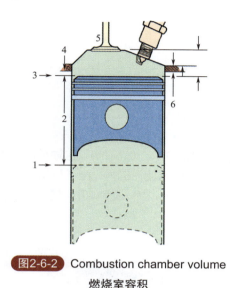

1. piston top at BDC 活塞顶在下止点
2. stroke 冲程
3. piston top at TDC 活塞顶在上止点
4. deck height 缸体面高度
5. combustion chamber volume 燃烧室容积
6. compressed head gasket 压缩后的气缸盖垫

图2-6-2　Combustion chamber volume 燃烧室容积

6.3 Compression ratio 压缩比（图2-6-3）

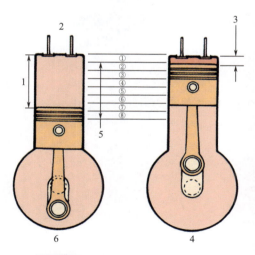

1. cylinder volume 气缸容积
2. compression ratio=8∶1 压缩比=8∶1，气缸总容积与燃烧室容积之比称为压缩比
3. clearance volume 余隙容积（燃烧室容积），活塞位于上止点时，活塞顶面以上气缸盖底面以下所形成的空间称为燃烧室，其容积称为燃烧室容积，也叫压缩容积
4. top dead center 上止点
5. piston displacement 活塞排量
6. bottom dead center 下止点

注：①～⑧表示气缸总容积分成八等份。

图2-6-3　Compression ratio 压缩比

PART2 Engine 发动机

Chapter 7
Block group 机体组

7.1 Overview 概述

现代汽车发动机机体组主要由机体、气缸盖、气缸盖罩、气缸衬垫、主轴承盖以及油底壳等组成（图2-7-1）。机体组是发动机的支架，是曲柄连杆机构、配气机构和发动机各系统主要零部件的装配基体。气缸盖用来封闭气缸顶部，并与活塞顶和气缸壁一起形成燃烧室。

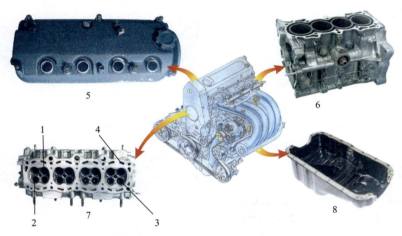

图2-7-1 Block group components 机体组部件

1. intake valve port 进气门孔
2. exhaust valve port 排气门孔
3. spark plug hole 火花塞孔
4. engine cooling passage 发动机冷却水道
5. valve cover 气门盖罩
6. cylinder block 气缸体，下部为上曲轴箱
7. cylinder head 气缸盖，其上附装配气机构部件
8. oil pan 油底壳，与气缸体结合而形成曲轴箱

7.2 Cylinder head 气缸盖

气缸盖用来封闭气缸并构成燃烧室（图2-7-2）。气缸盖铸有水套、进水孔、出水孔、火花塞孔、螺栓孔、燃烧室等。

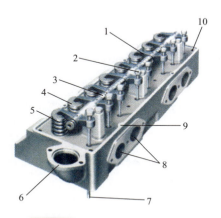

图2-7-2 Cylinder head 气缸盖

1. rocker arm pivots to open valve 开启气门的摇臂支撑轴
2. valve clearance adjuster 气门间隙调整螺钉
3. rocker shaft 摇臂轴
4. valve retainer 气门锁块
5. springs close valve 气门关闭弹簧
6. housing for thermostat 节温器壳体
7. pushrod moves up and down to pivot rocker arm 推杆上下运动，使摇臂摆动
8. intake ports 进气口
9. threaded hole bolting the rocker arm chamber cover to cylinder head 连接摇臂室罩和气缸盖的螺纹孔
10. stud hole 螺栓孔

7.3 Cylinder block 气缸体

气缸体是发动机的主体，它将各个气缸和曲轴箱连成一体，是安装活塞、曲轴以及其他零件和附件的支撑骨架（图2-7-3）。

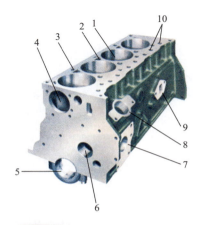

图2-7-3 Cylinder block 气缸体

1. cylinder bores 气缸缸径
2. coolant passage 冷却液通道
3. threaded stud hole 有螺纹的螺栓孔
4. mounting for water pump 水泵支座
5. main bearing supports crankshaft 主轴承支撑曲轴
6. camshaft bearing 凸轮轴轴承
7. mounting for oil filter 机油滤清器支座
8. mounting for distributor 分电器支座
9. mounting for fuel pump 燃油泵支座
10. holes for pushrods 推杆孔

7.4 Cylinder gasket 气缸垫

气缸垫位于气缸盖与气缸体之间,其功用是填补气缸体和气缸盖之间的微观孔隙,保证结合面处有良好的密封性,进而保证燃烧室的密封,防止气缸漏气和水套漏水(图2-7-4)。

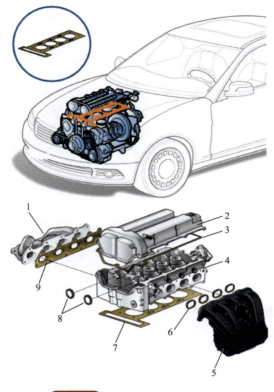

图2-7-4 Cylinder gasket 气缸垫

1. exhaust manifold 排气歧管
2. valve cover 气门罩
3. valve cover gasket 气门罩垫
4. cylinder head 气缸盖
5. intake manifold 进气歧管
6. intake manifold gasket 进气歧管垫
7. cylinder head gasket 气缸盖垫
8. camshaft seals 凸轮轴密封
9. exhaust manifold gasket 排气歧管垫

Chapter 8
Piston and connecting rod assembly 活塞连杆组件

8.1 Overview 概述

活塞连杆组是发动机的传动件，它把燃烧气体的压力传给曲轴，使曲轴旋转并输出动力。活塞连杆组主要由活塞、活塞环、活塞销及连杆等组成（图2-8-1）。

图2-8-1 Piston and connecting rod assembly 活塞连杆组件

1. piston ring 活塞环
2. bearing insert 连杆轴瓦
3. connecting rod 连杆
4. connecting rod cap 连杆盖
5. connecting rod bolt 连杆螺栓
6. piston pin 活塞销
7. piston 活塞
8. piston crown 活塞顶

PART2　Engine 发动机

8.2　Piston 活塞

活塞的主要功用是承受燃烧气体压力，并将此力通过活塞销传给连杆以推动曲轴旋转，此外活塞顶部与气缸盖、气缸壁共同组成燃烧室（图2-8-2）。活塞是发动机中工作条件最严酷的零件，作用在活塞上的有气体力和往复惯性力。

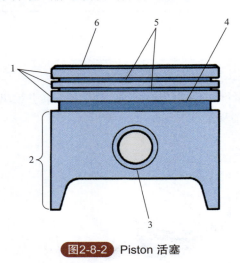

1. ring land 活塞环岸
2. skirt 活塞裙部
3. wrist pin boss 活塞销座
4. oil ring groove 油环槽
5. compression ring grooves 压缩环槽
6. crown 活塞顶

图2-8-2　Piston 活塞

8.3　Connecting rod 连杆

连杆组包括连杆体、连杆盖、连杆螺栓和连杆轴承等零件。连杆组的功用是将活塞承受的力传给曲轴，并将活塞的往复运动转变为曲轴的旋转运动（图2-8-3）。连杆小头与活塞销连接，同活塞一起做往复运动；连杆大头与曲柄销连接，同曲轴一起做旋转运动，因此在发动机工作时连杆在做复杂的平面运动。

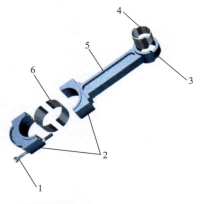

1. rod bolt 连杆螺栓
2. rod big end 连杆大端
3. rod small end 连杆小端
4. bushing 衬套
5. I-beam 工字梁杆身
6. bearing insert 轴瓦

图2-8-3　Connecting rod 连杆

Chapter 9
Crankshaft and flywheel assembly 曲轴飞轮组

9.1 Overview 概述

曲轴飞轮组包括曲轴、飞轮、扭转减振器、平衡轴。曲轴飞轮组的作用是把活塞的往复运动转变为曲轴的旋转运动，为汽车的行驶和其他需要动力的机构输出转矩；同时还储存能量，用以克服非做功行程的阻力，使发动机运转平稳（图2-9-1）。

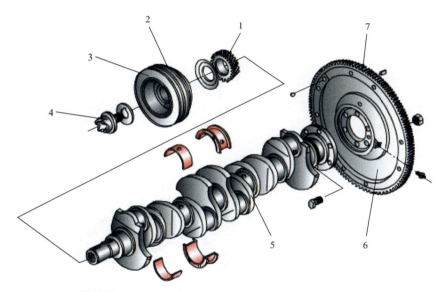

图2-9-1　Crankshaft and flywheel assembly 曲轴飞轮组

1. timing gear 正时齿轮
2. belt wheel 带轮
3. torsional vibration damper 扭转减振器
4. starting dog 启动爪
5. crankshaft 曲轴
6. flywheel 飞轮
7. ring gear 齿圈

PART2 Engine 发动机

9.2 Crankshaft function 曲轴的功用

曲轴的功用是把活塞、连杆传来的气体力转变为转矩，用以驱动汽车的传动系统和发动机的配气机构以及其他辅助装置（图2-9-2）。曲轴在周期性变化的气体力、惯性力及其力矩的共同作用下工作，承受弯曲和扭转交变载荷。

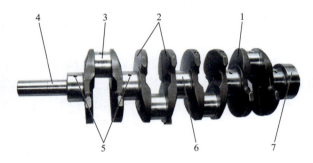

图2-9-2　Crankshaft 曲轴

1. crank 曲柄
2. balance weight 平衡块
3. connecting rod journal 连杆轴颈
4. front end 前端
5. oil passage 润滑油孔（道）
6. main journal 主轴颈
7. output end 输出端

曲轴术语如图2-9-3所示。

图2-9-3　Crankshaft terms 曲轴术语

1. mounting for camshaft drive sprocket 用于安装凸轮轴传动链轮
2. crank nose for pulley and/or vibration damper mounting 曲柄端头，用于安装带轮和/或减振器
3. main bearing journal 主轴承轴颈
4. main journal 主轴颈
5. counter weight 平衡重
6. crankpin oil hole 曲柄销油孔
7. flywheel mounting flange 安装飞轮的法兰盘
8. crankpin journal 曲柄销轴颈
9. web 曲柄
10. main journal oil way to lubricate crankpin journal 主轴颈油道，用于润滑曲柄销轴颈

9.3 Crankshaft mounting position 曲轴的安装位置（图2-9-4）

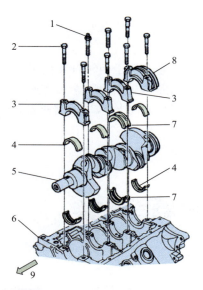

1. stud 双头螺栓
2. bolt 螺栓
3. cap 主轴承盖
4. main bearing insert 主轴承轴瓦
5. crankshaft 曲轴
6. cylinder block 气缸体
7. thrust bearing insert 止推轴承瓦
8. rear cap 后端轴承盖
9. front 前

图2-9-4 Crankshaft mounting position 曲轴的安装位置

9.4 Crankshaft bearing cap 曲轴轴承盖（图2-9-5）

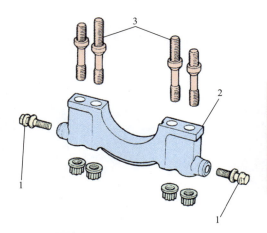

1. cross bolt 十字螺栓
2. bearing cap 轴承盖
3. studs screw into block 双头螺栓，拧入缸体

图2-9-5 Crankshaft bearing cap 曲轴轴承盖

PART2 Engine 发动机

9.5 How a crankshaft works 曲轴工作原理

我们都知道，气缸内活塞做的是上下的直线运动，但要输出驱动车轮前进的旋转力，是怎样把直线运动转化为旋转运动的呢？其实这个与曲轴的结构有很大关系。曲轴的连杆轴与主轴是不在同一直线上的，而是对立布置的。

这个运动原理其实跟我们踩自行车非常相似，两个脚相当于相邻的两个活塞，脚踏板相当于连杆轴，而中间的大飞轮就是曲轴的主轴。左脚向下用力蹬时（活塞做功或吸气向下做运动），右脚会被提上来（另一活塞压缩或排气做向上运动）。这样周而复始，就有直线运动转化为旋转运动了（图2-9-6）。

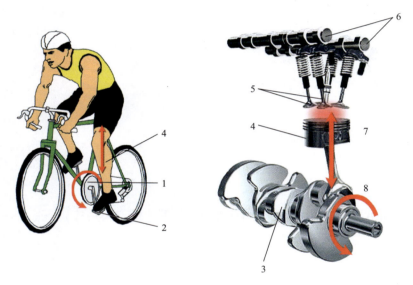

图2-9-6 How a crankshaft works 曲轴工作原理

1. crankshaft main shaft 曲轴主轴
2. crankshaft connecting shaft 曲轴连杆轴
3. crankshaft 曲轴
4. piston 活塞
5. valve 气门
6. camshaft 凸轮轴
7. the up and down movement of the piston 活塞的上下运动
8. the rotation of the crankshaft 曲轴旋转运动

9.6 Balance shafts 平衡轴

平衡轴简单地说是一个装有偏心重块并随曲轴同步旋转的轴，利用偏心重块所产生的反向振动力，使发动机获得良好的平衡，降低发动机的振动（图2-9-7）。两个相反方向旋转的平衡轴用于平衡发动机的振动。

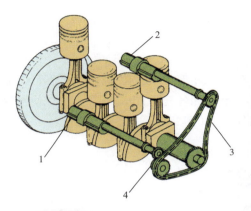

1. balance shaft rotating in the opposite direction to the crankshaft 与曲轴反方向旋转的平衡轴
2. balance shaft rotating in the same direction to the crankshaft 与曲轴同方向旋转的平衡轴
3. drive chain 传动链
4. oil pump gears reverse the direction of rotation 反方向旋转的机油泵

图2-9-7 Balance shafts 平衡轴

9.7 Engine flywheel 发动机飞轮

飞轮是一个质量较大的铸铁惯性圆盘，它贮蓄能量，供给非做功行程，带动整个曲连杆结构越过上、下止点，保证发动机曲轴旋转的惯性旋转的均匀性和输出转矩的均匀性，借助于本身旋转的惯性力，帮助克服启动时气缸中的压缩阻力和维持短期超载时发动机的继续运转（图2-9-8）。

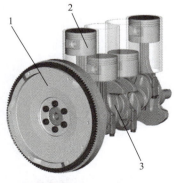

1. flywheel 飞轮
2. piston 活塞
3. crankshaft 曲轴

图2-9-8 Flywheel 飞轮

PART2 Engine 发动机

Chapter 10
Valve train 配气机构

10.1 Overview 概述

配气机构主要包括正时齿轮系、凸轮轴、气门传动组件（气门、推杆、摇臂等），主要的作用是根据发动机的工作情况，适时地开启和关闭各气缸的进、排气门，以使得新鲜混合气体及时充满气缸，废气得以及时排出气缸外（图2-10-1）。

图2-10-1 Valve train 配气机构示意图

1. intake camshaft pulley 进气凸轮轴带轮
2. timing belt 正时皮带
3. tension pulley 皮带张紧轮
4. crankshaft pulley 曲轴带轮
5. crankshaft balance weight 曲轴平衡块
6. crankshaft 曲轴
7. piston 活塞
8. exhaust valve 排气门
9. exhaust camshaft 排气凸轮轴
10. intake camshaft 进气凸轮轴
11. the crankshaft drives the camshaft by the belt 曲轴通过皮带带动凸轮轴转动

10.2 Valve train components 配气机构组成（图2-10-2）

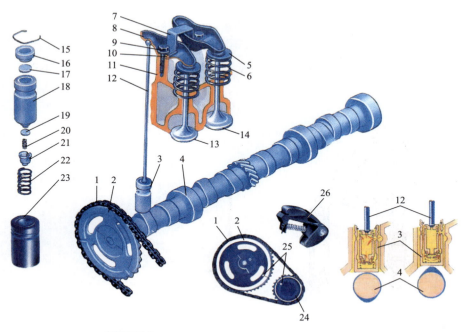

图2-10-2 Valve train components 配气机构组成

1. timing chain 正时链
2. camshaft sprocket 凸轮轴传动链轮
3. hydrualic tappet 液力挺柱（杆）
4. camshaft 凸轮轴
5. spring seat 弹簧座
6. valve spring 气门弹簧
7. bridge 过桥
8. rocker arm 摇臂
9. screw 螺钉
10. pivot assembly 枢轴
11. cylinder head 气缸盖
12. tappet 挺杆
13. exhuast valve 排气门
14. intake valve 进气门
15. snap ring 卡环
16. tappet seat 挺杆座
17. metering valve 限流阀
18. plunger 液力挺柱柱塞
19. check valve 单向阀
20. check valve spring 单向阀弹簧
21. check valve retainer 单向阀保持架
22. plunger return spring 柱塞回位弹簧
23. tappet body 挺柱体
24. crankshaft sprocket 曲轴链轮
25. timing mark 正时标记
26. tensioner 张紧器

10.3 Types of valve train 配气机构类型

按照凸轮轴的位置可分为底置凸轮轴式和顶置凸轮轴式。底置凸轮轴式就是凸轮轴布置在气缸底部；顶置凸轮轴式是指凸轮轴布置在气缸的顶部。OHV（Overhead valve）是指顶置气门底置凸轮轴（图2-10-3）。OHC（Overhead camshaft）是指顶置凸轮轴。如果气缸顶部只有一根凸轮轴同时负责进、排气门的开、关，称为单顶置凸轮轴SOHC（Single overhead camshaft）。

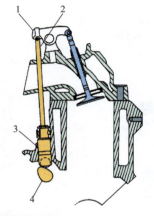

图2-10-3 Overhead valve engines
顶置气门发动机

1. rocker arm 摇臂
2. pushrod 推杆
3. lifter 挺杆
4. camshaft 凸轮轴

如果在顶部有两根凸轮轴分别负责进气门和排气门的开关，则称为双顶置凸轮轴（Double overhead camshaft，DOHC）。在DOHC下，凸轮轴有两根，一根可以专门控制进气门，另一根则专门控制排气门，这样可以增大进气门面积，改善燃烧室形状，而且提高了气门运动速度，非常适合高速汽车使用（图2-10-4）。

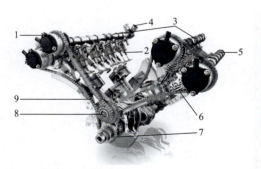

图2-10-4 Double overhead camshaft
双顶置凸轮轴

1. actuator 执行器
2. valve 气门
3. intake camshaft 进气凸轮轴
4. high pressure pump driver rod 高压泵驱动杆
5. exhaust camshaft 排气凸轮轴
6. high performance chain 高性能链条
7. primary drive 主传动
8. intermediate shaft 中间轴
9. high performance chain 高性能链条

OHV 与 SOHC 的结构比较如图 2-10-5 所示。

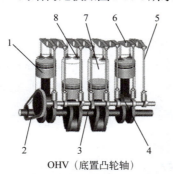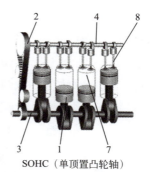

OHV（底置凸轮轴）　　SOHC（单顶置凸轮轴）

图2-10-5　OHV and SOHC的结构比较

1. piston 活塞
2. timing belt 正时皮带
3. crankshaft 曲轴
4. camshaft 凸轮轴
5. pushrod 顶杆
6. rocker arm 摇臂
7. cylinder 气缸
8. valve 气门

10.4 Valve timing 气门正时

所谓气门正时，可以简单理解为气门开启和关闭的时刻。理论上在进气行程中，活塞由上止点移至下止点时，进气门打开、排气门关闭；在排气行程中，活塞由下止点移至上止点时，进气门关闭、排气门打开（图2-10-6）。

正时的目的其实在实际的发动机工作中，为了增大气缸内的进气量，进气门需要提前开启、延迟关闭；同样地，为了使气缸内的废气排得更干净，排气门也需要提前开启、延迟关闭，这样才能保证发动机有效地运行。

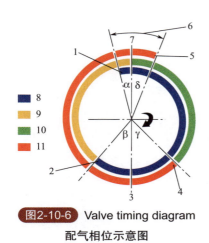

图2-10-6　Valve timing diagram
配气相位示意图

1. intake valve open 进气门打开
2. intake valve close 进气门关闭
3. bottom dead center 下止点
4. exhaust valve open 排气门打开
5. exhaust valve close 排气门关闭
6. valve overlap（α+δ）气门重叠角（α+δ）
7. top dead center 上止点
8. intake 进气
9. compression 压缩
10. power 做功
11. exhaust 排气

α.intake advance angle 进气提前角
β.intake retard angle 排气延迟角
γ.exhaust advance angle 排气提前角
δ.exhaust retard angle 排气延迟角

PART2 Engine 发动机

10.5 Valve train components 配气机构部件

10.5.1 Camshaft 凸轮轴

凸轮轴主要负责进、排气门的开启和关闭。凸轮轴在曲轴的带动下不断旋转，凸轮便不断地下压气门，从而实现控制进气门和排气门开启和关闭的功能（图2-10-7）。

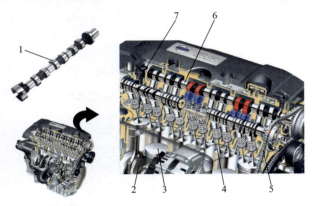

图2-10-7 Camshaft configuration 凸轮轴构造

1. cam 凸轮
2. crankshaft 曲轴
3. piston 活塞
4. intake valve 进气门
5. timing chain 正时链条

6. exhaust camshaft 排气凸轮轴，负责排气门的开、关
7. intake camshaft 进气凸轮轴，负责进气门的开、关

凸轮轴术语见图2-10-8。

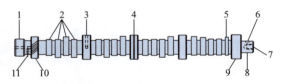

图2-10-8 Camshaft terms 凸轮轴术语

1. rear bearing 后轴承
2. cams 凸轮
3. oil holes 机油孔
4. oil groove 油槽
5. eccentric（for fuel pump if used）偏心轮（若有，则用于机油泵）
6. keyway 键槽

7. topped hole 螺纹孔
8. gear fit 齿轮配合面
9. front bearing 前轴承
10. driving gear for distributor（oil pump）用于分电器（机油泵）的驱动齿轮
11. oil holes 机油孔

10.5.2　Valve 气门

气门的作用是专门负责向发动机内输入燃料并排出废气（图2-10-9）。

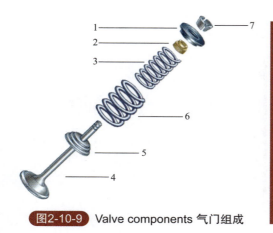

1. upper valve spring seat 上气门弹簧座
2. valve oil seal 气门油封
3. inner valve spring 内气门弹簧
4. valve 气门
5. lower valve spring seat 下气门弹簧座
6. outer valve spring 外气门弹簧
7. valve keeper 气门锁块

图2-10-9　Valve components 气门组成

气门术语如图2-10-10所示。

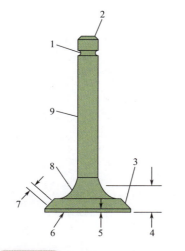

1. keeper groove 锁块槽
2. valve tip 气门杆头
3. valve face 气门面
4. valve head 气门头
5. margin 边线
6. combustion surface 燃烧面
7. proper seat contact area 适当的气门座接触面积（气门锥面）
8. fillet 过渡圆角
9. stem 杆

图2-10-10　Valve terms 气门术语

10.5.3 Valve spring 气门弹簧

气门弹簧的作用是依靠其弹簧的张力使开启的气门迅速回到关闭的位置，并防止气门在发动机的运动过程中因惯性力量而产生间隙，确保气门在关闭状态时能紧密贴合，同时也防止气门在振动时因跳动而破坏密封性（图2-10-11）。

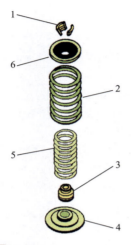

1. keepers 锁块
2. outer valve spring 外气门弹簧
3. seal 油封
4. spring seat 弹簧座
5. inner valve spring 内气门弹簧
6. retainer 挡圈

图2-10-11　Typical valve spring and related components 典型气门弹簧与相关部件

10.5.4 Insert for valve seat 气门座圈

气门座圈是气门和气缸盖之间的接触面。气门和气门座圈用于燃烧室的密封，以调节进排气（图2-10-12）。

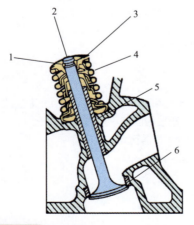

1. valve keeper 气门锁块
2. valve 气门
3. retainer 挡圈
4. valve spring 气门弹簧
5. valve guide 气门导管
6. insert for valve seat 气门座圈

图2-10-12　Insert for valve seat 气门座圈

10.5.5 Valve clearance 气门间隙

发动机在冷态下,当气门处于关闭状态时,气门与传动件之间的间隙称为气门间隙。图2-10-13(a)表示通过螺钉调整气门间隙,图2-10-13(b)表示通过垫片调整气门间隙。

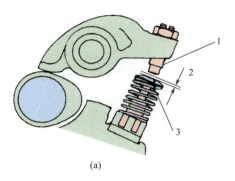
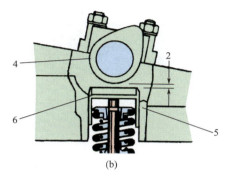

图2-10-13 Valve clearance 气门间隙

1. adjusting screw 调节螺钉
2. valve clearance 气门间隙
3. valve stem 气门杆
4. cam lobe heel 凸角跟部(基圆)
5. cam follower 凸轮随动件
6. adjusting shim 调节垫片

10.5.6 Hydraulic tappet 液力挺杆

液压挺杆主要由挺杆体、柱塞、球头柱塞(推杆支座)、单向阀、单向阀弹簧及回位弹簧等零件组成(图2-10-14)。利用液压挺杆内部独特的结构设计,可自动调节配气机构传动间隙、传递凸轮升程变化、准时开闭气门。

其工作原理是:当凸轮在升程阶段,凸轮压缩柱塞,单向阀关闭,高压腔中的油液从挺杆体与柱塞按偶件配合的间隙中泄出少量,这时液压挺杆可近似被看作一个不被压缩的刚体,在"刚体"的支撑作用下,将进、排气门打开。在凸轮回程阶段,柱塞的受力被解除,在回位弹簧作用下柱塞恢复上升,气门在气门弹簧的作用下自动关闭,完成一个工作循环,达到自动调节气门间隙的目的。

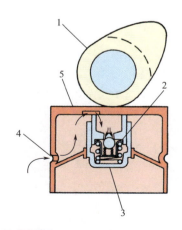

图2-10-14 Hydraulic tappet 液力挺杆

1. camshaft 凸轮轴
2. hydraulic adjuster 液压调节器
3. valve stem contacts here 在这接触气门杆
4. oil enters here 在这进油
5. lifter 挺柱

10.5.7 Rocker arm 摇臂

摇臂是顶压气门的杠杆机构,用于驱动气门开启和关闭(图2-10-15)。

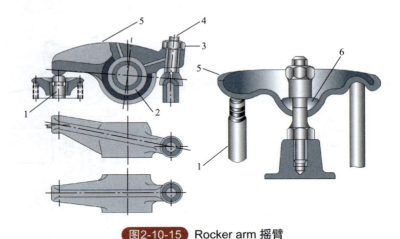

图2-10-15 Rocker arm 摇臂

1. valve 气门
2. rocker arm bushing 摇臂衬套
3. locked nut 锁紧螺母
4. valve clearance adjust screw 气门间隙调整螺钉
5. rocker arm 摇臂
6. rocker arm pivot seat 摇臂支点球座

10.5.8 Rocker shaft 摇臂轴

有些发动机利用摇臂轴支撑摇臂,如图2-10-16所示。

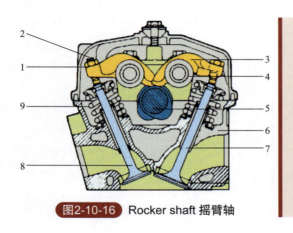

图2-10-16 Rocker shaft 摇臂轴

1. locknut 锁止螺母
2. adjustment screw 调整螺钉
3. rocker arm 摇臂
4. rocker shaft 摇臂轴
5. camshaft 凸轮轴
6. cylinder head 气缸盖
7. intake valve 进气门
8. exhaust valve 排气门
9. valve spring 气门弹簧

Chapter 11

Variable valve timing and variable valve lift 可变气门正时与可变气门升程

11.1 Overview 概述

可变气门正时和可变气门升程可以根据发动机转速和工况的不同而进行调节，使得发动机在高低速下都能获得理想的进、排气效率。

11.1.1 Variable valve timing 可变气门正时

如图2-11-1所示，利用液压控制凸轮轴正时齿轮内部内转子，可以实现一定范围内的角度提前或延迟。

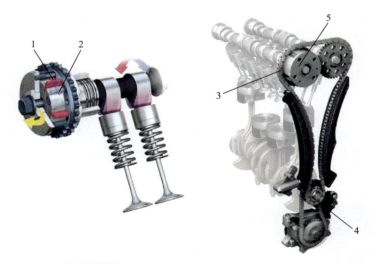

图2-11-1　Variable valve timing 可变气门正时

1. advance 提前
2. retard 延迟
3. timing chain 正时链条
4. crankshaft timing gear 曲轴正时齿轮
5. camshaft timing gear 凸轮轴正时齿轮

PART2 Engine 发动机

11.1.2 Variable valve lift 可变气门升程

图2-11-2表示可变气门升程系统主要通过切换凸轮轴上的低角度凸轮和高角度凸轮，来实现气门的可变升程。

图2-11-2 Variable valve lift 可变气门升程

1. low angle of the cam 低角度凸轮
2. high angle of the cam 高角度凸轮

11.2 Toyota variable valve timing intelligence（VVT-i）丰田智能可变气门正时系统

丰田的可变气门正时系统已广泛应用，主要的原理是在凸轮轴上加装一套液力机构，通过ECU的控制，在一定角度范围内对气门的开启、关闭的时间进行调节，或提前、或延迟、或保持不变（图2-11-3）。

凸轮轴的正时齿轮的外转子与正时链条（皮带）相连，内转子与凸轮轴相连。外转子可以通过机油间接带动内转子，从而实现一定范围内的角度提前或延迟。

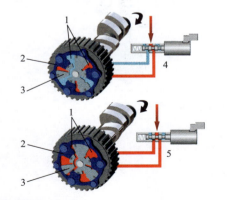

图2-11-3 Toyota variable valve timing intelligence 丰田智能可变气门正时系统

1. oil 机油
2. outer rotor 外转子
3. inner rotor 内转子
4. when filled with blue oil, the angle advances 当充满蓝色油液时，角度提前
5. when filled with red oil, the angle retards 当充满红色油液时，角度延迟

11.3 Honda variable valve timing and lift electronic control （VTEC）本田智能可变气门正时和升程电子控制

本田的VTEC可变气门升程系统可以看作在原来的基础上加了第三根摇臂和第三个凸轮轴。通过三根摇臂的分离与结合一体，来实现高低角度凸轮轴的切换，从而改变气门的升程（图2-11-4）。

当发动机处于低负荷时，三根摇臂处于分离状态，低角度凸轮两边的摇臂来控制气门的开闭，气门升程量小；当发动机处于高负荷时，三根摇臂结合为一体，由高角度凸轮驱动中间摇臂，气门升程量大。

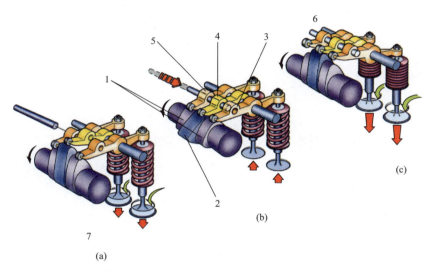

图2-11-4　Honda VTEC system 本田VTEC系统

1. normal operaion 正常运转（低转速）
2. high performance camshaft 高性能凸轮轴
3. primary rocker arm 主摇臂
4. mid rocker arm 中摇臂
5. secondary rocker arm 次摇臂
6. high performance operaion（high rpm）高性能运转（高转速）
   For higher engine power output the valves follow the larger center camshaft lobe 为获得较大的发动机功率输出，气门跟随较大的凸轮轴凸角运动
7. normal operaion（low rpm）正常运转（低转速）
   For good fuel economy and smooth operation both valves follow the smaller camshaft lobes 为获得较好的燃油经济性和运转平稳，气门跟随较小的凸轮轴凸角运动

11.4 Audi valve lift system（AVS）奥迪气门升程系统

奥迪的AVS可变气门升程系统，主要通过切换凸轮轴上两组高度不同的凸轮来实现气门升程的改变，其原理与本田的VTEC非常相似，只是AVS系统是通过安装在凸轮轴上的螺旋沟槽套筒，来实现凸轮轴的左右移动，进而切换凸轮轴上的高低凸轮。在电磁驱动器的作用下，通过螺旋沟槽可以使凸轮轴向左或向右移动，从而实现不同凸轮间的切换（图2-11-5）。

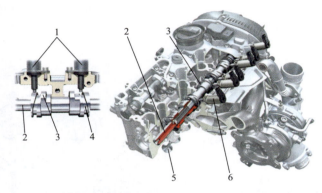

图2-11-5 Audi valve lift system 奥迪气门升程系统

1. solenoid actuator 电磁驱动器
2. camshaft 凸轮轴
3. cam 凸轮
4. spiral groove 螺旋沟槽
5. valve 气门
6. solenoid actuator 电磁阀驱动器

发动机处于高负荷时，电磁驱动器使凸轮轴向右移动，切换到高角度凸轮，从而增大气门的升程（图2-11-6）。

图2-11-6 AVS operation（high load） AVS工作原理（高负荷）

1. solenoid actuator 电磁阀驱动器
2. camshaft 凸轮轴

当发动机处于低负荷时，电磁驱动器使凸轮轴向左移动，切换到低角度凸轮，以减少气门的升程（图2-11-7）。

1. solenoid actuator 电磁驱动器
2. camshaft 凸轮
3. spiral slot 螺旋沟槽
4. valve 气门
5. valve spring 气门弹簧
6. cam 凸轮
7. camshaft 凸轮轴

图2-11-7　AVS operation（low load）AVS工作原理（低负荷）

11.5　BMW Valvetronic variable valve lift system 宝马Valvetronic可变气门升程系统

宝马的Valvetronic可变气门升程系统，主要是通过在其配气机构上增加偏心轴、伺服电机和中间推杆等部件来改变气门升程。当电动机工作时，蜗轮蜗杆机构会驱动偏心轴发生旋转，再通过中间推杆和摇臂推动气门。偏心轮旋转的角度不同，凸轮轴通过中间推杆和摇臂推动气门产生的升程也不同，从而实现对气门升程的控制（图2-11-8）。

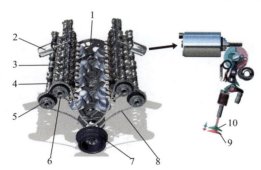

图2-11-8　BMW engine variable valve 宝马发动机可变气门

1. flywheel 飞轮
2. variable valve mechanism servo motor 可变气门机构伺服电动机
3. intake camshaft 进气凸轮轴
4. exhuast camshaft 排气凸轮轴
5. exhuast camshaft sprocket 排气凸轮轴链轮
6. intake camshaft sprocket 进气凸轮轴链轮
7. crankshaft pulley 曲轴带轮
8. timing chain 正时链条
9. valve opening when in high speed 高速时气门开度
10. valve opening when in low speed 低速时气门开度

PART2 Engine 发动机

Chapter 12

Fuel supply system 燃料供给系统

12.1 Overview 概述

发动机燃料系统的功能是把发动机所需的燃油与空气按照机器自身的设计方式混合成一定浓度的气体供给燃烧室，并将燃烧后的废气排掉，如图2-12-1所示。燃料供给系统可分为汽油机燃料供给系统和柴油机燃料供给系统。

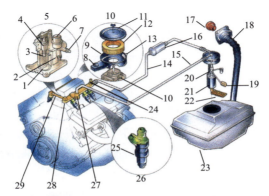

图2-12-1 Fuel supply system 燃料供给系统

1. throttle plate 节气门阀板
2. fuel return 回油管
3. fuel injection nozzle 喷油嘴
4. solenoid 电磁阀
5. throttle body 节气门体
6. fuel pressure regulator 油压调节器
7. fuel inlet 进油口
8. vacuum motor 真空马达
9. air cleaner 空气滤清器
10. carburetor 化油器
11. cover 滤清器盖
12. air filter 空气滤芯
13. crankcase breather element 曲轴箱通风部件
14. fuel feed line 供油管
15. fuel return line 回油管
16. inline fuel filter 管路中的燃油滤清器
17. fuel cap 加油盖
18. filler pipe 加油管
19. float 浮子
20. fuel level gauge sensor 油面仪表传感器
21. in-tank fuel pump 箱内燃油泵
22. in-tank fuel filter 箱内燃油滤清器
23. fuel tank 油箱
24. Schrader valve 施克拉德阀（维修阀）
25. fuel injector 喷油器
26. fuel injection 燃油喷射
27. fuel pressure regulator 油压调节器
28. fuel rail and injector 油轨和喷油器
29. fuel crossover line 输油管

12.2 Gasoline engine fuel supply system 汽油机燃料供给系统

　　汽油机燃料供给系统的任务是根据发动机各种不同工况的要求，配制出一定数量和浓度的可燃混合气，供入气缸，使之在临近压缩终了时点火燃烧而膨胀做功。供给系统还应将燃烧产物——废气排入大气中（图2-12-2）。

　　汽油机燃料供给系统分为化油器式燃料供给系统和电子燃油喷射式供给系统。

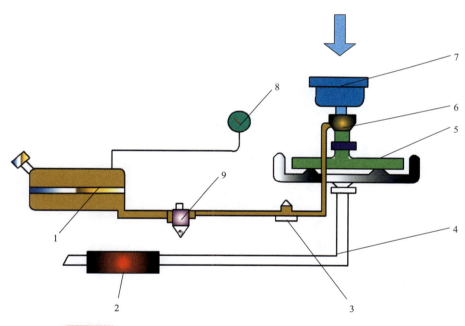

图2-12-2　Carburetor fuel supply system 化油器式燃料供给系统

1. fuel tank 油箱
2. exhaust silencer 排气消声器
3. gasoline pump 汽油泵
4. exhaust manifold 排气管
5. intake manifold 进气管
6. carburetor 化油器
7. air cleaner 空气滤清器
8. gasoline gauge 汽油表
9. gasoline filter 汽油滤清器

PART2 Engine 发动机

Chapter 13

Gasoline engine electronic fuel injection (EFI) system 汽油机电子控制燃油喷射系统

13.1 Overview 概述

电子控制燃油喷射系统简称为"电控燃油喷射系统"、"电喷系统"或"EFI"，是以电控单元为控制中心，并利用安装在发动机上的各种传感器测出发动机的各种运行参数，再按照电脑中预存的控制程序精确地控制喷油器的喷油量，使发动机在各种工况下都能获得最佳空燃比的可燃混合气（图2-13-1）。

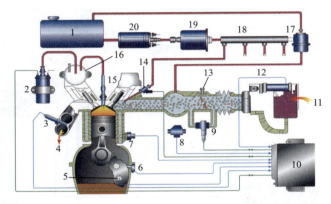

图2-13-1 Electronic control gasoline injection system 电子控制汽油喷射系统

1. fuel tank 油箱
2. ignition coil 点火线圈
3. oxygen sensor 氧传感器
4. exhaust out 废气排出
5. camshaft position sensor 凸轮轴位置传感器
6. crankshaft position sensor 曲轴位置传感器
7. water temperature sensor 水温传感器
8. throttle position sensor 节气门位置传感器
9. idle speed control valve 怠速控制阀
10. ECU（electronic control unit）电控单元
11. fresh air 新鲜空气
12. air flow meter 空气流量计
13. idle speed adjustment screw 怠速调节螺钉
14. injector 喷油器
15. igniter 点火器
16. distributor 分电器
17. fuel pressure regulator 油压调节器
18. fuel rail 燃油分配管
19. fuel filter 燃油滤清器
20. fuel pump 燃油泵

13.2 Electronic fuel injection system components 电子燃油喷射系统组成（图2-13-2）

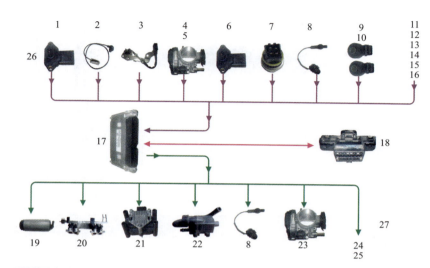

图2-13-2 Electronic fuel injection system components 电子燃油喷射系统组成

1. air flow sensor 空气流量传感器
2. crankshaft position sensor 曲轴位置传感器
3. camshaft location sensor 凸轮轴位置传感器
4. throttle position sensor 节气门位置传感器
5. idle speed switch 怠速开关
6. intake air temperature sensor 进气温度传感器
7. coolant temperature sensor 冷却温度传感器
8. O_2 sensor 氧传感器
9. No.1 detonation sensor No.1爆震传感器
10. No.2 detonation sensor No.2爆震传感器
11. additional signals 附加信号：ignition switch signal 点火开关信号
12. starter switch signal 启动开关信号
13. battery voltage signal 电源电压信号
14. air conditioning signal 空调信号
15. vehicle speed signal 车速信号
16. neutral start switch signal 空挡安全开关信号
17. engine control unit ECU 发动机控制单元
18. troubleshooting communication connector 故障诊断通信接口
19. fuel pump 汽油泵
20. injector 喷油器
21. ignition controller and ignition coil 点火控制器与点火线圈
22. canister solenoid 活性碳罐电磁阀
23. idle speed control motor 怠速控制电动机
24. air conditioning drive signal 空调驱动信号
25. ignition feedback signal 点火反馈信号
26. sensor 传感器
27. actuator 执行器

13.3 Electronic fuel injection system construction 电子燃油喷射系统结构（图2-13-3）

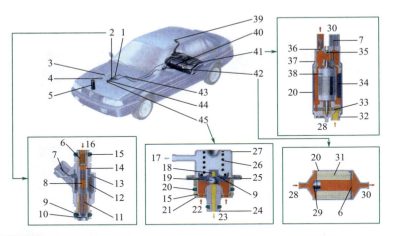

图2-13-3 Electronic fuel injection system construction 电子燃油喷射系统结构

1. fuel supply pipe 供油管
2. injector 喷油器
3. fuel tank 燃油箱油气排放管
4. canister solenoid 活性碳罐电磁阀
5. canister 活性碳罐
6. screen 滤网
7. connector 插头
8. spring 弹簧
9. valve seat 阀座
10. orifice plate 喷孔板
11. needle valve 阀针
12. solenoid 电磁线圈
13. injector case 喷油器壳体
14. inlet line and valve body assembly 进油管与阀体组件
15. O-ring O形密封圈
16. fuel 燃油
17. to intake manifold 接进气歧管
18. small spring 小弹簧
19. valve ball 阀球
20. case 壳体
21. lower cap 下盖
22. from fuel rail 从燃油分配管来
23. fuel return 回油
24. fuel return nozzle 回油管嘴
25. diaphragm 膜片
26. big spring 大弹簧
27. upper cap 上盖
28. fuel inlet port 进油口
29. plug 油塞
30. fuel outlet port 出油口
31. filter element 滤芯
32. bottom cap 下端盖
33. vane 叶轮
34. magnet 磁铁
35. safe valve 安全阀
36. fuel outlet valve 出油阀
37. upper cap 上端盖
38. armature 电枢
39. fuel filler port 加燃油口
40. fuel tank 燃油箱
41. electric fuel pump 电动燃油泵
42. fuel filter 燃油滤清器
43. fuel return line 回油管
44. fuel rail 燃油分配管（油轨）
45. fuel pressure regulator 燃油压力调节器

13.4 EFI main components EFI 主要部件

13.4.1 Injector 喷油器

多点喷射系统的喷油器位于进气口处，见图2-13-4。

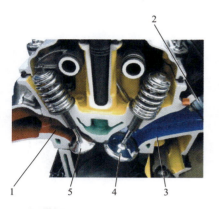

1. exhaust port 排气口
2. fuel injector 喷油器
3. intake port 进气口
4. intake valve 进气门
5. exhaust valve 排气门

图2-13-4　A port-injected engine 进气口喷射发动机

喷油器的作用是接受ECU送来的喷油脉冲信号，精确地控制燃油喷射量（图2-13-5）。

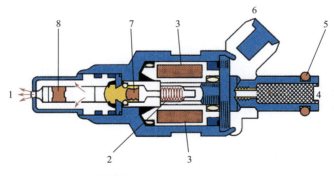

图2-13-5　Injector 喷油器结构

1. injection 喷油
2. plunger spring（closes needle valve）柱塞弹簧（关闭针阀）
3. coil winding 线圈绕组
4. inlet 进油口
5. O-ring seal O 形密封圈
6. wiring terminal 接线端子
7. plunger 柱塞
8. needle valve 针阀

13.4.2 Air flow meter 空气流量计

空气流量计将吸入的空气流量转换成电信号送至电控单元（ECU），作为决定喷油的基本信号之一，是用来测定吸入发动机的空气流量的传感器（图2-13-6）。

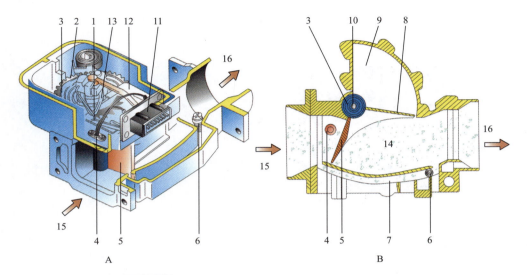

图2-13-6 Vane type air flow meter 翼片式空气流量计

A. structure diagram 结构图
B. cutaway view 剖视图
1. fuel pump switch contact 油泵触点
2. adjusting sector 调节齿扇
3. return spring 复位弹簧
4. intake air sensor 进气温度传感器
5. measuring blade 测量叶片
6. CO adjustment screw CO调节螺钉
7. air by-pass 旁通空气道
8. chamber vane 缓冲叶片
9. damper chamber 缓冲室
10. potentiometer shaft 电位计转轴
11. connector 接线插座
12. print board 印刷电路板
13. potentiometer sliding contact 电位计滑动触点
14. air main passage 空气主通道
15. air filter 空气滤清器
16. intake manifold 进气歧管

13.4.3 Oxygen sensor 氧传感器

氧传感器是利用陶瓷敏感元件测量汽车排气管道中的氧电势,由化学平衡原理计算出对应的氧浓度,达到监测和控制燃烧空燃比的目的,以保证产品质量及尾气排放达标的测量元件。

汽车上的氧传感器工作原理与干电池相似,传感器中的氧化锆起类似电解液的作用。其基本工作原理是:在一定条件下,利用氧化锆内外两侧的氧浓度差,产生电位差,且浓度差越大,电位差越大(图2-13-7)。

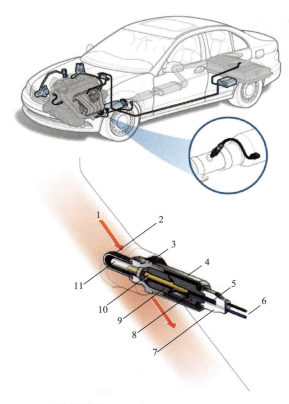

图2-13-7　Oxygen sensor 氧传感器

1. exhaust gas 废气
2. tube cover with slots 有通孔的管盖
3. sensor housing 传感器壳
4. stainless steel shell 不锈钢壳
5. reference air 参考空气
6. wire leads 导线
7. cable connector 接线端
8. heater contact 加热器触点
9. insulating bushing 绝缘衬套
10. heater 加热器
11. zirconium dioxide ceramic thimble sensing element 氧化锆陶瓷敏感元件

PART2 Engine 发动机

13.4.4 Electronic throttle valve 电子节气门

节气门主要的作用就是控制进入气缸的混合气量大小,如图2-13-8所示。

1. intake manifold 进气歧管
2. inlet to every cylinder 通往各气缸连接口
3. throttle valve 节气门
4. throttle body 节气门体
5. when the accelerator pedal is depressed, the throttle valve opening will change 当踩下油门踏板时,节气门开度将发生变化

图2-13-8 Electronic throttle valve 电子节气门

传统拉线油门是通过钢丝一端与油门踏板相连,另一端与节气门相连,它的传输比例是1∶1,这种方式控制精度不理想。而现在的电子节气门,是通过位置传感器,将踩踏油门踏板动作的力量、幅度等数据传输到控制单元进行分析,然后总结出驾驶者踩油门的意图,再由ECU计算实际节气门开合度并发出指令控制节气门电机工作,从而实现对节气门的精准控制,见图2-13-9。

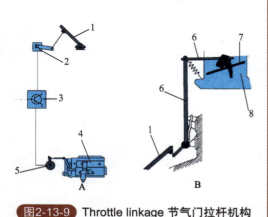

A. electronic throttle valve 电子节气门
B. conventional throttle valve 传统节气门
1. accelerator pedal 油门踏板
2. pedal position sensor 踏板位置传感器
3. ECU（electronic control unit）电子控制单元
4. throttle valve gear 节气门机构
5. motor 电动机
6. linkage 拉杆
7. throttle valve 节气门
8. intake manifold 进气管道

图2-13-9 Throttle linkage 节气门拉杆机构

13.5 Gasoline direct-injection（GDI）system 汽油缸内直喷系统

　　汽油缸内直喷是将喷油嘴安装在燃烧室内，将汽油直接喷注在气缸燃烧室内，空气则通过进气门进入燃烧室与汽油混合成混合气被点燃做功，这种形式与直喷式柴油机相似（图2-13-10）。

　　目前一般汽油发动机上所用的汽油电控喷射系统，是将汽油喷入进气歧管或进气管道中，与空气混合成混合气后再通过进气门进入气缸燃烧室内被点燃做功。

图2-13-10　Gasoline direct-injection system schematic 汽油缸内直喷系统示意图

1. exhaust valve 排气门
2. piston 活塞
3. combustion chamber 燃烧室
4. injector 喷油器
5. intake valve 进气门
6. air 空气
7. spark plug 火花塞
8. high pressure injector 高压喷油器

PART2 Engine 发动机

13.5.1　A typical direct-injection system operation 典型汽油缸内直喷系统原理

图2-13-11所示的汽油缸内直喷系统采用两个油泵，油箱内的低压电动泵和由凸轮轴驱动的高压油泵。

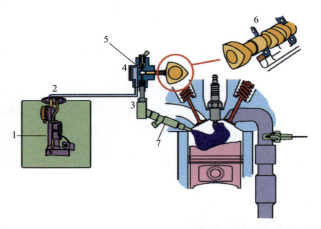

图2-13-11　A typical direct-injection system operation 典型汽油缸内直喷系统原理

1. low pressure fuel pump 低压燃油泵
2. fuel tank 油箱
3. common rail 共轨
4. pressure regulator 压力调节器
5. high pressure fuel pump 高压燃油泵
6. the high pressure pump driving lobe is located on the engine camshaft 高压油泵驱动凸角压靠在发动机凸轮轴上
7. injector 喷油器

13.5.2　Direct-injection system main components 汽油缸内直喷系统结构主要部件（图2-13-12）

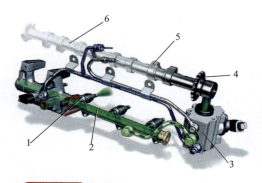

1. injector 喷油器
2. fuel injection rail 燃油喷射管道
3. injection pump 高压油泵
4. camshaft sprocket 凸轮轴链轮
5. cam 凸轮
6. camshaft 凸轮轴

图2-13-12　Direct-injection system main components 汽油缸内直喷系统结构主要部件

Chapter 14
Diesel engine fuel supply system 柴油机燃料供给系统

14.1 Overview 概述

柴油机燃料供给系统的功用是：不断供给发动机经过滤清的清洁燃料和空气，根据柴油机不同工况的要求，将一定量的柴油以一定压力喷入燃烧室，使其与空气迅速混合并燃烧，做功后将燃烧废气排出气缸（图2-14-1）。

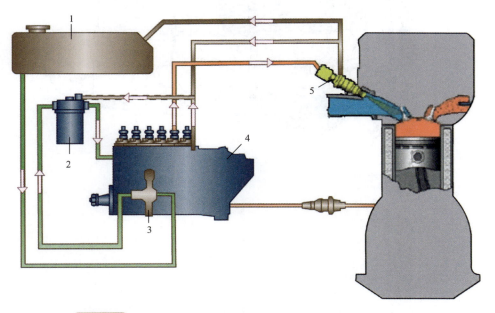

图2-14-1 Diesel engine fuel supply system 柴油机燃料供给系统

1. tank 油箱
2. filter 滤清器
3. fuel delivery pump 输油泵
4. fuel injection pump 高压油泵
5. fuel injector 喷油器

· 65 ·

PART2 Engine 发动机

14.2 Fuel injection pump 高压油泵

在汽车柴油机上得到广泛应用的有直列柱塞式喷油泵和转子分配式喷油泵。

14.2.1 Plunger type injection pump 柱塞式喷油泵

柱塞式喷油泵由泵油机构、供油量调节机构、驱动机构和喷油泵体等部分组成（图2-14-2）。

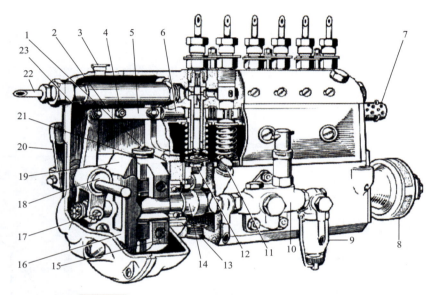

图2-14-2 Plunger type injection pump 柱塞式喷油泵

1. adjusting nut 调整螺母
2. outer link fork 外拉杆叉
3. oil lubricator 机油润滑器
4. screw for link forks 拉杆叉螺钉
5. inner link fork 内拉杆叉
6. control rod 控制杆
7. control rod stop 控制杆止停块
8. drive coupling 传动耦合器
9. preliminary filter 初级滤清器
10. plunger type feed pump 柱塞式输油泵
11. oil dipstick 机油尺
12. tappet screw 锥形螺钉
13. closing plug 密封塞
14. camshaft 凸轮
15. flyweights 飞块
16. bell crank pin retaining cage 曲柄销保持架
17. coupling cross-head pin 联轴器十字头销
18. eccentric 偏心块
19. bell crank lever 直角杠杆
20. control lever 控制杆
21. governor spring 调速器弹簧
22. fuel inlet connection 进油管接头
23. floating lever 浮动杠杆

14.2.2 Volume control of plunger type injection pump 柱塞式喷油泵油量控制

当供油量调节机构的调节齿杆拉动柱塞转动时，柱塞上的螺旋槽与柱塞套油孔之间的相对位置发生变化，从而改变了柱塞的有效行程。当柱塞上的直槽对正柱塞套油孔时，柱塞有效行程为零，这时喷油泵不供油，如图2-14-3。

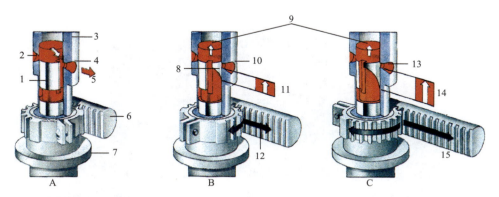

图2-14-3 Volume control of plunger type injection pump 柱塞式喷油泵油量控制

A. no flow 无流量

B. partial flow 有部分流量

C. full flow 流量最大

1. piston 活塞
2. inlet 进油
3. pump cylinder 泵缸
4. hole open 油孔打开
5. fuel return 回油
6. control rod 控制杆
7. regulator housing 调节器壳体
8. angled edge 斜边
9. to the injector valve（consumable volume）到喷油器阀（可消耗的燃油量）
10. hole partially open 油孔部分打开
11. partial flow amount 部分流量
12. movement of the control rod 控制杆的运动
13. full throttle 全节流（关闭）
14. full flow amount 最大流量
15. control rod at full throttle 控制杆在全节流位置

PART2 Engine 发动机

14.2.3　Distributor pump 分配泵

分配式喷油泵简称分配泵，有转子式和单柱塞式两大类。按压缩方式分有径向压缩式和轴向压缩式。分配泵主要由驱动机构、输油泵、高压分配泵头和油量控制阀等部分组成（图2-14-4）。

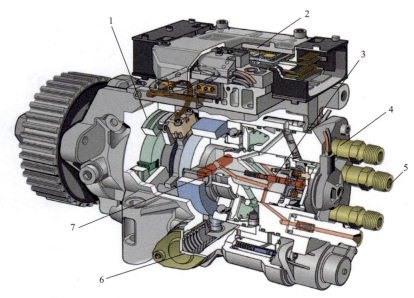

图2-14-4　Solenoid valve-controlled radial-piston distributor pump 电磁阀控制的径向活塞分配泵

---

1. sensor（position/ timing）传感器（位置/正时）
2. ECU 电控单元
3. high-pressure solenoid valve needle 高压电磁阀针阀
4. solenoid 电磁阀
5. outlets to injectors 喷油器出口
6. timing device（ignition advance mechanism）正时装置（点火提前机构）
7. radial-piston high-pressure pump 径向活塞高压泵

14.3 Diesel electronic control high pressure common rail system
柴油机电控高压共轨系统

高压共轨电喷技术是指在高压油泵、压力传感器和电子控制单元（ECU）组成的闭环系统中，将喷射压力的产生和喷射过程彼此完全分开的一种供油方式（图2-14-5）。它是由高压油泵将高压燃油输送到公共供油管（油轨），通过公共供油管内的油压实现精确控制，使高压油管压力大小与发动机的转速无关，可以大幅度减小柴油机供油压力随发动机转速变化的程度。

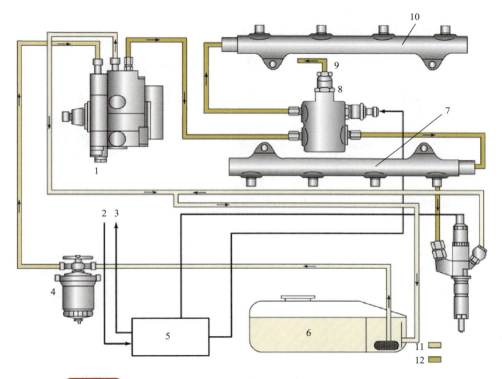

图2-14-5　High pressure common rail components 高压共轨系统组成

1. high pressure pump 高压泵
2. sensors 传感器
3. actuators 执行器
4. filter with water separator and integrated hand pump 过滤器，带油水分离器和整体式手动泵
5. electronic control module 电控模块
6. tank 油箱
7. common rail（right bank）共轨（右排）
8. rail pressure sensor 油轨压力传感器
9. pressure limiting valve 限压阀
10. common rail（left bank）共轨（左排）
11. high pressure 高压
12. low pressure 低压

14.4 High pressure common rail system principle 高压共轨系统原理

高压共轨系统利用较大容积的共轨腔将油泵输出的高压燃油蓄积起来，并消除燃油中的压力波动，然后再输送给每个喷油器，通过控制喷油器上的电磁阀实现喷射的开始和终止（图2-14-6）。

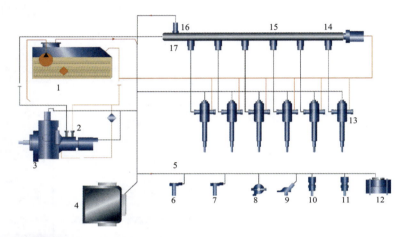

图2-14-6 High pressure common rail system principle 高压共轨系统原理

1. electric fuel pump with primary filter 带初级过滤器的电动燃油泵
2. filter 过滤器
3. high pressure pump with pressure regulator 带压力调节阀的高压泵
4. electronic control unit 电子控制单元
5. sensor 传感器
6. engine rpm sensor 发动机转速传感器
7. engine timing sensor 发动机相位传感器
8. accelerator pedal sensor 加速踏板传感器
9. charging sensor 增压传感器
10. air temperature sensor 空气温度传感器
11. coolant temperature sensor 冷却液温度传感器
12. intake air-mass flow sensor 进气质量流量传感器
13. injector 喷油器
14. pressure limiting valve 压力限制阀
15. common rail 共轨
16. rail pressure sensor 油轨压力传感器
17. flow limiter 流量限制器

Chapter 15
Exhaust system 排气系统

15.1 Overview 概述

汽车的排气系统主要包括排气歧管、三元催化转换器、消声器和排气管道等，主要的作用就是将气缸内燃烧的废气收集并且排出到大气中（图2-15-1）。

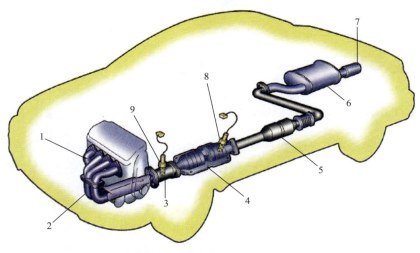

图2-15-1 Exhaust system 排气系统

1. exhaust manifold 排气歧管
2. exhaust pipe A 排气管A
3. mid pipe 中间管
4. three way catalytic converter 三元催化转换器
5. exhaust pipe B 排气管B
6. muffler 消声器
7. exhaust pipe tip 排气管头
8. secondary heated O_2 sensor 辅加热式氧传感器
9. primary heated O_2 sensor 主加热式氧传感器

15.2 Exhaust manifold 排气歧管

排气歧管是与发动机气缸体相连的，将各缸的排气集中起来导入排气总管的，带有分歧的管路。为了防止排气口间的废气产生相互干涉或回流的现象，排气歧管设计得很"怪异"，但也是有原则的，以防止出现紊流。如各缸排气歧管尽可能独立，长度尽可能长且相等，管内表面尽可能光滑（图2-15-2）。

1. O₂ sensor 氧传感器
2. ports leading to each cylinder 通往各气缸连接口

图2-15-2　Exhaust manifold 排气歧管

15.3 Exhaust gas recirculation（EGR）废气再循环

废气再循环系统用于降低废气中的氧化氮（NO_x）的排出量。氮和氧只有在高温高压条件下才会发生化学反应，发动机燃烧室内的温度和压力满足了上述条件，在强制加速期间更是如此。

当发动机在负荷下运转时，EGR阀开启，使少量的废气进入进气歧管，与可燃混合气一起进入燃烧室。怠速时EGR阀关闭，几乎没有废气再循环至发动机。汽车废气是一种不可燃气体（不含燃料和氧化剂），在燃烧室内不参与燃烧。它通过吸收燃烧产生的部分热量来降低燃烧温度和压力，以减少氧化氮的生成量。进入燃烧室的废气量随着发动机转速和负荷的增加而增加（图2-15-3）。

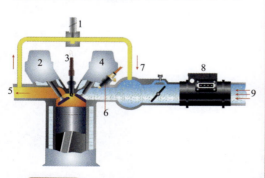

1. exhaust gas recirculation valve 废气再循环控制阀（EGR 阀）
2. exhaust valve 排气门
3. spark plug 火花塞
4. intake valve 进气门
5. exhaust gas 排气
6. injector 喷油器
7. idle speed adjustment screw 怠速调整螺钉
8. hot wire air flow meter（LH type EFI）热线式空气流量计（LH 型 EFI）
9. intake gas 进气

图2-15-3　EGR valve working principle EGR阀工作原理

15.3.1　EGR valve EGR阀

当EGR阀打开时，废气通过阀门，进入进气歧管内的通道（图2-15-4）。

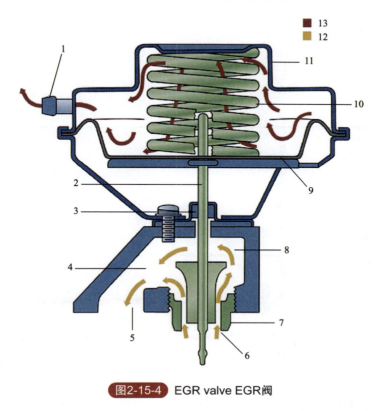

图2-15-4　EGR valve EGR阀

1. controlled vacuum connection 可控的真空连接口
2. valve shaft 阀轴
3. seal 密封
4. valve chamber 阀室
5. to intake manifold 到进气歧管
6. exhaust gas port inlet 废气入口
7. valve seat 阀座
8. valve open 阀开启
9. actuating diaphragm 活动膜片
10. spring 弹簧
11. diaphragm cover 膜片盖
12. vacuum 真空
13. exhaust 排气

PART2 Engine 发动机

15.3.2 Engine EGR control system 发动机废气再循环控制系统

发动机废气再循环控制系统中，EGR阀工作时，ECU根据存储器内存储的不同工作条件下理想的EGR阀开度控制EGR阀。EGR阀开度传感器检测EGR阀的开度并将信号传递至ECU，然后ECU将此开度与根据输入信号计算出的理想开度进行对比，如果他们之间不同，ECU将减小EGR阀控制电磁阀的电流，因此减小施加到EGR阀的真空，结果使EGR阀再循环的废气量改变（图2-15-5）。

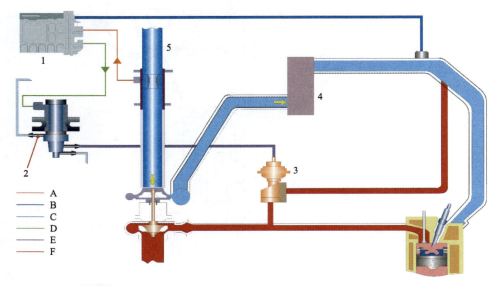

图2-15-5 Engine EGR control system 发动机废气再循环控制系统

1. ECU 电控单元
2. exhaust gas recirculation control valve 废气再循环控制阀
3. EGR（exhaust gas recirculation）valve EGR 阀
4. intake air intercooler 进气中冷器
5. air flow meter 空气流量计
A. sensor electronic signal 传感器电信号
B. intake pressure 进气压力
C. atmospheric pressure 大气压力
D. solenoid control signal 电磁阀控制电信号
E. control pressure 控制压力
F. exhaust gas 排气

15.4 Evaporative emission control system 汽油蒸发控制系统

汽油箱和化油器浮子室中的汽油随时都在蒸发气化，若不加以控制或回收，则当发动机停机时，汽油蒸气将逸入大气，造成对环境的污染。汽油蒸发控制系统的功用便是将这些汽油蒸气收集和储存在碳罐内，在发动机工作时再将其送入气缸进行燃烧（图2-15-6）。

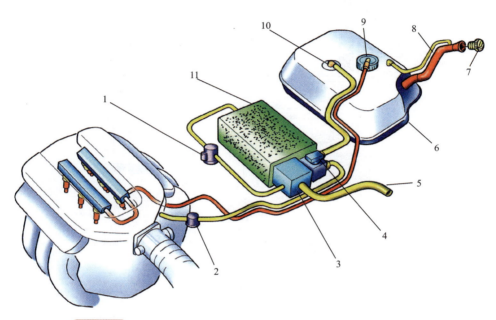

图2-15-6　Evaporative emission control system 汽油蒸发控制系统

1. evaporative two-way valve 蒸发双向阀
2. evaporative canister purge valve 蒸发碳罐净化阀
3. canister vent valve 活性碳罐通风阀
4. fuel tank pressure sensor 油箱压力传感器
5. vent hose 通风软管
6. fuel tank 油箱
7. fuel fill cap 加油盖
8. vapor recirculation tube 燃油蒸气再循环管
9. fuel pump 燃油泵
10. fuel tank vapor control valve 燃油蒸气控制阀
11. evaporative emission canister 蒸发排放活性碳罐

PART2 Engine 发动机

蒸发控制系统（EVAP system）原理：当计算机将碳罐净化电磁阀打开时，歧管真空将存储在碳罐的蒸气吸入发动机。歧管真空也作用到压力控制阀，当该阀打开，油箱中的汽油蒸气也被吸入到碳罐，最终进入到发动机。当电磁阀关闭（或发动机停转，没有真空），压力控制阀在弹簧作用下关闭，油箱内的蒸气无法进入大气中（图2-15-7）。

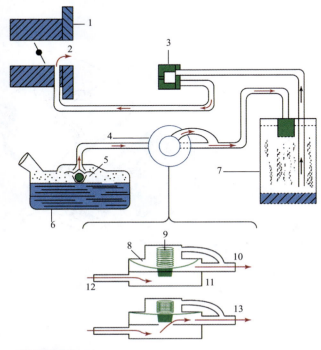

图2-15-7　EVAP system operation 蒸发控制系统原理

1. throttle body 节气门体
2. manifold vacuum 歧管真空
3. canister purge solenoid 碳罐净化电磁阀
4. pressure control valve 压力控制阀
5. rollover check valve 侧倾单向阀
6. fuel tank 油箱
7. charcoal canister 活性碳罐
8. rubber diaphragm 橡胶膜片
9. spring 弹簧
10. valve closed 阀关闭
11. to canister 到碳罐
12. from tank 从油箱
13. valve open 阀打开

15.5 Three way catalytic converter 三元催化转换器

三元催化转换器，是安装在汽车排气系统中最重要的机外净化装置，也称作催化净化转换器。利用催化剂的作用将排气中的CO、HC和NO_x转换为对人体无害的气体，可同时减少CO、HC和NO_x的排放，它以排气中的CO和HC作为还原剂，把NO_x还原为氮（N_2）和氧（O_2），而CO和HC在还原反应中被氧化为CO_2和H_2O（图2-15-8）。

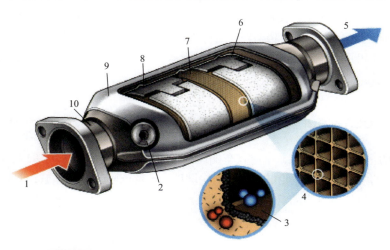

图2-15-8　Three way catalytic converter 三元催化转换器

1. exhaust gas 废气
   HC（hydrocarbons）碳氢化合物
   CO（carbon monoxide）一氧化碳
   NO_x（nitrogen oxide）氮氧化物
2. position for oxygen sensor plug 氧传感器塞体的位置
3. major reaction 主要反应
   $CO+1/2O_2=CO_2$
   $H_4C_2+3O_2=2CO_2+2H_2O$
   $CO+NO_x=CO_2+N_2$
4. catalytic active material 催化活性物质
   alumina oxide Al_2O_3 氧化铝
   cerium oxide CeO_2 氧化铈
   rare earth stabilizers 稀土稳定剂
   metals Pt/Pd/Rh 金属：铂/钯/铑
5. tail pipe emissions 排气管排放物
   H_2O（water）水
   CO_2（carbon dioxide）二氧化碳
   N_2（nitrogen）氮气
6. oxidation catalyst to eliminate carbon monoxide（CO）and unburned hydrocarbons（HC）氧化剂，消除一氧化碳和未燃碳氢化合物
7. cerium and ceramic honeycomb catalyst configuration 铈和陶瓷的蜂窝式催化剂结构
8. reduction catalyst to eliminate NO_x 还原剂，消除NO_x
9. heat shield 隔热罩
10. stainless steel catalytic converter body 不锈钢催化转换器壳体

PART2 Engine 发动机

Chapter 16

Charger 增压器

增压器是发动机借以增加气缸进气压力的装置。进入发动机气缸前的空气先经增压器压缩以提高空气的密度，使更多的空气充填到气缸里，从而增大发动机功率。装有增压器的发动机除能输出较大的功率外，还可改善发动机的高密度特性。

汽车发动机进气增压器，主要包括三种形式：废气涡轮增压器、机械涡轮增压器、双涡轮增压器。

16.1 Turbocharger 涡轮增压器

涡轮增压大家并不陌生，平时在车的尾部都可以看到诸如1.4T、2.0T等字样，这说明了这辆车的发动机是带涡轮增压的。涡轮增压（turbocharger）简称Turbo或T。涡轮增压是利用发动机的废气带动涡轮来压缩进气，从而提高发动机的功率和转矩，使车更有劲（图2-16-1）。

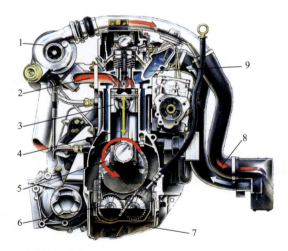

图2-16-1　Turbocharger location 涡轮增压器的位置

1. turbocharger 涡轮增压器
2. exhaust manifold 排气管道
3. piston 活塞
4. cylinder 气缸
5. crankshaft sprocket 曲轴链轮
6. oil pump sprocket 机油泵链轮
7. oil 机油
8. exhaust gas recirculation direction 废气再循环方向
9. intake manifold 进气管道

16.1.1 Turbocharger principle 涡轮增压原理

涡轮增压器主要由涡轮机和压缩机两部分组成，它们之间通过一根传动轴连接。涡轮的进气口与发动机排气歧管相连，排气口与排气管相连；压缩机的进气口与进气管相连，排气口则接在进气歧管上。到底是怎样实现增压的呢？主要是通过发动机排出的废气冲击涡轮高速运转，从而带动同轴的压缩机高速转动，强制地将增压后的空气压送到气缸中，提高发动机的功率（图2-16-2）。

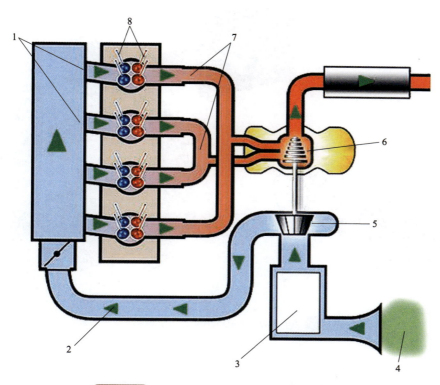

图2-16-2 Turbocharger principle 涡轮增压原理

1. intake manifold 进气歧管
2. air flow indicator 气体流向指示
3. air cleaner 空气滤清器
4. fresh air 新鲜空气
5. compressor blade 压缩机叶片
6. turbine blade 涡轮叶片
7. exhaust manifold 排气歧管
8. valve 气门

PART2 Engine 发动机

16.1.2　Air flow in turbocharger 涡轮增压空气流动

　　涡轮增压主要是利用发动机废气的能量带动压缩机来实现对进气的增压，整个过程中基本不会消耗发动机的动力，拥有良好的加速持续性，但是在低速时涡轮不能及时介入，带有一定的滞后性。空气经空气滤清器后，被涡轮增压器加压到中冷器，进入进气歧管、进气门、气缸、排气门、排气歧管（图2-16-3）。

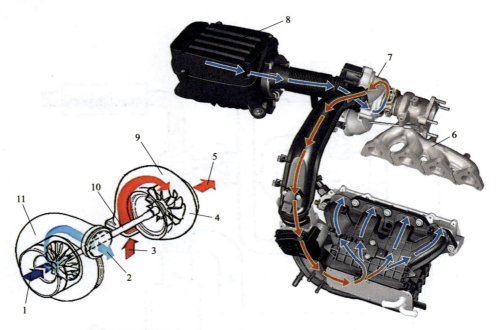

图2-16-3　Air flow in turbocharger 涡轮增压空气流动

1. compressor inlet 压缩机进气口
2. compressor outlet 压缩机排气口
3. turbine exhaust gas inlet 涡轮废气入口
4. turbine 涡轮
5. turbine exhaust gas outlet 涡轮废气出口
6. exhaust manifold 排气歧管
7. turbocharger 涡轮增压器
8. air cleaner 空气滤清器
9. turbine cover 涡轮壳体
10. shaft 转轴
11. compressor cover 压缩机壳体

16.2 Supercharger 机械增压器

相对于涡轮增压,机械增压的原理则有所不同。机械增压主要是通过曲轴的动力带动一个机械式的空气压缩机旋转来压缩空气的。与涡轮增压不同的是,机械增压工作过程中会对发动机输出的动力造成一定程度的损耗(图2-16-4)。

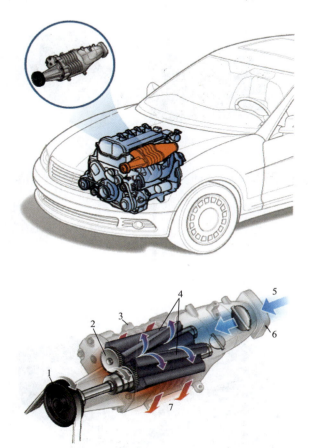

图2-16-4　Supercharger type engine 机械增压器发动机

1. pulley 皮带轮
2. gears 齿轮
3. housing 壳体
4. rotors 转子
5. air intake 进气
6. inlet 入口
7. compressed air to intake manifold 进入进气歧管的压缩空气

PART2　Engine 发动机

由于机械增压器是直接由曲轴带动的，发动机运转时，增压器也就开始工作了，所以在低转速时，发动机的转矩输出表现也十分出色，而且空气压缩量是按照发动机转速线性上升的，没有涡轮增压发动机介入那一刻的唐突，也没有涡轮增压发动机的低速迟滞。但是在发动机高速运转时，机械增压器对发动机动力的损耗也是很大的，动力提升不太明显（图2-16-5）。

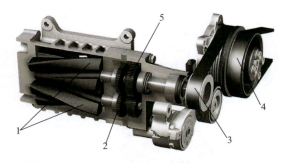

图2-16-5　Supercharger configuration 机械增压器的结构

1. compressor rotor 压缩机转子
2. meshed gear 同步齿轮
3. compressor wheel 压缩机轮
4. driving wheel 驱动轮
5. drive gear 传动齿轮

图2-16-6为带有中冷器的机械增压器。

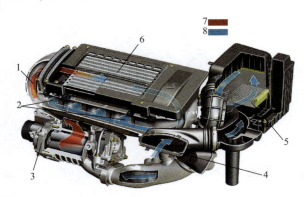

图2-16-6　Supercharger with the intercooler 带有中冷器的机械增压器

1. the compressed air is cooled by the intercooler 压缩后的空气进入中冷器进行冷却
2. to cylinder 进入气缸
3. supercharger 机械增压器
4. intake port 进气管口
5. air cleaner 空气滤清器
6. intercooler 中冷器
7. the red indicates the high temperature air 红色表示温度较高的空气
8. the blue indicates the low temperature air 蓝色表示温度较低的空气

16.3 Twin turbocharger type engine 双增压发动机

双增压发动机，是指一台发动机上装有两个增压器。如宝马3.0L直列六缸发动机，采用的就是两个涡轮增压器（图2-16-7）。

1. exhaust manifold 1 排气歧管组1
2. exhaust manifold 2 排气歧管组2
3. two turbochargers 双涡轮增压器

图2-16-7　Twin turbocharger type engine 双增压发动机

双增压发动机原理：涡轮增压器在低转速时有迟滞现象，但高速时增压值大，发动机动力提升明显，而且基本不消耗发动机的动力；而机械增压器，是发动机运转直接驱动涡轮，没有涡轮增压的迟滞，但是损耗部分动力、增压值较低，许多现代汽车将二者结合在一起实现了优势互补（图2-16-8）。

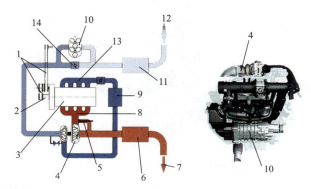

图2-16-8　Twin turbocharger type engine operation 双增压发动机原理

1. power transmission 动力传递
2. crankshaft 曲轴
3. engine 发动机
4. turbocharger 涡轮增压器
5. exhaust gas throttle valve 废气节流阀
6. three way catalytic converter 三元催化转化器
7. exhaust gas outlet 废气排出
8. exhaust manifold 排气歧管
9. intercooler 中冷器
10. supercharger 机械增压器
11. air cleaner 空气滤清器
12. fresh air 新鲜空气
13. intake manifold 进气歧管
14. throttle valve 节流阀

Chapter 17
Engine lubrication system 发动机润滑系统

17.1 Overview 概述

润滑系统的功用就是在发动机工作时连续不断地把数量足够、温度适当的洁净机油输送到全部传动件的摩擦表面，并在摩擦表面之间形成油膜，实现液体摩擦，从而减小摩擦阻力、降低功率消耗、减轻机件磨损，以达到提高发动机工作可靠性和耐久性的目的（图2-17-1）。

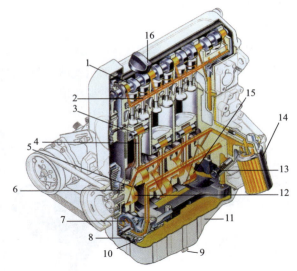

图2-17-1 Lubrication system 润滑系统

1. camshaft bearing journal 凸轮轴轴颈
2. head main oil gallery 气缸盖主油道
3. piston pin 活塞销
4. connecting rod oil passage 连杆油道
5. crankshaft oil passage 曲轴油道
6. crankshaft sprocket 曲轴链轮
7. oil pump 机油泵
8. oil pump sprocket 机油泵链轮
9. oil pan drain plug 油底壳放油螺栓
10. oil pump drive chain 机油泵传动链条
11. oil pan 油底壳
12. crankshaft main bearing journal 曲轴主轴颈
13. oil pressure regulating valve 机油压力调节阀
14. oil filter 机油滤清器
15. crankpin bearing journal 曲柄销轴颈
16. oil filler cap 加机油口盖

17.2 Engine lubrication system operation 发动机润滑系统工作原理

机油主要存储在油底壳中，当发动机运转后带动机油泵，利用泵的压力将机油压送至发动机各个部位。润滑后的机油会沿着缸壁等途径回到油底壳中，重复循环使用（图2-17-2）。

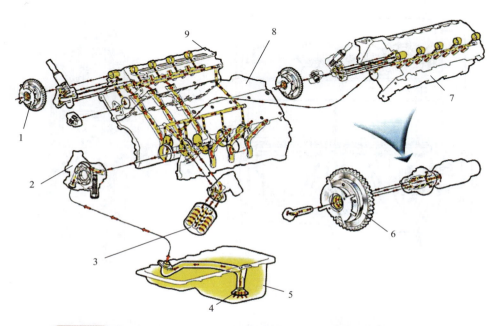

图2-17-2　Engine lubrication oil flow schematic 发动机润滑油流向示意图

1. camshaft gear 凸轮轴齿轮
2. oil pump 机油泵
3. oil filter 机油滤清器
4. oil screen 机油滤网
5. oil pan 油底壳
6. cam timing sprocket 凸轮正时链轮
7. cylinder 气缸
8. cylinder block 气缸体
9. cylinder head 气缸盖

PART2 Engine 发动机

17.3 Lubricating oil passage 发动机润滑油路

如图2-17-3所示为典型的发动机润滑系统结构，采用压力和飞溅润滑。机油在压力下经过油道到达发动机顶端，随后机油流回油底壳，来润滑其他部件，或将飞溅到部件上。

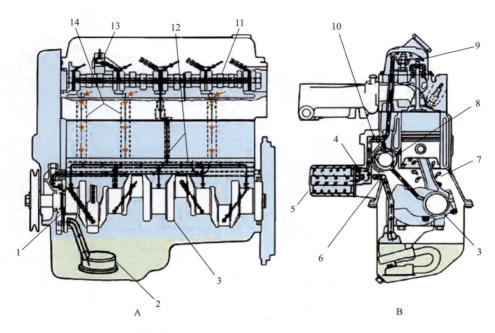

图2-17-3　Lubricating oil passage 发动机润滑油路

A. side view 侧视图
B. end view 端视图
1. oil pump 机油泵
2. pickup tube and screen 集滤管和滤网
3. crankshaft 曲轴
4. filter bypass valve 滤清器旁通阀
5. oil filter 机油滤清器
6. filter feed gallery 滤清器进油油道
7. splash oiling to cylinder walls 向气缸壁的飞溅润滑
8. camshaft 凸轮轴
9. splash oiling and return to sump 飞溅润滑和到油底壳的回油
10. pressure oiling to crankshaft, camshaft and rocker arms 压力油送往曲轴、凸轮轴和摇臂
11. overhead camshaft 顶置式凸轮轴
12. oil galleries 机油油道
13. hydraulic valve lifter (cam follower) 液力气门挺杆（凸轮随动件）
14. oil returns 回油油路

· 86 ·

17.4 Oil pump 机油泵

机油泵的功用是保证机油在润滑系统内循环流动，并在发动机任何转速下都能以足够高的压力向润滑部位输送足够数量的机油（图2-17-4）。

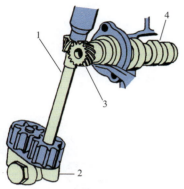

1. distributor shaft 分电器轴
2. oil pump 机油泵
3. drive gear for distributor and oil pump 分电器和机油泵的传动齿轮
4. camshaft 凸轮轴

图2-17-4　Oil pump 机油泵

17.5 Dry sump system 干式油底壳

干式油底壳取消了在发动机底部安装容器，而是在外部独立安装一个机油箱，采用机油泵对曲轴和连杆系统进行压力润滑（图2-17-5）。

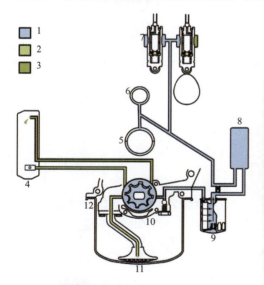

1. main pressure 主压力
2. suction 吸油
3. return to oil tank 回到油箱
4. oil tank 油箱
5. crank bearing 曲柄轴承
6. cam bearing 凸轮轴承
7. valve lifter 气门挺杆
8. oil cooler 油冷器
9. oil filter 机油滤清器
10. relief valve 泄压阀
11. oil pickup 机油集滤器
12. oil pump 油泵

图2-17-5　A dry sump system as used in a Chevrolet Corvette 雪佛兰科尔维特的干式油底壳

PART2 Engine 发动机

Chapter 18
Engine cooling system 发动机冷却系统

18.1 Overview 概述

冷却系统的主要功用是把受热零件吸收的部分热量及时散发出去，保证发动机在最适宜的温度状态下工作。

发动机冷却方式有水冷和风冷两种。水冷系统均为强制循环水冷系统，即利用水泵提高冷却液的压力，强制冷却液在发动机中循环流动（图2-18-1）。

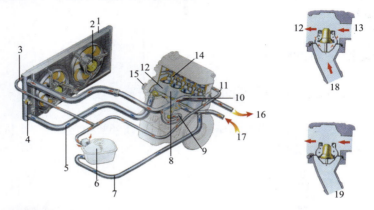

图2-18-1 Engine cooling system schematic 发动机冷却系统示意图

1. radiator 散热器
2. electric fan 电动风扇
3. overheat vapor 过热蒸气
4. electric fan twin-speed thermo switch 电动风扇双速热敏开关
5. inlet hose 进水管
6. coolant expanding tank 冷却液膨胀箱
7. lower coolant rubber hose 冷却液下橡胶软管
8. cylinder block water jacket 气缸体水套
9. throttle valve hot water hose 节气门热水管
10. upper coolant rubber hose 冷却液上橡胶软管
11. engine water jacket outlet 发动机水套排水管
12. water pump 水泵
13. coolant circulation passage 循环水道
14. cylinder head water jacket 气缸盖水套
15. cogged belt pulley 齿形带带轮
16. to A/C heating exchanger 到空调暖风热交换器
17. from heating device 自暖风装置
18. when water temperature is high 水温高时
19. when water temperature is low 水温低时

18.2 Cooling system operation 冷却系统工作原理

发动机是怎么进行冷却的呢？主要通过水泵使环绕在气缸水套中的冷却液加快流动，通过行驶中的自然风和电动风扇，使冷却液在散热器中进行冷却，冷却后的冷却液再次引入到水套中，周而复始，实现对发动机的冷却。

冷却系统除了对发动机有冷却作用外，还有"保温"的作用，因为"过冷"或"过热"，都会影响发动机的正常工作。这个过程主要是通过节温器实现发动机冷却系统"大小循环"的切换。什么是冷却系统的大小循环？可以简单理解为：小循环的冷却液是不通过散热器的，而大循环的冷却液是通过散热器的（图2-18-2和图2-18-3）。

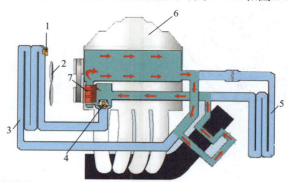

图2-18-2 Short circulation of cooling system 冷却系统小循环

1. thermo-switch 热敏开关
2. cooling fan 冷却风扇
3. radiator 散热器
4. thermostat 节温器
5. heater exchanger 暖风装置热交换器
6. engine 发动机
7. water pump 水泵

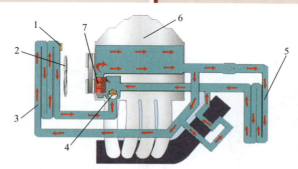

图2-18-3 Full circulation of cooling system 冷却系统大循环

1. thermo-switch 热敏开关
2. cooling fan 冷却风扇
3. radiator 散热器
4. thermostat 节温器
5. heater exchanger 暖风装置热交换器
6. engine 发动机
7. water pump 水泵

PART2 Engine 发动机

18.3 Thermostat 节温器

当冷却液温度低于规定值时，节温器感温体内的石蜡呈固态，节温器阀在弹簧的作用下关闭发动机与散热器间的通道，进行小循环。当冷却液温度达到规定值后，石蜡开始熔化逐渐变成液体，体积随之增大并压迫橡胶管使其收缩，在橡胶管收缩的同时对推杆作用以向上的推力。由于推杆上端固定，推杆对橡胶管和感温体产生向下的反推力使阀门开启，这时冷却液经由散热器和节温器阀，再经水泵流回发动机，进行大循环（图2-18-4）。

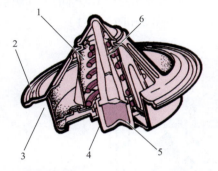

1. spring 弹簧
2. upper housing 上壳体
3. lower housing 下壳体
4. copper cup 铜杯
5. wax pellet 石蜡体
6. piston 活塞

图2-18-4 A cross section of a typical wax-actuated thermostat 蜡式节温器剖面图

18.4 Radiator 散热器

发动机水冷系统中的散热器由进水室、出水室及散热器芯三部分构成。冷却液在散热器芯内流动，空气在散热器芯外通过。热的冷却液由于向空气散热而变冷，冷空气则因为吸收冷却液散出的热量而升温，所以散热器是一个热交换器（图2-18-5）。

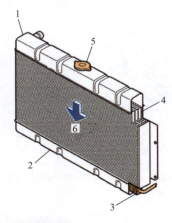

1. top tank 上水室
2. bottom tank 下水室
3. transmission oil cooler 变速器油冷器
4. tubes 冷却管
5. radiator cap 散热器盖
6. coolant flow 冷却液流动方向

图2-18-5 Radiator 散热器

18.5 Radiator cap 散热器盖

散热器盖的作用是密封水冷系统并调节系统的工作压力。当发动机工作时,冷却液的温度逐渐升高。由于冷却液容积膨胀使冷却系统内的压力增高,当压力超过预定值时,压力阀开启,一部分冷却液经溢流管流入补偿水桶,以防止冷却液胀裂散热器。当发动机停机后,冷却液的温度下降,冷却系统内的压力也随之降低。当压力降到大气压力以下出现真空时,真空阀开启,补偿水桶内的冷却液部分地流回散热器,可以避免散热器被大气压力压坏(图2-18-6)。

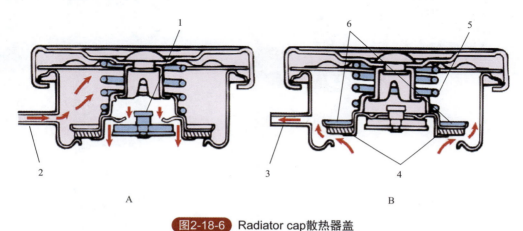

图2-18-6 Radiator cap 散热器盖

A. vacuum valve operation 真空阀原理
B. pressure valve operation 压力阀原理
1. vacuum valve 真空阀
2. overflow tube coolant flow from recovery tank 溢流管冷却液,来自溢流(膨胀)箱
3. overflow tube coolant flow to recovery tank 溢流管冷却液,到溢流(膨胀)箱
4. seal gasket 密封垫
5. pressure spring 压力阀弹簧
6. pressure valve 压力阀

PART 3

Chassis 底盘

- Chapter 1　Chassis introduction 底盘概述
- Chapter 2　Drive train 传动系统
- Chapter 3　Clutch 离合器
- Chapter 4　Manual transmission 手动变速器
- Chapter 5　Automatic transmission 自动变速器
- Chapter 6　Continuously variable transmission 无级变速器
- Chapter 7　Dual clutch transmission 双离合器变速器
- Chapter 8　Propeller shaft 传动轴
- Chapter 9　Four wheel drive 四轮驱动
- Chapter 10　Differential 差速器
- Chapter 11　Suspension system 悬架系统
- Chapter 12　Tire 轮胎
- Chapter 13　Steering system 转向系统
- Chapter 14　Brake system 制动系统

Chassis introduction 底盘概述

　　底盘由传动系统、行驶系统、转向系统和制动系统四部分组成,用以支撑、安装汽车发动机及其各部件的总成,形成汽车的整体造型,并接受发动机的动力,使汽车产生运动,保证正常行驶(图3-1-1)。

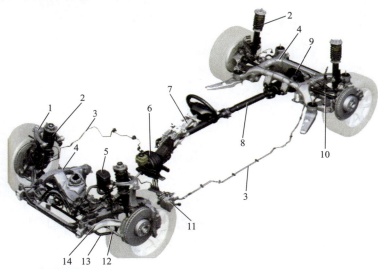

图3-1-1　A typical passenger car chassis 典型乘用车底盘

1. suspension upper fork arm 悬架上叉臂
2. shock absorber and spring 减振器和减振器弹簧
3. brake fluid pipe 制动液管
4. subframe 副车架
5. power-assisted steering fluid reservoir 转向助力储液罐
6. vacuum booster 真空助力器
7. steering column 转向柱
8. propeller shaft 传动轴
9. rear differential 后差速器
10. half shaft 半轴
11. brake master cylinder 制动主缸
12. steering linkages 转向拉杆
13. stabilizer bar 稳定杆
14. suspension link 悬架连杆

PART3 Chassis 底盘

典型货车底盘如图3-1-2所示。

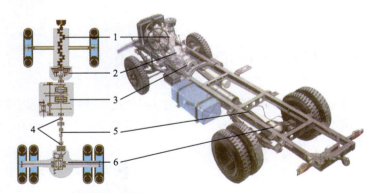

图3-1-2　A typical truck chassis 典型货车底盘

1. engine crankshaft 发动机曲轴
2. clutch 离合器
3. transmission 变速器
4. universal joints 万向节
5. propeller shaft 传动轴
6. driving axle 驱动桥

1.1 Drive line 传动系统

汽车传动系统是指从发动机到驱动车轮之间所有动力传递装置的总称，其功用是将发动机的动力传给驱动车轮（图3-1-3）。

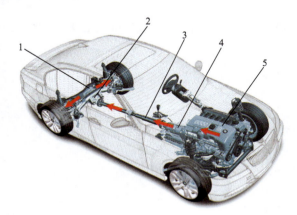

图3-1-3　Automotive power flow process 汽车动力传递流程

1. rear driving axle 后驱动桥
2. rear differential 后差速器
3. propeller shaft 传动轴
4. transmission 变速器
5. engine 发动机

1.2 Running gear 行驶系统

汽车行驶系统一般由车架、悬架、车桥和车轮等组成。汽车行驶系统的作用是将汽车构成一个整体，支撑汽车的总质量；将传动系统传来的转矩转化为汽车行驶的驱动力；承受并传递路面对车轮的各种反力及力矩；减振缓冲，保证汽车平顺行驶；与转向系统配合，正确控制汽车的行驶方向（图3-1-4）。

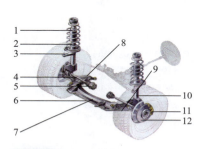

图3-1-4　Automotive running gear 汽车行驶系统

1. coil spring 螺旋弹簧
2. telescopic shock absorber 筒式减振器
3. steering arm 转向臂
4. propeller shaft 传动轴
5. constant velocity universal joint 等速万向节
6. transverse stabilizer bar 横向稳定杆
7. subframe 副车架
8. fork swing arm 叉形摆臂
9. control arm 摇臂
10. front suspension part 前悬架部件
11. brake caliper 制动钳
12. brake disc 制动盘

1.3 Steering system 转向系统

转向系统的功用是保证汽车能够按照驾驶员选定的方向行驶，主要由转向操纵机构、转向器、转向传动机构组成。现在的汽车普遍采用动力转向装置（图3-1-5）。

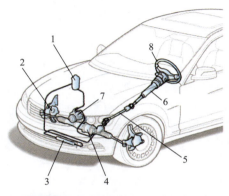

图3-1-5　Steering system 转向系统

1. power steering fluid reservoir 动力转向储液罐
2. steering knuckle 转向节
3. fluid cooler 转向液冷却器
4. rack&pinion steering gear 齿轮齿条式转向器
5. intermediate shaft 中间轴
6. steering column 转向柱
7. power steering pump 动力转向泵
8. steering wheel 方向盘

PART 3 Chassis 底盘

1.4 Braking system 制动系统

制动系统的功用是使汽车减速、停车并能保证可靠地驻停。汽车制动系统一般包括行车制动系统和驻车制动系统等两套相互独立的制动系统，每套制动系统都包括制动器和制动传动机构（图3-1-6）。现在汽车的行车制动系统一般都装配有制动防抱死系统（ABS）。

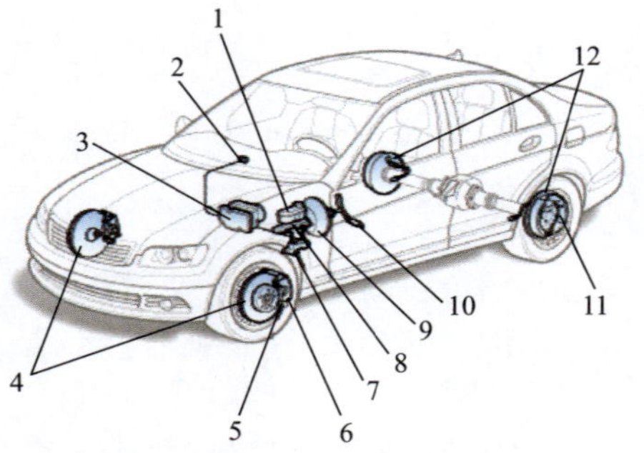

1. brake fluid reservoir 制动液存储罐
2. brake warning light 制动报警灯
3. ABS pump ABS 泵
4. disc brakes 盘式制动
5. brake pad 制动踏板
6. brake caliper 制动钳
7. combination valve 组合阀
8. master cylinder 主缸
9. brake booster 制动增压器
10. brake pedal 制动踏板
11. brake shoe 制动蹄
12. drum brakes 鼓式制动

图3-1-6 Braking system 制动系统

Chapter 2

Drive train 传动系统

2.1 Overview 概述

发动机输出的动力，先经过离合器，由变速器变矩和变速后，经传动轴把动力传递到主减速器上，最后通过差速器和半轴把动力传递到驱动轮上（图3-2-1）。

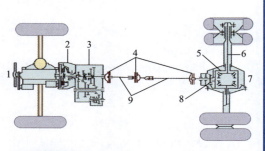

1. front 前端
2. clutch 离合器
3. transmission 变速器
4. universal joint 万向节
5. differential 差速器
6. half shaft 半轴
7. rear 后端
8. final reduction 主减速器
9. propeller shaft 传动轴

图3-2-1 Truck drive train 货车传动系统

2.2 Clutch 离合器

离合器是汽车传动系统中直接与发动机相连接的部件，它负责动力与传动系统之间的切断和结合，所以能够保证汽车起步时平稳起步，也能保证换挡时的平顺，也防止了传动系统过载（图3-2-2）。

1. pilot bearing 导向轴承
2. release bearing 分离轴承
3. input shaft 输入轴
4. release fork 分离叉
5. pressure plate 压盘
6. clutch disk 离合器从动盘
7. flywheel 飞轮
8. crankshaft 曲轴

图3-2-2 Clutch 离合器

2.3 Transmission 变速器

汽车变速器是一套用来协调发动机的转速和车轮的实际行驶速度的变速装置，用于发挥发动机的最佳性能。变速器可以在汽车行驶过程中，在发动机和车轮之间产生不同的变速比，通过换挡可以使发动机在其最佳的动力性能状态下工作（图3-2-3）。

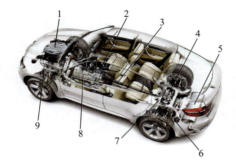

1. engine 发动机
2. transmission lever 变速杆
3. propeller shaft 传动轴
4. differential 差速器
5. silencer 消声器
6. rear suspension 后悬挂
7. rear driving axle 后驱动桥
8. transmission 变速器
9. front suspension 前悬挂

图3-2-3 Transmission location diagram 变速器位置示意图

2.3.1 Manual transmission（MT）手动变速器

手动变速器又称机械式变速器，即必须用手拨动变速杆才能改变变速器内的齿轮啮合位置，改变传动比，从而达到变速的目的（图3-2-4）。

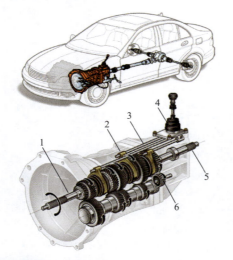

1. input shaft 输入轴
2. shift fork 换挡拨叉
3. shift rod 换挡杆
4. gear shift 换挡机构
5. output shaft 输出轴
6. idler gear 空转轮

图3-2-4　Manual transmission 手动变速器

2.3.2 Automatic transmission（AT）自动变速器

自动变速器，亦称自动变速箱，台湾称自排变速箱，香港称自动波，通常来说是一种可以在车辆行驶过程中自动改变齿轮传动比的汽车变速器，从而使驾驶员不必手动换挡（图3-2-5）。

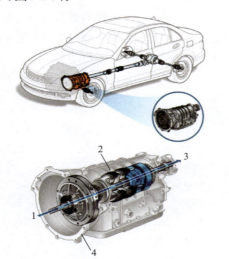

1. power from engine 来自发动机的动力
2. automatic shifting devices 自动换挡装置
3. power to differential 到差速器的动力
4. transmission housing 变速器壳

图3-2-5　Automatic transmission 自动变速器

2.4 Propeller shaft and universal joints 传动轴和万向节

传动轴是由轴管、伸缩套和万向节组成。伸缩套能自动调节变速器与驱动桥之间距离的变化。万向节是保证变速器输出轴与驱动桥输入轴两轴线夹角的变化，并实现两轴的等角速传动（图3-2-6）。

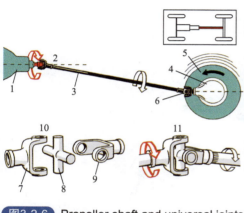

图3-2-6 Propeller shaft and universal joints 传动轴和万向节

1. transmission 变速器
2. forward universal joint 前万向节
3. propeller shaft 传动轴
4. differential 差速器
5. rear wheel 后轮
6. rear universal joint 后万向节
7. driving yoke 主动叉
8. cross 十字轴
9. driven yoke 从动叉
10. parts of universal joints 万向节部件
11. universal joint assembled 装配在一起的万向节

2.5 Final reduction 主减速器

主减速器在汽车传动系统中将动力传给差速器，并实现降速增矩作用，从而得到较大的驱动力。对发动机纵置的汽车来说，主减速器还利用锥齿轮传动以改变动力方向（图3-2-7）。

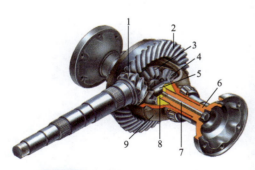

图3-2-7 Final reduction 主减速器

1. final reduction driving bevel gear 主减速器主动锥齿轮
2. final reduction driven bevel gear 主减速器从动锥齿轮
3. half shaft gear 半轴齿轮
4. planetary pinion 行星齿轮
5. planetary pinion shaft 行星齿轮轴
6. half shaft and flange 半轴及凸缘
7. half shaft bolt 半轴螺栓
8. lock nut 防转螺母
9. differential case 差速器壳

2.6 Differential and half shaft 差速器与半轴

　　汽车差速器的作用就是在向两边半轴传递动力的同时，允许两边半轴以不同的转速旋转，满足两边车轮尽可能以纯滚动的形式做不等距行驶，减少轮胎与地面的摩擦。半轴将差速器的动力传给驱动车轮（图3-2-8）。差速器由行星齿轮、行星轮架（差速器壳）、半轴齿轮等零件组成。

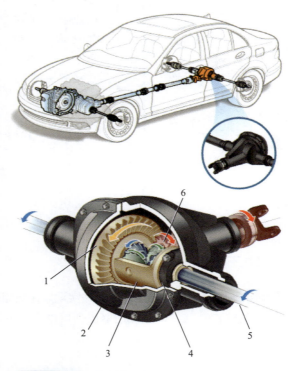

图3-2-8　Differential and half shaft 差速器与半轴

1. ring gear 齿圈
2. differential cover 差速器盖
3. differential housing 差速器壳
4. cap 端盖
5. drive shaft 半轴
6. drive pinion 主动小齿轮

Chapter 3
Clutch 离合器

3.1 Overview 概述

离合器位于发动机与变速器之间的飞轮壳内，被固定在飞轮的后平面上，另一端连接变速器的输入轴。离合器相当于一个动力开关，可以传递或切断发动机向变速器输入的动力，主要是为了使汽车平稳起步，适时中断到传动系统的动力以配合换挡，还可以防止传动系统过载（图3-3-1）。

图3-3-1　Clutch 离合器

1. flywheel ring gear 飞轮齿圈
2. flywheel 飞轮
3. pressure plate 压盘
4. diaphragm spring 膜片弹簧
5. friction disc 摩擦片
6. torsional spring 减振弹簧

PART3 Chassis 底盘

3.2 Clutch components 离合器组成

离合器主要由四部分组成，具体如下。

（1）主动部分：飞轮、离合器盖、离合器主动盘（压盘）。

（2）从动部分：离合器从动盘（俗称离合器片）。

（3）压紧机构：膜片弹簧或螺旋弹簧。

（4）操纵机构：离合器踏板、离合器总泵、离合器分泵、离合器分离拨叉、分离轴承、轴承座等组成（图3-3-2）。

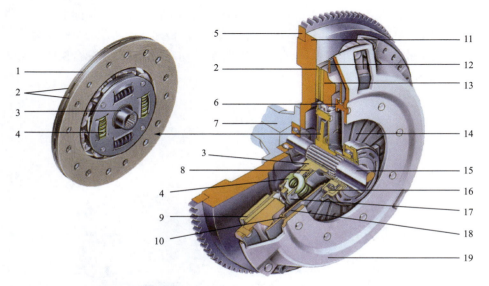

图3-3-2　Clutch components 离合器组成

1. cushion plate 波形片
2. friction plate 摩擦片
3. spine hub 花键轴套
4. damper spring 减振弹簧
5. flywheel ring gear 飞轮齿圈
6. rivet 限位铆钉
7. crankshaft 曲轴
8. damping plate 阻尼片
9. clutch driven disc 离合器从动盘
10. clutch cover 离合器盖
11. flywheel 飞轮
12. steel belt 传动钢带
13. pressure plate 压盘
14. disc spring 碟形（膜片）弹簧
15. transmission input shaft 变速器输入轴
16. clutch release bearing 离合器分离轴承
17. driven wheel cover 从动盘盖板
18. clutch diaphragm spring 离合器膜片弹簧
19. support ring 支撑环

离合器从动盘也可以叫后压盘，就是从后面给离合器摩擦片一个力，让摩擦片轻微前移和主动盘（前压盘、飞轮）压紧，以传递动力。离合器控制的就是从动盘，通过其前后移动来压紧和放开离合器摩擦片，达到动力的切断和接合（图3-3-3）。

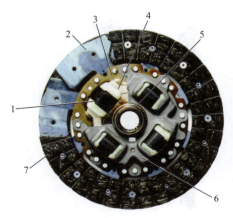

1. torsion damper 扭振器
2. cushion plate 缓冲盘
3. disc plate 从动盘
4. hub flange 离合器毂法兰盘
5. hub 离合器毂
6. cover plate 盖板
7. facing 衬面

图3-3-3 Clutch driven disc 离合器从动盘

3.3 Clutch operation 离合器原理

离合器盖通过螺钉固定在飞轮的后端面上，离合器内的摩擦片在弹簧的作用力下被压盘压紧在飞轮面上，而摩擦片是与变速器的输入轴相连。通过飞轮及压盘与从动盘接触面的摩擦作用，将发动机发出的转矩传递给变速器（图3-3-4）。

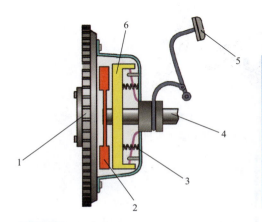

1. flywheel 飞轮
2. friction disc 摩擦盘
3. compression spring 压紧弹簧
4. transmission input shaft 变速器输入轴
5. clutch pedal 离合器踏板
6. pressure plate 压盘

图3-3-4 Friction type clutch 摩擦式离合器

PART3 Chassis 底盘

如图3-3-5所示，踩下离合器前，摩擦盘（红色）在压盘（黄色）的作用下，迫使摩擦盘与飞轮一起转动，传递动力。踩下离合器后，在分离机构的作用下，摩擦盘与飞轮分离，中断传递动力。

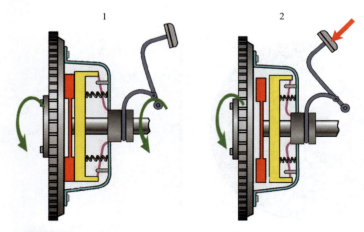

图3-3-5 Friction type clutch principle 摩擦式离合器工作原理

1. before depressed 踩离合器前
2. after depressed 踩离合器后

3.4 Clutch control system 离合器操纵机构

离合器操纵机构始于驾驶室内的离合器踏板，终于离合器内的分离轴承，作用是将踏板上的人力变为推动分离套筒的推力（图3-3-6）。

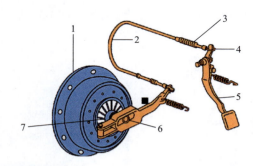

图3-3-6 Clutch control system 离合器操纵机构

1. clutch cover 离合器壳
2. clutch release cable 离合器分离钢索
3. cable adjustment location 离合器调整位置
4. clutch release lever 离合器分离杠杆
5. clutch pedal 离合器踏板
6. clutch fork 离合器叉
7. throwout（release）bearing 离合器止推（分离）轴承

Chapter 4
Manual transmission 手动变速器

4.1 Overview 概述

手动变速器就是必须用手拨动变速器杆,才能改变传动比的变速器。手动变速器主要由壳体、传动组件(输入输出轴、齿轮、同步器等)、操纵组件(换挡拉杆、拨叉等)(图3-4-1)。

图3-4-1 Manual transmission configuration 手动变速器构造

1. shifting linkage 换挡拉杆
2. driving gear 主动齿轮
3. driving shaft 主动轴
4. driven shaft 从动轴
5. driven gear 从动齿轮
6. synchronizer 同步器
7. shifting york 换挡拨叉
8. transmission case 变速器壳体

PART3 Chassis 底盘

4.2 Transmission principle 变速器原理

变速器为什么可以调整发动机输出的转矩和转速呢？其实这里蕴含了齿轮和杠杆的原理。变速器内有多个不同的齿轮，通过不同大小的齿轮组合在一起，就能实现对发动机转矩和转速的调整。用低转矩可以换来高转速，用低转速则可以换来高转矩（图3-4-2）。

变速器的作用主要表现在三方面：第一，改变传动比，扩大驱动轮的转矩和转速的变化范围；第二，在发动机转向不变的情况下，实现汽车倒退行驶；第三，利用空挡，可以中断发动机动力传递，使得发动机可以启动、怠速。

图3-4-2 Transmission principle 变速器原理

1. speed：A > B 转速：A > B
drive force: A < B 驱动力：A < B

2. speed：A < B 转速：A < B
drive force: A > B 驱动力：A > B

4.3 Manual transmission operation 手动变速器原理

手动变速器的工作原理，就是通过拨动变速杆，切换中间轴上的主动齿轮，通过大小不同的齿轮组合与动力输出轴结合，从而改变驱动轮的转矩和转速。

发动机的动力输入轴是通过一根中间轴，间接与动力输出轴连接的。如图3-4-3所示，中间轴的两个齿轮（红色）与动力输出轴上的两个齿轮（蓝色）是随着发动机输出一起转动的。但是如果没有同步器（紫色）的接合，两个齿轮（蓝色）只能在动力输出轴上空转（即不会带动输出轴转动）。图中同步器位于中间状态，相当于变速器挂了空挡。

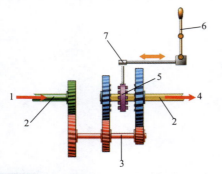

1. engine 发动机
2. output shaft 动力输出轴
3. countershaft 中间轴
4. differential 差速器
5. synchronizer 同步器
6. shifting lever 变速杆
7. shifting fork 换挡叉

图3-4-3 Simple transmission configuration
简单变速器结构

4.4 5 speed manual transmission 5挡手动变速器

4.4.1 5 speed manual transmission operation 5挡手动变速器原理（图3-4-4）

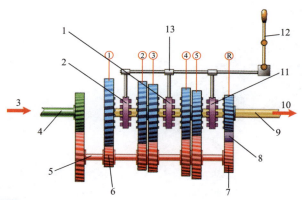

图3-4-4 5 speed manual transmission operation 5挡手动变速器原理

1. 3rd，4th gear synchronizer 3、4挡同步器
2. 1st，2nd gear synchronizer 1、2挡同步器
3. engine power 发动机动力
4. power input 动力输入轴
5. countershaft 主动轴
6. 1st driving gear 1挡主动齿轮
7. reverse driving gear 倒挡主动齿轮
8. reverse immediate gear 倒挡中间齿轮
9. power output shaft 动力输出轴
10. to differential 至差速器
11. 5th，reverse gear synchronizer 5挡、倒挡同步器
12. shift lever 换挡杆
13. shift fork 换挡叉

5挡手动变速器剖面图显示出变速器的主要部件（图3-4-5）。

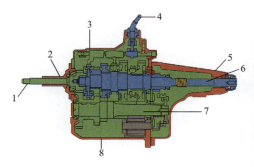

图3-4-5 Cross section of a five-speed manual transmission 5挡手动变速器剖面图

1. input shaft 输入轴
2. front bearing retainer 前轴承盖
3. shift cover assembly 换挡盖总成
4. shift lever 换挡杆
5. extension housing 加长壳体
6. output shaft 输出轴
7. countershaft 中间轴
8. transmission case 变速器壳

5挡手动变速器组成如图3-4-6所示。

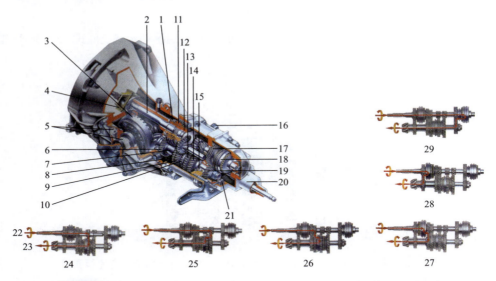

图3-4-6　5 speed manual transmission components 5挡手动变速器组成

1. driving shaft 4th gear 主动轴4挡齿轮
2. driving shaft with 1st/2nd gear 主动轴（含1/2挡齿轮）
3. differential assembly with driven bevel gear 差速器组件（带从动锥齿轮）
4. clutch release fork 离合器分离板
5. speedometer drive gear set 车速里程表传动齿轮组
6. driven shaft 4th gear 从动轴4挡齿轮
7. driven shaft with driving bevel gear 从动轴（带主动锥齿轮）
8. driven shaft 3rd gear 从动轴3挡齿轮
9. driven shaft 2nd gear 从动轴2挡齿轮
10. 1st/2nd gear synchronizer 1/2挡同步器
11. 2nd/3rd gear synchronizer 2/3挡同步器
12. driving shaft 3rd gear 主动轴3挡齿轮
13. reverse gears 倒挡齿轮组
14. driven shaft 1st gear 从动轴1挡齿轮
15. double row tapered roller bearings 双列圆锥滚子轴承
16. reverse gear fork alignment block 倒挡拨叉定位挡
17. driving shaft 5th gear 主动轴5挡齿轮
18. 5th gear synchronizer 5挡同步器
19. driven shaft 5th gear 从动轴5挡齿轮
20. rear cover assembly 后盖总成
21. shaped magnets 异形磁铁
22. input 输入
23. output 输出
24. reverse 倒挡
25. 1st gear 1挡
26. 2nd gear 2挡
27. 3rd gear 3挡
28. 4th gear 4挡
29. 5th gear 5挡

4.4.2 Shift mechanism 换挡机构

换挡机构不仅增强驾驶员换挡感觉，而且可以防止同时挂入两个挡位（图3-4-7）。

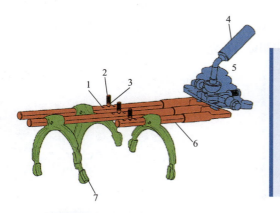

1. notch 卡槽
2. spring 弹簧
3. detent ball 锁定球
4. shift lever 换挡杆
5. ball socket 球座
6. shift fork shaft 换挡拨叉轴
7. shift fork 换挡拨叉

图3-4-7　Shift mechanism 换挡机构

4.5 Synchronizer 同步器

变速器在进行换挡操作时，尤其是从高挡向低挡的换挡很容易产生轮齿或花键齿间的冲击。为了避免齿间冲击，在换挡装置中都设置同步器。同步器有常压式和惯性式两种，目前大部分同步式变速器上采用的是惯性同步器，它主要由接合套、同步锁环等组成，主要是依靠摩擦作用实现同步（图3-4-8）。

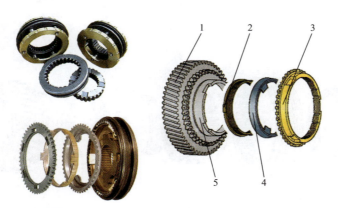

图3-4-8　Synchronizer configuration 同步器结构

1. speed gear 换挡齿轮
2. inner synchronizer ring 内同步环
3. outer synchronizer ring 外同步环
4. outer cone 外锥环
5. synchronizer inner cone 同步器内锥面

· 109 ·

4.5.1 Synchronizer working principle 同步器工作原理

当同步锁环内锥面与待接合齿轮齿圈外锥面接触后，在摩擦力矩的作用下齿轮转速迅速降低（或升高）到与同步锁环转速相等，两者同步旋转，齿轮相对于同步锁环的转速为零，因而惯性力矩也同时消失，这时在作用力的推动下，接合套不受阻碍地与同步锁环齿圈接合，并进一步与待接合齿轮的齿圈接合而完成换挡过程（图3-4-9）。

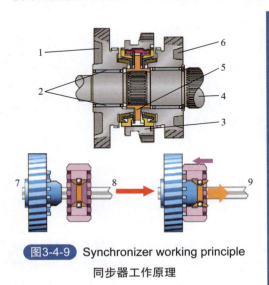

图3-4-9 Synchronizer working principle 同步器工作原理

1. 1st gear 1挡换挡齿轮
2. needle bearing 滚针轴承
3. sliding sleeve 滑套
4. power output 动力输出轴
5. 1st，2nd gear synchronizer 1、2挡同步器
6. 2nd gear 2挡换挡齿轮
7. the shifting gear is idling on the output shaft before mesh 接合前，换挡齿轮在输出轴上空转
8. mesh 接合
9. the power transmits to the output shaft through the synchronizer after mesh 接合后，动力通过同步器把动力传递到输出轴上

4.5.2 Synchronizer components 同步器部件（图3-4-10）

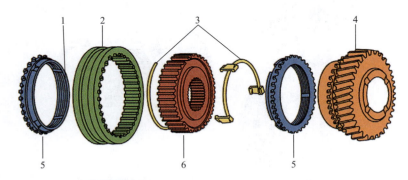

图3-4-10 Synchronizer components 同步器部件

1. ring grooves 环槽
2. synchronizer sleeve 同步器衬套
3. key springs 卡簧
4. speed gear 换挡齿轮
5. synchronizer ring 同步器闭锁环
6. clutch hub 离合器毂

Chapter 5
Automatic transmission 自动变速器

5.1 Overview 概述

　　汽车自动变速器常见的有四种形式，分别是液力自动变速器（hydraulic automatic transmissions，HAT）、无级变速器（continuously variable transmission，CVT）、电控机械式自动变速器（automated mechanical transmission，AMT）、双离合自动变速器（dual clutch transmission，DCT）。

　　轿车普遍使用的是液力自动变速器，本章中的自动变速器指的也是液力自动变速器（HAT）。自动变速器主要由液力变矩器、行星齿轮和液压操纵系统组成，通过液力传递和齿轮组合的方式来达到变速变矩（图3-5-1）。

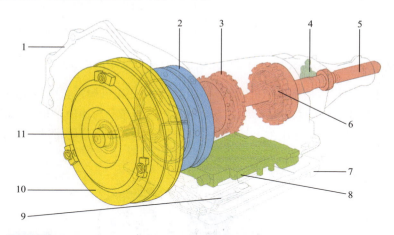

图3-5-1 Automatic transmission main components 自动变速器主要部件

1. case 壳体
2. oil pump 油泵
3. clutch plate 离合器片
4. speed sensor 速度传感器
5. output shaft 输出轴
6. planetary gear transmission 行星齿轮变速器
7. bottom case 底壳
8. electronic hydraulic control system 电子液压控制系统
9. filter 滤清器
10. torque converter 变矩器
11. input shaft 输入轴

PART3 Chassis 底盘

5.2 Hydraulic torque converter 液力变矩器

液力变矩器一般是由泵轮、导轮、涡轮以及锁止离合器组成（图3-5-2）。动力传递路径：壳体→泵轮→涡轮→变速器。

图3-5-2 Hydraulic torque converter configuration 液力变矩器的结构

1. power to transmission 传递到变速器的动力
2. impeller 泵轮
3. stator 定叶轮（子）
4. turbine 涡轮
5. lock-up clutch 锁止离合器
6. case 壳体
7. the power from engine 来自发动机的动力
8. drive interface 驱动接口

5.2.1 Hydraulic torque converter operation 液力变矩器的工作原理

液力变矩器的作用是将发动机的动力输出传递到变速机构，它里面充满了传动油，当与动力输入轴相连接的泵轮转动时，它会通过传动油带动与输出轴相连的涡轮一起转动，从而将发动机动力传递出去，其原理就像一把插电的风扇能够带动一把不插电的风扇的叶片转动一样（图3-5-3）。

图3-5-3 Hydraulic torque converter operation 液力变矩器的工作原理

1. the engine drives the impeller wheel rotation 发动机带动泵轮旋转
2. the stator guides the AT fluid pumped by the impeller 定子对泵轮泵过来的变速器油起导向作用
3. the turbine is pushed by the AT fluid from the pump 涡轮被泵轮泵过来的变速器油推动

5.2.2 Hydraulic torque converter components 液力变矩器组成部件（图3-5-4）

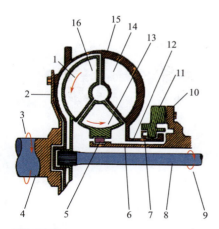

图3-5-4 Hydraulic torque converter components 液力变矩器组成部件

1. direction of oil flow 液流方向
2. flex plate 柔性盘
3. engine rotation 发动机旋转
4. engine crankshaft 发动机曲轴
5. stator one-way overrunning clutch 定子单向超越离合器
6. stator support（reaction shaft）定子支撑轴（反作用轴）
7. front seal 前油封
8. transmission input shaft 变速器输入轴
9. input shaft rotation 输入轴旋转
10. stator support assembly 定子支撑总成
11. oil pump 油泵
12. converter hub 变矩器毂
13. stator 定子
14. impeller 泵轮
15. torque converter housing 变矩器壳体
16. turbine 涡轮

5.3 Planetary gear drive 行星齿轮传动

行星齿轮组包括行星架、齿圈以及太阳轮，当这三个部件中的一个被固定后，动力便会在其他两个部件之间传递（图3-5-5）。

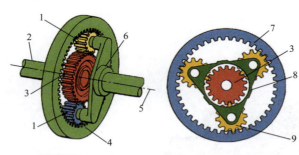

图3-5-5 Planetary gear drive 行星齿轮传动

1. planet pinion gear 行星齿轮
2. input shaft 输入轴
3. sun gear 太阳轮
4. internal ring gear 内齿圈
5. power flow axis 动力输出轴
6. planet carrier assembly 行星架总成
7. ring gear（annulus or internal gear）齿圈（内环齿或内齿）
8. planet carrier 行星架
9. planet pinion 行星齿轮

行星齿轮变速器原理如图3-5-6所示。

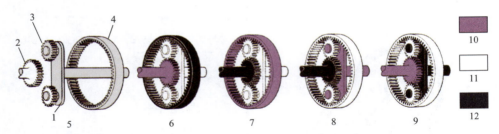

图3-5-6 Planetary gear transmission operation 行星齿轮变速器原理

1. planet carrier 行星架
2. sun gear 太阳轮
3. pinions or planet gears 小齿轮，即行星轮
4. ring gear 齿圈
5. parts unassembled 分解件
6. low speed 低速
7. second speed 中速
8. high speed and overdrive 高速和超速
9. reverse 倒挡
10. driving member 主动件
11. driven member 从动件
12. stationary member 固定件

5.4 AT shift mechanism 自动变速器换挡执行机构

换挡执行机构主要是用来改变行星齿轮中的主动元件或限制某个元件的运动，改变动力传递的方向和速比，主要由离合器、制动器和单向离合器等组成。

离合器的作用是把动力传给行星齿轮机构的某个元件使之成为主动件（图3-5-7）。

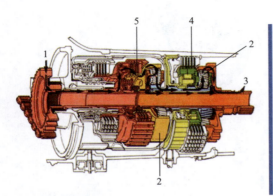

图3-5-7 Clutch operation 离合器原理

1. power from hydraulic torque converter 由液力变矩器传来的动力
2. planetary gear set 行星齿轮组
3. power output 输出动力
4. one-way clutch mesh 单向离合器接合
5. forward clutch mesh 前进离合器接合

5.4.1　Multi-plate clutch 多片离合器

离合器的摩擦片是在变速器油中工作，且用油压推动活塞进行工作。如图3-5-8所示，压力油进入离合器壳体，对离合器活塞施加作用力。离合器活塞迫使钢片和摩擦片挤压在一起，完成换挡。

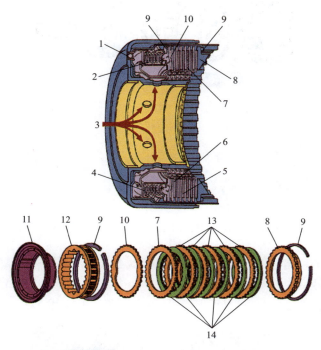

图3-5-8　Multi-plate clutch 多片离合器

1. retainer and ball assembly 保持架和球总成
2. release spring and apply ring 分离弹簧和工作环
3. clutch apply fluid 离合器工作液
4. piston with seal 带密封的活塞
5. plate assembly 钢片总成
6. clutch apply reaction plate（tapered）离合器工作反作用片（锥形）
7. reaction plate 反作用片
8. backing plate 挡板
9. snap ring 卡环
10. wave plate 波形片
11. clutch piston 离合器活塞
12. spring assembly 弹簧总成
13. steel plates 钢片
14. friction plates 摩擦片

PART3 Chassis 底盘

5.4.2 Brake band 制动带

制动器的作用是将行星齿轮机构中的某个元件抱住，使之不动（图3-5-9）。

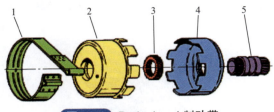

图3-5-9 Brake band 制动带

1. intermediate band 中间制动带
2. high-reverse clutch drum 高–倒挡离合器毂
3. front sun gear 前太阳轮
4. input shell 输入壳体
5. rear sun gear 后太阳轮

5.5 Automatic transmission shift control 自动变速器换挡控制

自动变速器的换挡控制方式如图3-5-10所示。变速器控制电脑通过电信号控制电磁阀的动作，从而改变变速器油在阀体油道的走向。当作用在多片式离合片上的油压达到制动压力时，多片式离合片接合从而促使相应的行星齿轮组输出动力。

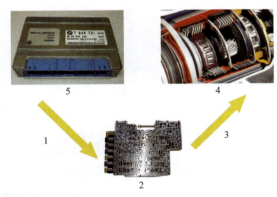

图3-5-10 Transmission control computer 变速器控制电脑

1. electronic signal to control solenoids 控制电磁阀的电信号
2. solenoids and valve body oil passages 电磁阀及阀体油道
3. hydraulic pressure to control clutches 控制离合器的液压力
4. multi-plate clutch 多片式离合器
5. transmission control computer 变速器控制电脑

5.5.1 Valve body 阀体

液压自动操纵系统通常由供油、手动选挡、参数调节、换挡时刻控制、换挡品质控制等部分组成。供油部分根据节气门开度和选挡杆位置的变化，将油泵输出油压调节至规定值，形成稳定的工作液压。

在液控液动自动变速器中，参数调节部分主要有节气门压力调节阀（简称节气门阀）和速控调压阀（又称调速器）。节气门压力调节阀使输出液压的大小能够反映节气门开度；速控调压阀使输出液压的大小能够反映车速的大小。换挡时刻控制部分用于转换通向各换挡执行机构（离合器和制动器）的油路，从而实现换挡控制。锁定信号阀受电磁阀的控制，使液力变矩器内的锁止离合器适时地接合与分离。

自动变速器采用阀体内的各种电子阀来控制管路压力，开启和关闭阀体内的油道，实现换挡（图3-5-11）。

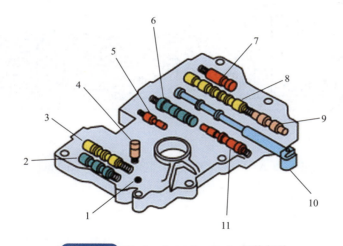

图3-5-11　Parts of a valve body 阀体部件

1. cooler check valve 油冷器单向阀
2. lock-up control valve 锁止控制阀
3. lock-up shift valve 锁止换挡阀
4. torque converter check valve 变矩器单向阀
5. shift valve E 换挡阀E
6. shift valve D 换挡阀D
7. modulator valve 调节阀
8. shift valve C 换挡阀C
9. reverse CPC valve 倒挡CPC（clutch pressure control，离合器压力控制）阀
10. manual valve 手动阀
11. servo control valve 伺服控制阀

5.5.2 Power flow 动力流程

通用4L60-E变速器在1挡时力矩（动力）流程如图3-5-12所示。

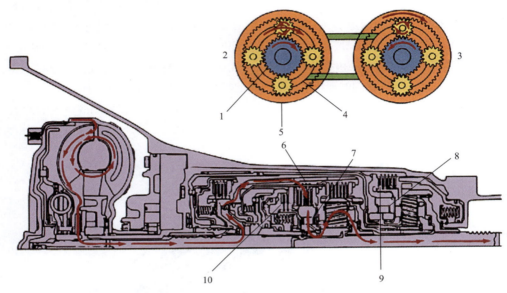

图3-5-12　A GM 4L60-E torque（power）flow in first gear
通用4L60-E变速器1挡力矩（动力）流程

1. input 输入
2. input gearset 输入齿轮组
3. reaction gearset 反作用齿轮组
4. output 输出
5. held 结合
6. forward clutch applied 施加前进挡离合器
7. forward sprag clutch holding on acceleration 加速时前进挡超越离合器结合
8. low roller clutch holding on acceleration 加速时低挡滚子离合器结合
9. low-reverse clutch applied（manual low）施加低倒挡离合器（手动低挡）
10. overrun clutch applied（manual first）施加超越离合器（手动1挡）

Chapter 6
Continuously variable transmission 无级变速器

6.1 Overview 概述

CVT（continuously variable transmission），直接翻译就是连续可变传动，也就是我们常说的无级变速器，顾名思义就是没有明确具体的挡位，操作上类似自动变速器，但是速比的变化却不同于自动变速器的跳挡过程，而是连续的，因此动力传输持续而顺畅，如图3-6-1所示。

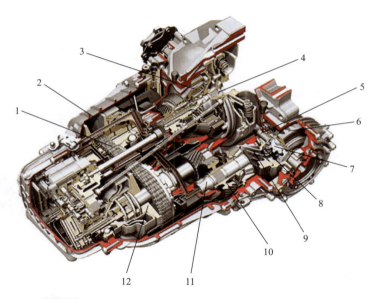

图3-6-1 Continuously variable transmission 无级变速器

1. metal belt 金属带
2. driving pulley 主动滑轮
3. starter clutch 启动离合器
4. power input shaft 动力输入轴
5. half shaft 半轴
6. power output driven gear 动力输出从动齿轮
7. differential pinion 差速器行星齿轮
8. differential side gear 差速器侧齿轮
9. power output driving gear 动力输出主动齿轮
10. immediate driven gear 中间传动从动齿轮
11. driven shaft 从动轴
12. driven pulley 从动滑轮

6.2 CVT operation CVT原理

CVT传动系统里，传统的齿轮被一对滑轮和一只钢制带所取代，每个滑轮其实是由两个锥形盘组成的V形结构，发动机轴连接小滑轮，透过钢制皮带带动大滑轮。CVT的传动滑轮构造比较奇怪，分成活动的左右两半，可以相对接近或分离。锥形盘可在液压的推力作用下收紧或张开，挤压钢片链条以此来调节V形槽的宽度。当锥形盘向内侧移动收紧时，钢片链条在锥盘的挤压下向圆心以外的方向（离心方向）运动，相反会向圆心以内运动。这样，钢片链条带动的圆盘直径增大，传动比也就发生了变化（图3-6-2）。

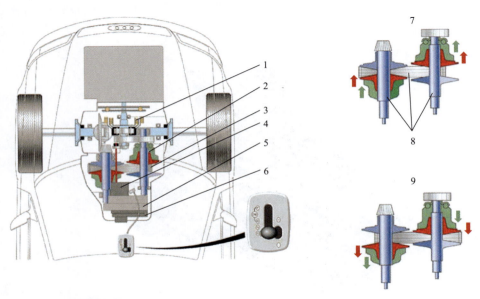

图3-6-2 CVT transmission schematic CVT变速器系统简图

1. starter clutch 启动离合器
2. pulley mechanism 滑轮机构
3. metal belt 金属带
4. hydraulic pump 液压油泵
5. hydraulic control 液压控制
6. electronic control 电子控制
7. push outward（down shift）向外推动（低挡位）
8. transmission with chain belt and chain 使用链板链条的变速器
9. push inward（up shift）向里拉近（高挡位）

6.3 CVT pulley control mechanism CVT滑轮控制机构

汽车开始起步时,主动滑轮的工作半径较小,变速器可以获得较大的传动比,从而保证驱动桥能够有足够的转矩来保证汽车有较高的加速度。随着车速的增加,主动滑轮的工作半径逐渐增大,从动滑轮的工作半径相应减小,CVT的传动比下降,使得汽车能够以更高的速度行驶(图3-6-3)。

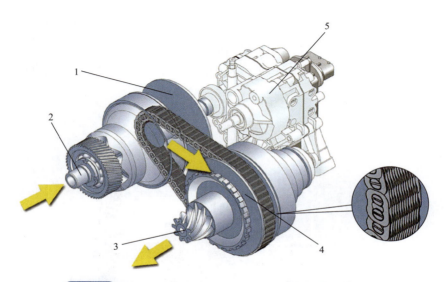

图3-6-3 CVT pulley control mechanism CVT滑轮控制机构

1. driving pulley 主动滑轮
2. power input shaft 动力输入轴
3. power output shaft 动力输出轴
4. driven pulley 从动滑轮
5. pulley control module 滑轮控制模块

PART3 Chassis 底盘

Chapter 7
Dual clutch transmission 双离合器变速器

7.1 Dual clutch transmission principle 双离合器变速器原理

7.1.1 Dual clutch transmission basic design 双离合器变速器基本结构

双离合器变速器有两组离合器，分别由电子控制并由液压系统推动，而两组离合器分别对应两组齿轮，这样传动轴也相应复杂地被分为两部分，实心传动轴负责一组齿轮，而空心传动轴负责另一组（图3-7-1）。

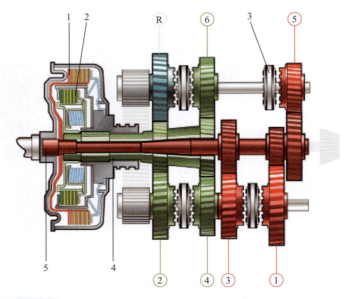

图3-7-1　6 speed transmission configureation 6速变速器结构

1. clutch 1 离合器1
2. clutch 2 离合器2
3. gear selector 挡位选择器
4. outer transmission shaft 外变速器轴
5. inner transmission shaft 内变速器轴

7.1.2　Dual clutch transmission arrangement 双离合器变速器布置形式

如图3-7-2所示，离合器1负责2挡、3挡，离合器2负责1挡、3挡和5挡；挂上奇数挡时，离合器2结合，内输入轴工作，离合器1分离，外输入轴不工作，即在变速器的工作过程中总是有2个挡位是结合的，一个正在工作，另一个则为下一步做好准备。

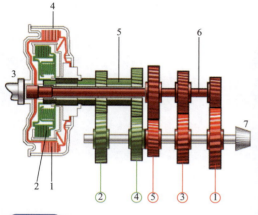

1. clutch 2 离合器2
2. clutch 1 离合器1
3. from engine 来自发动机
4. clutch case 离合器壳
5. outer transmission shaft 外变速器轴
6. inner transmission shaft 内变速器轴
7. to differential 到差速器

图3-7-2　Dual clutch transmission arrangement 双离合器变速器布置形式

7.1.3　Multi-plate wet clutch 多片湿式离合器

离合器有干式和湿式两种，干式离合器内是空气，湿式离合器内是液压油，如图3-7-3所示。湿式多片离合器和变矩器一样，都是使用液压来驱动齿轮。

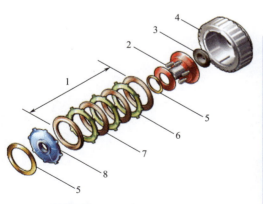

1. clutch pack 离合器组件
2. piston and return springs 活塞和回位弹簧
3. seal 油封
4. clutch drum 离合器毂
5. snap ring 卡簧
6. clutch plate 离合器片
7. friction disc 摩擦盘
8. pressure plate 压板

图3-7-3　A multi-plate wet clutch 多片湿式离合器

7.2 Volkswagen DSG transmission 大众DSG变速器

7.2.1 Volkswagen 6 speed DSG transmission operation 大众6速DSG变速器原理

DSG（direct shift gearbox）中文字面意思为"直接换挡变速器"，DSG只是大众对自己买断的双离合技术专有的称谓而已。两个离合器与变速器装配在同一机构内，其中离合器1负责挂1、3、5挡和倒挡，离合器2负责挂2、4、6挡。当驾驶员挂上1挡起步时，换挡拨叉同时挂上1挡和2挡，但离合器1结合，离合器2分离，动力通过1挡的齿轮输出动力，2挡齿轮空转。当驾驶员换到2挡时，换挡拨叉同时挂上2挡和3挡，离合器1分离的同时离合器2结合，动力通过2挡齿轮输出，3挡齿轮空转。其余各挡位的切换方式均与此类似。这样就解决了换挡过程中动力传输中断的问题（图3-7-4）。

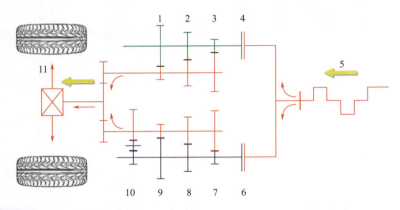

图3-7-4 Volkswagen 6 speed DSG transmission operation 大众6速DSG变速器原理

1. 6th gear 6挡
2. 4th gear 4挡
3. 2nd gear 2挡
4. clutch 2 离合器2
5. power input 动力输入
6. clutch 1 离合器1
7. 1st gear 1挡
8. 3rd gear 3挡
9. 5th gear 5挡
10. reverse gear 倒挡
11. power output 动力输出

7.2.2 Volkswagen 6 speed DSG transmission configuration 大众6速DSG变速器结构（图3-7-5）

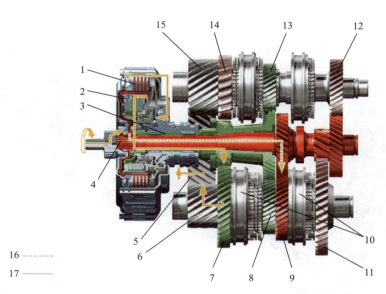

图3-7-5 Volkswagen 6 speed DSG transmission configuration 大众6速DSG变速器结构

1. clutch 1（disengagement）离合器1（分离）
2. clutch2（engagement）离合器2（接合）
3. input shaft 2 输入轴2
4. input shaft 1 输入轴1
5. differential 差速器
6. power output（even gear）动力输出（偶数挡）
7. 2nd gear（operating）2挡（工作中）
8. 4th gear 4挡
9. 3rd gear（pre-selected）3挡（预选挡）
10. gear synchronizer 齿轮同步器
11. 1st gear 1挡
12. 5th gear 5挡
13. 6th gear 6挡
14. reverse gear 倒挡
15. power output（odd gear）动力输出（奇数挡）
16. no power output 不输出动力
17. power output 输出动力

7.2.3 Volkswagen 7 speed DSG transmission 大众7速DSG变速器

大众7速DSG双离合变速器的工作原理与6速类似。离合器1负责控制1、3、5、7挡，离合器2负责控制2、4、6挡和倒挡（图3-7-6）。

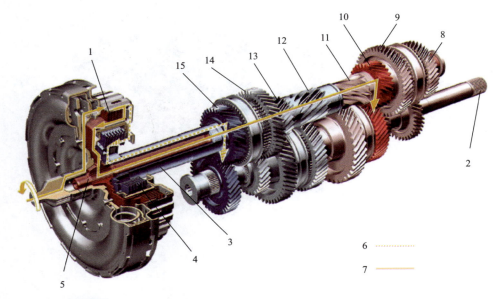

图3-7-6 Volkswagen 7 speed DSG transmission 大众7速DSG变速器

1. clutch 1 离合器1
2. power output to differential 动力输出到差速器
3. input shaft 2 输入轴2
4. clutch 2 离合器2
5. input shaft 1 输入轴1
6. no power output 不输出动力
7. power output 输出动力
8. 5th gear 5挡
9. 7th gear 7挡
10. 3rd gear 3挡
11. 1st gear 1挡
12. reserve gear 倒挡
13. 2nd gear 2挡
14. 6th gear 6挡
15. 4th gear 4挡

Four wheel drive 四轮驱动

8.1 Overview 概述

四轮驱动，顾名思义就是采用四个车轮作为驱动轮。如果在一些复杂路段出现前轮或后轮打滑时，另外两个轮子还可以继续驱动汽车行驶，不至于无法动弹。特别是在冰雪或湿滑路面行驶时，更不容易出现打滑现象，比一般的两驱车更稳定（图3-8-1）。

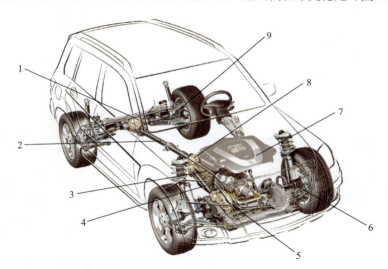

图3-8-1　A four wheel drive car 四轮驱动汽车

1. rear differential 后差速器
2. rear propeller shaft 后传动轴
3. transmission 变速器
4. front propeller shaft 前传动轴
5. front differential 前差速器
6. front half shaft 前半轴
7. engine 发动机
8. transfer case 分动器
9. rear half shaft 后半轴

8.2 Part time four wheel drive 分时四驱

分时四驱可以简单理解为根据不同路况驾驶员可以手动切换两驱或四驱模式。如在湿滑草地、泥泞、沙漠等复杂路况行驶时，可切换至四驱模式，提高车辆通过性；如在公路上行驶，可切换至两驱模式，避免转向时车辆发生干涉现象，降低油耗等（图3-8-2）。

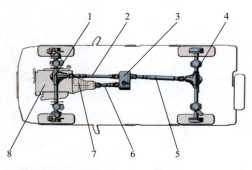

1. front differential 前差速器
2. front propeller shaft 前传动轴
3. switchable transfer 可切换的分动器
4. rear differential 后差速器
5. rear propeller shaft 后传动轴
6. propeller shaft 传动轴
7. transmission 变速器
8. engine 发动机

图3-8-2 A part time four wheel drive car 分时四驱汽车

8.3 Real time four wheel drive 适时四驱

适时四驱，又称为实时四驱，只有在适当的时候才会转换为四轮驱动，而在其他情况下仍然是两轮驱动的驱动系统。系统会根据车辆的行驶路况自动切换为两驱或四驱模式，不需要人为操作（图3-8-3）。

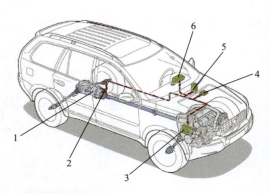

1. electronically controlled coupling/differential unit 电子控制耦合/差速器
2. DEM（differential electronic module）差速器电子模块
3. ECM（engine control module）发动机控制模块
4. BCM（brake control module）制动控制模块
5. CEM（central electronic module）中央电子处理模块
6. DIM（driver's information module）驾驶信息模块

图3-8-3 A real time four wheel drive car 适时四驱汽车

8.4 Full time four wheel drive 全时四驱

全时四驱就是指汽车的四个车轮时时刻刻都能提供驱动力。全时四驱汽车传动系统中，设置了一个中央差速器，发动机动力先传递到中央差速器，将动力分配到前后驱动桥（图3-8-4）。

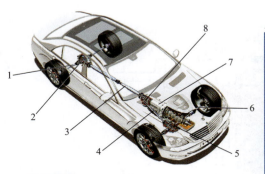

1. rear half shaft 后半轴
2. rear differential 后差速器
3. rear propeller shaft 后传动轴
4. front propeller shaft 前传动轴
5. front differential 前差速器
6. front half shaft 前半轴
7. transmission 变速器
8. transfer case 分动器

图3-8-4 A full time four wheel drive car 全时四驱汽车

8.5 Transfer case 分动器

在多轴驱动的汽车上设有分动器，它位于变速器与驱动桥之间的传动链中，用来增大变速器输出的转矩，以扩大变速范围，并将转矩分配给各驱动桥（图3-8-5）。

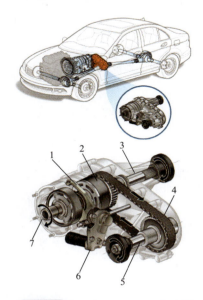

1. clutch lever 离合器分离杆
2. clutch assembly 离合器总成
3. rear output shaft 后输出轴
4. drive chain 传动链
5. front output shaft 前输出轴
6. transfer case encoder motor 分动器编码电机
7. input shaft 输入轴

图3-8-5 A transfer case 分动器

PART3 Chassis 底盘

分动器原理：带轴间差速器的分动器在前、后输出轴和之间有一个行星齿轮式轴间差速器。两根输出轴可以不同的转速旋转，并按一定的比例将转矩分配给前、后驱动桥，既可使前桥经常处于驱动状态，又可保证各车轮运动协调（图3-8-6）。

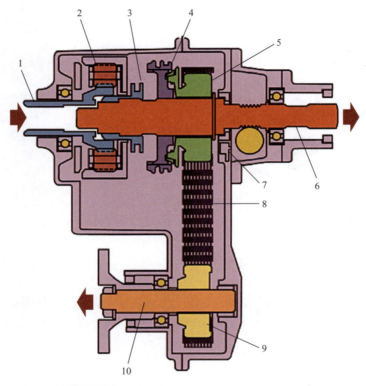

图3-8-6　The transfer case operation 分动器原理

1. input gear 输入齿轮
2. helical planetary assembly 斜行星轮总成
3. range clutch 选挡离合器
4. mode synchronizer assembly 挡位模式同步器总成
5. drive sprocket 传动链轮
6. rear output shaft 后输出轴
7. oil pump 油泵
8. chain 链条
9. drive sprocket 传动链轮
10. front output shaft 前输出轴

Chapter 9
Propeller shaft 传动轴

9.1 Overview 概述

传动轴是由轴管、伸缩套和万向节组成，也称drive shaft。传动轴的作用是与变速器、驱动桥一起将发动机的动力传递给车轮，使汽车产生驱动力（图3-9-1）。

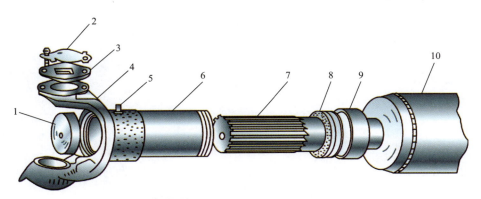

图3-9-1 A propeller shaft 传动轴

1. cap 盖子
2. plate 盖板
3. gasket 盖垫
4. universal joint yoke 万向节叉
5. grease nozzle 滑脂嘴
6. release sleeve 伸缩套
7. sliding spline shaft 滑动花键轴
8. seal 油封
9. seal boot 油封盖
10. propeller shaft tube 传动轴管

PART3 Chassis 底盘

9.2 Universal joint 万向节

万向节是指利用球形等装置来实现不同方向的轴动力输出，位于传动轴的末端，起到连接传动轴和驱动桥、半轴等机件的作用。

9.2.1　Cardin universal joint 十字轴万向节

十字轴万向节由一个十字轴、两个万向节叉（传动轴叉和套筒叉）和四个滚针轴承等组成。两个万向节叉上的孔分别套在十字轴的两对轴颈上，这样，当主动轴转动时，从动轴既可随之转动，又可绕十字轴中心在任意方向摆动（图3-9-2）。

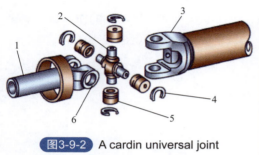

图3-9-2　A cardin universal joint 十字轴万向节

1. sleeve 套筒
2. cross 十字轴
3. propeller shaft fork 传动轴叉
4. snap clip 卡环
5. bearing outer 轴承外圈
6. sleeve fork 套筒叉

9.2.2　Rzeppa constant velocity universal joint 球笼式等速万向节

球笼式等速万向节是奥地利人A.H.Rzeppa于1926年发明，利用若干钢球分别置于与两轴连接的内、外星轮槽内，以实现两轴转速同步的万向节（图3-9-3）。

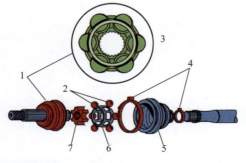

图3-9-3　Rzeppa constant velocity universal joint 球笼式等速万向节

1. fixed joint housing 固定的万向节壳
2. balls 球
3. end view 端视
4. clamps 夹
5. boot 防尘套
6. cage 球笼（保持架）
7. inner race 内圈

Chapter 10
Differential 差速器

10.1 Overview 概述

　　差速器由行星齿轮、行星轮架（差速器壳）、半轴齿轮等零件组成。发动机的动力经传动轴进入差速器，直接驱动行星轮架，再由行星轮带动左、右两条半轴，分别驱动左、右车轮。通过差速器把动力分别传递给两个驱动轮，可以实现左、右两个车轮间转速的不同（图3-10-1）。

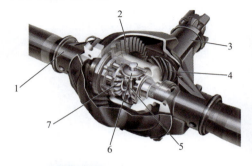

1. half shaft 半轴
2. driven gear（ring gear）从动齿轮（环齿轮）
3. propeller shaft 传动轴
4. driving gear 主动齿轮
5. planetary gear shaft 行星齿轮轴
6. planetary gear 行星齿轮
7. side gear 侧齿轮

图3-10-1　Differential 差速器

10.2 Differential operation 差速器原理

　　传动轴传过来的动力通过主动齿轮传递到环齿轮上，环齿轮带动行星齿轮轴一起旋转，同时带动侧齿轮转动，从而推动驱动轮前进。当车辆直线行驶时，动力通过环形齿轮，传递到行星齿轮，由于两侧驱动轮受到的阻力相同，行星齿轮不发生自转，通过半轴把动力传到两侧车轮（相当于刚性连接，两侧车轮转速相等）（图3-10-2）。

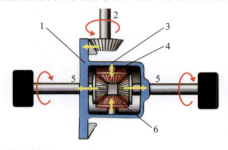

1. ring gear 环形齿轮
2. power input 动力输入
3. differential case 差速器外壳
4. planetary gear 行星齿轮
5. half shaft 半轴
6. no rotation 不自转

图3-10-2　Differential working principle（1）
　　　　　差速器工作原理示意图（1）

· 133 ·

当车辆转弯时，左、右车轮受到的阻力不一样，行星齿轮绕着半轴转动并同时自转，从而吸收阻力差，使车轮能够有不同的旋转速度，保证汽车顺利过弯，如图3-10-3所示。

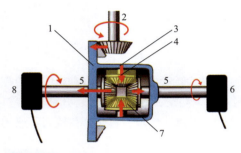

图3-10-3 Differential working principle（2）
差速器工作原理示意图（2）

1. ring gear 环形齿轮
2. power input 动力输入
3. differential case 差速器外壳
4. planetary gear 行星齿轮
5. half shaft 半轴
6. corner inner end 转弯内侧
7. rotation absorption resistance difference 自转吸收阻力差
8. corner outer end 转弯外侧

10.3 Limited slip differential 限滑差速器

限滑差速器主要通过摩擦片来实现动力的分配，其壳体内有多片离合器，一旦某组车轮打滑，利用车轮差的作用，会自动把部分动力传递到没有打滑的车轮，从而摆脱困境。不过在长时间重负荷、高强度越野时，会影响它的可靠性（图3-10-4）。

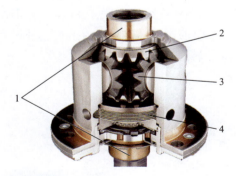

图3-10-4 Limited slip differential with frictional discs 带摩擦片的限滑差速器

1. drive shaft 传动轴
2. side gear 侧齿轮
3. planetary pinion 行星齿轮
4. friction disc 摩擦片

Chapter 11
Suspension system 悬架系统

汽车悬架是汽车中带有弹性的、连接车架与车轴的装置，它一般由弹性元件、导向机构、减振器等部件构成，主要任务是缓和由不平路面传给车架的冲击，以提高乘车的舒适性。常见的悬架有麦弗逊式悬架、双叉臂式悬架、多连杆悬架等。

11.1 Overview 概述

典型的悬架系统主要包括弹性元件、导向机构以及减振器等部分。弹性元件又有钢板弹簧、空气弹簧、螺旋弹簧以及扭杆弹簧等形式，而现代轿车悬架系统多采用螺旋弹簧和扭杆弹簧，个别高级轿车则使用空气弹簧（图3-11-1）。

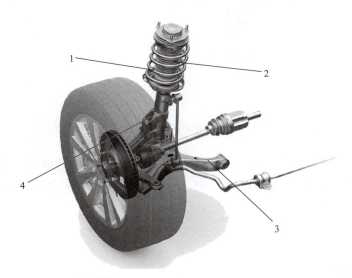

图3-11-1 Suspension configuration 悬架结构

1. coil spring 螺旋弹簧
2. shock absorber 减振器
3. lower arm 下摆臂
4. swing bearing 摆动轴承

· 135 ·

11.2 Suspension classification 悬架的类型

根据结构悬架不同可分为独立悬架和非独立悬架两种。

11.2.1 Independent suspension 独立悬架

独立悬架可以简单理解为是左、右两个车轮间没有通过实轴进行刚性连接的，一侧车轮的悬架部件全部都只与车身相连；而非独立悬架的两个车轮间不是相互独立的，之间有实轴进行刚性连接（图3-11-2）。

1. upper control arm 上摆臂
2. stabilizer 稳定杆
3. coil spring 螺旋弹簧
4. shock absorber 减振器
5. lower control arm 下摆臂
6. there is no solid connection between the two wheels in the independent suspension 独立悬挂中，两个车轮间没有硬性连接

图3-11-2 Independent suspension 独立悬架

11.2.2 Dependent suspension 非独立悬架

从结构上看，独立悬架由于两个车轮间没有干涉，可以有更好的舒适性和操控性；而非独立悬架的两个车轮间有硬性连接物，会发生相互干涉，但其结构简单，有更好的刚性和通过性（图3-11-3）。

1. shock absorber 减振器
2. leaf spring 钢板弹簧
3. there is solid connection between the two wheels in the dependent suspension 非独立悬挂中，两个车轮间有硬性连接

图3-11-3 Dependent suspension 非独立悬架

11.3 Macpherson suspension 麦弗逊式悬架

麦弗逊式悬架是一种最为常见的独立悬架，主要由A字形叉臂和减振机构组成。叉臂与车轮相连，主要承受车轮下端的横向力和纵向力。减振机构的上部与车身相连，下部与叉臂相连，承担减振和支持车身的任务，同时还要承受车轮上端的横向力（图3-11-4）。

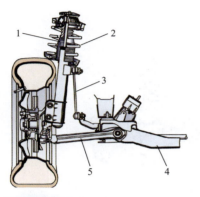

1. shock absorber 减振器
2. coil spring 螺旋弹簧
3. anti-roll link 防倾杆连接杆
4. subframe 副车架
5. lower control arm 下控制臂

图3-11-4　Macpherson suspension 麦弗逊式悬架

麦弗逊式悬架分解如图3-11-5所示。

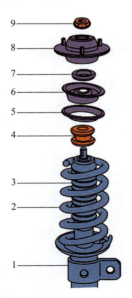

1. strut 支柱
2. spring 弹簧
3. shield 护罩
4. bumper 缓冲垫
5. insulator 隔离垫
6. spring seat 弹簧座
7. bearing 轴承
8. strut mounting assembly 支柱安装总成
9. nut 螺母

图3-11-5　Macpherson strut suspension exploded view 麦弗逊式悬架分解图

11.4 Double wishbone suspension 双叉臂式悬架

双叉臂式悬架（双A臂、双横臂式悬架）由上、下两根不等长V字形或A字形控制臂以及支柱式液压减振器构成，通常上控制臂短于下控制臂。上控制臂的一端连接着支柱减振器，另一端连接着车身；下控制臂的一端连接着车轮，而另一端则连接着车身（图3-11-6）。

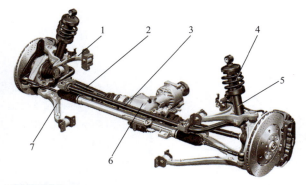

图3-11-6 Double wishbone suspension 双叉臂式悬架

1. upper control arm 上摆臂
2. driving half shaft 驱动半轴
3. stabilizer bar 稳定杆
4. coil spring 螺旋弹簧
5. shock absorber 减振器
6. final reduction 主减速器
7. lower control arm 下摆臂

11.5 Torsion beam axle type suspension 扭转梁式悬架

扭转梁式悬架的结构中，两个车轮之间没有硬轴直接相连，而是通过一根扭转梁进行连接，扭转梁可以在一定范围内扭转。但如果一个车轮遇到非平整路面时，两车轮之间的扭转梁仍然会对另一侧车轮产生一定的干涉，严格地说，扭转梁式悬架属于半独立式悬架（图3-11-7）。

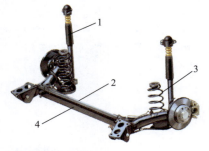

图3-11-7 Torsion beam axle type suspension 扭转梁式悬架

1. shock absorber 减振器
2. torsion beam 扭转梁
3. coil spring 螺旋弹簧
4. torsion beam can twist within a certain range 扭转梁可在一定范围内扭转

11.6 Stabilizer bar 稳定杆

稳定杆也叫平衡杆，主要是用来防止车身侧倾，保持车身平衡的。稳定杆的两端分别固定在左、右悬架上，当汽车转弯时，外侧悬架会压向稳定杆，稳定杆发生弯曲，由于变形产生的弹力可防止车轮抬起，从而使车身尽量保持平衡（图3-11-8）。

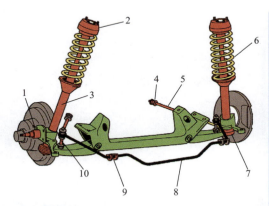

1. spindle 心轴
2. upper mount assembly 上安装组件
3. strut assembly 支柱总成
4. strut rod bushing 支撑杆衬套
5. strut rod 支撑杆
6. coil spring 螺旋弹簧
7. ball joint 球铰
8. stabilizer bar（anti-sway bar） 稳定杆（防横摆杆）
9. stabilizer bar bushing 稳定杆衬套
10. stabilizer bar link 稳定杆连杆

图3-11-8 Stabilizer bar position 稳定杆位置

11.7 Multi-link suspension 多连杆悬架

多连杆悬架就是指由三根或三根以上连杆拉杆构成的悬架结构，以提供多个方向的控制力，使车轮具有更加可靠的行驶轨迹。常见的有三连杆、四连杆、五连杆等（图3-11-9）。

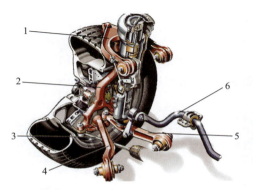

1. upper control arm 上控制臂
2. alignment arm 定位臂
3. steering tie rod 转向拉杆
4. front control arm 前控制臂
5. lower control arm 下控制臂
6. stabilizer bar 稳定杆

图3-11-9 Multi-link suspension 多连杆悬架

PART3 Chassis 底盘

11.8 Air suspension 空气悬架

空气悬架是指采用空气减振器的悬架，相对于传统的钢制悬架系统来说，空气悬架具有很多优势。如车辆高速行驶时，悬架可以变硬，以提高车身稳定性；而低速或颠簸路面行驶时，悬架可以变软来提高舒适性（图3-11-10）。

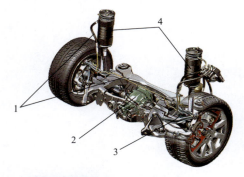

1. air line 充气管
2. differential 差速器
3. upper control arm 上控制臂
4. air shock absorber 空气减振器

图3-11-10 Air suspension 空气悬架

空气悬架控制系统主要是通过空气泵来调整空气减振器的空气量和压力，可改变空气减振器的硬度和弹性系数。通过调节泵入的空气量，可以调节空气减振器的行程和长度，可以实现底盘的升高或降低（图3-11-11）。

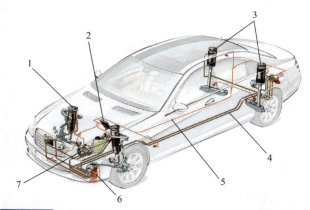

图3-11-11 Air suspension control system 空气悬架控制系统

1. front air shock absorber 前空气减振器
2. electronic control unit 控制单元
3. rear air shock absorber 后空气减振器
4. air tube 空气管道
5. control wire 控制线路
6. dynamic chassis control unit 动态底盘控制单元
7. air pump 空气泵

11.9 Shock absorber 减振器

在悬架的减振机构中，除了减振器还会有弹簧。当车辆行驶在不平路面时，弹簧受到地面冲击后发生形变，而弹簧需要恢复原形时会出现来回振动的现象，这样显然会影响汽车的操控性和舒适性。而减振器对弹簧起到阻尼的作用，抑制弹簧来回摆动，这样，在汽车通过不平路段时，才不至于不停地颤动（图3-11-12）。

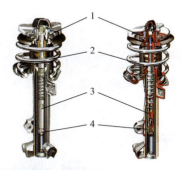

1. oil seal 油封
2. coil spring 螺旋弹簧
3. piston bar 活塞杆
4. piston 活塞

图3-11-12　Shock absorber 减振器

减振器原理：当车架（或车身）和车桥间振动而出现相对运动时，减振器内的活塞上下移动，减振器腔内的油液便反复地从一个腔经过不同的孔隙流入另一个腔内，此时孔壁与油液间的摩擦和油液分子间的内摩擦对振动形成阻尼力，使汽车振动能量转化为油液热能，再由减振器吸收散发到大气中。

典型双管减振器的剖面如图3-11-13（a）和（b）所示，表示在伸展和压缩期间进油和压缩阀的位置。

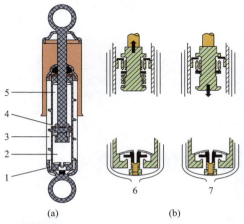

1. compression intake valve 压缩进油阀
2. compression chamber 压缩室
3. reserve chamber 储油室
4. rebound intake valve 回弹进油阀
5. rebound chamber 回弹室
6. rebound（extension）回弹（伸展）
7. jounce（compression）上跳（压缩）

图3-11-13　A cutaway drawing of a typical double-tube shock absorber
典型双管减振器的剖面图

PART3 Chassis 底盘

Chapter 12
Tire 轮胎

12.1 Overview 概述

轮胎直接与路面接触，和汽车悬架共同来缓和汽车行驶时所受到的冲击，保证汽车有良好的乘坐舒适性和行驶平顺性；保证车轮和路面有良好的附着性，提高汽车的牵引性、制动性和通过性；承受着汽车的重量（图3-12-1）。

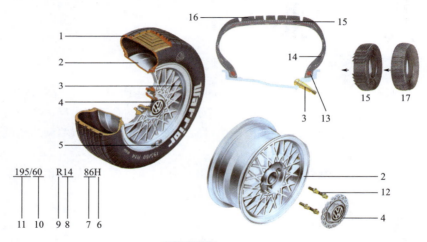

图3-12-1 Tire 轮胎

1. radial tire 子午线轮胎
2. aluminum alloy wheel rim 铝合金轮辋
3. valve nozzle 气门嘴
4. wheel trim 车轮饰板
5. balance weight clip 平衡块夹子
6. speed rating flag 车速级别标志
7. load index 负载指数
8. rim diameter（inch）轮辋直径（英寸）
9. radial construction flag 子午线结构标志
10. tire load surface aspect ratio(%series）轮胎截面高宽比（%系列）
11. tire load surface width（mm）轮胎截面宽度（mm）
12. wheel bolt 车轮螺栓
13. bead 钢线圈
14. inner liner 气密层
15. belt 带束层
16. tread layer 胎面层
17. radial carcass 子午线胎体

12.2 Wheel alignment 车轮定位

车轮定位就是汽车的每个车轮、转向节和车桥与车架的安装应保持一定的相对位置。车轮定位的作用：保持汽车直线行驶的稳定性，保证汽车转弯时转向轻便，且使转向轮自动回正，减少轮胎的磨损等。转向轮定位参数有：主销后倾、主销内倾、车轮外倾、前轮前束等。

12.2.1　Camber 车轮外倾

车轮旋转平面上略向外倾斜，称为车轮外倾（图3-12-2）。

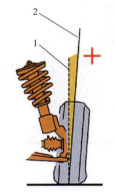

1. vertical reference 垂直参考线
2. angle of tire 轮胎角度

图3-12-2　Camber 车轮外倾

12.2.2　Caster 主销后倾

主销安装到前轴上，通过车轮中心的铅垂线和真实或假想的转向主销轴线在车辆纵向对称平面的投影线所夹锐角为主销后倾角，向前为负，向后为正（图3-12-3）。

主销后倾的作用是保持汽车直线行驶的稳定性，并使汽车转弯后能自动回正。简要地说，后倾角越大，车速越高，车轮的稳定性越强。

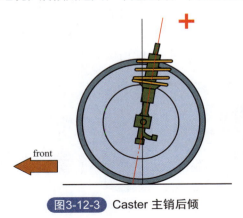

front 前

图3-12-3　Caster 主销后倾

12.2.3　Steering axis inclination 主销内倾

主销内倾是指主销向内倾斜与铅垂线间的夹角。它的作用是使车轮转向后能自动回正，且操纵轻便（图3-12-4）。

图3-12-4中的左图表示主销内倾角由穿过上下球铰之间的中心线确定，这表示前轮在转弯时的铰接点；右图表示主销内倾角由穿过上支柱轴承安装总成的轴线和下球铰的中心之间的连线确定。

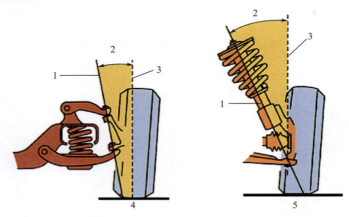

图3-12-4　Steering axis inclination 主销内倾

1. steering axis 转向轴
2. steering axis inclination（angle）主销内倾（角）
3. vertical reference 垂线
4. short/long arm suspension 长短臂悬架
5. strut suspension 支柱悬架

12.2.4　Toe-in 前束

俯视车轮，汽车的两个前轮的旋转平面并不完全平行，而是稍微带一些角度，这种现象被称为前轮前束。正确的前束角与外倾角配合能够减少车辆行进时对轮胎的磨损，它补偿了由于车轮外倾角使得地面对轮胎产生的侧向力，使驾驶稳定（图3-12-5）。

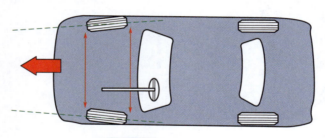

图3-12-5　Toe-in 前束

12.2.5　Scrub radius 主销偏距

　　主销偏距指由内倾角延长线至地面与轮胎中心线的差距。合适的主销偏距使车辆易于驾驶，既可以减小路面的冲击，又可以使方向盘有很好的回正能力（图3-12-6）。

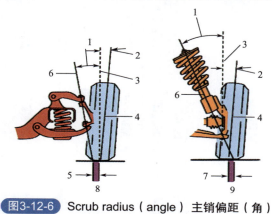

图3-12-6　Scrub radius（angle）主销偏距（角）

1. steering axis inclination（angle）主销内倾（角）
2. chamber angle 车轮外倾角
3. vertical reference 垂线
4. camber line 车轮外倾线
5. positive scrub radius 正主销偏距
6. steering axis 转向轴
7. negative scrub radius 负主销偏距
8. short/long arm suspension 长短臂悬架
9. strut suspension 支柱悬架

12.2.6　Toe-out on turns 转向时负前束

　　转向时负前束，缩写为TOT或TOOT，指转向时内轮相对外轮的前束差值，表示当向左右转向时，转向梯形臂的工作状态。通过转向时负前束的测量值，可以判断梯形是否变形（图3-12-7）。

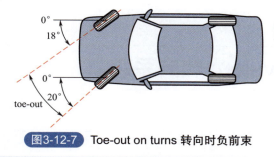

图3-12-7　Toe-out on turns 转向时负前束

toe-out 负前束

PART3 Chassis 底盘

12.2.7 Tire wear and wheel alignment 轮胎磨损与车轮定位

车轮定位不准会导致轮胎磨损，如图3-12-8所示。

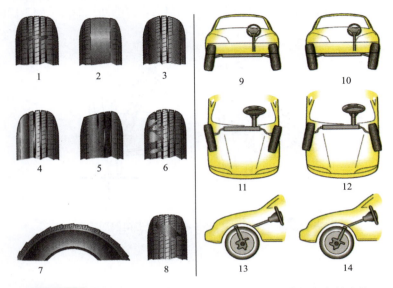

图3-12-8 Tire wear and wheel alignment 轮胎磨损与车轮定位

1. wear indicator 磨损指示标记
2. overinflation 充气过度
3. underinflation 充气不足
4. feathered wear（excessive toe in or out）羽毛形磨损（前束或反/负前束过大）
5. camber wear 外倾磨损
6. spotty/chopped wear（multiproblem）点状/切碎形磨损（多种问题）
7. diagonal wear/heel and toe wear 对角磨损/胎面边缘磨损
8. local wear 局部磨损
9. negative camber 负外倾
10. positive camber 正外倾
11. toe in 前束
12. toe-out 反/负前束
13. negative caster 负后倾
14. positive caster 正后倾

Chapter 13
Steering system 转向系统

13.1 Overview 概述

用来改变或保持汽车行驶或倒退方向的一系列装置称为汽车转向系统（图3-13-1）。

汽车转向系统的功能就是按照驾驶员的意愿控制汽车的行驶方向。日常接触最多的就是齿轮齿条和循环球式转向系统。

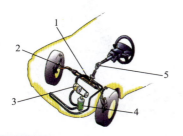

1. rack and pinion configuration 齿轮齿条结构
2. front tie rod 前横拉杆
3. steering power pump 转向助力泵
4. fluid reservoir 储油罐
5. universal joint 万向节

图3-13-1　Steering system 转向系统

13.2　Rack and pinion steering system 齿轮齿条式转向系统

齿轮齿条式转向系统主要由小齿轮、齿条、调整螺钉、外壳及齿条导块等组成，转向器小齿轮在转向主轴的下端，与转向齿条啮合。当旋转方向盘时，转向器中的小齿轮便开始转动，带动转向器中的齿条朝方向盘转动的方向移动（图3-13-2）。

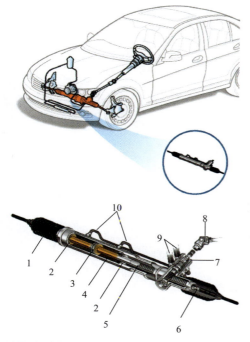

1. rack boot 齿条罩
2. end seal 堵头密封
3. hydraulic piston 液力活塞
4. power steering fluid 动力转向液
5. rack 齿条
6. inner tie rod 内横拉杆
7. pinion 齿轮
8. steering shaft 转向轴
9. power steering hoses 动力转向软管
10. fluid lines 转向液管

图3-13-2　Rack and pinion steering system 齿轮齿条式转向系统

PART3 Chassis 底盘

齿轮齿条式转向系统分解如图3-13-3所示。

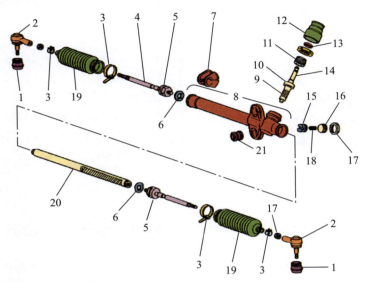

图3-13-3 Rack and pinion steering system exploded view 齿轮齿条式转向系统分解图

1. dust cover 防尘盖
2. outer tie rod end 外横拉杆端头
3. boot clamp 防尘罩夹
4. tie rod 横拉杆
5. inner tie rod end 内横拉杆端头
6. tab washer 有耳垫圈
7. rubber mounting pad 橡胶垫
8. steering gear housing 转向器壳体
9. pinion 齿轮
10. bearing 轴承
11. top cover 顶盖
12. U-joint shield extension 万向节护罩延长部分
13. oil seal 油封
14. steering gear input shaft 转向器输入轴
15. rack support 齿条支撑
16. rack support cover 齿条支撑盖
17. locknut 锁止螺母
18. rack support spring 齿条支撑弹簧
19. boot 防尘罩
20. rack 齿条
21. mounting bushing 安装衬套

齿轮齿条式转向器安装在防火墙凸缘上，其他部件安装到发动机体或车架上（图3-13-4）。

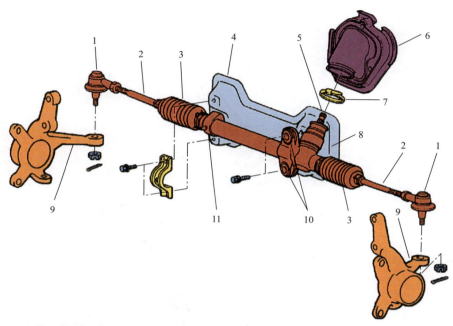

图3-13-4 Rack and pinion steering gear mounting 齿轮齿条式转向器安装

1. outer tie rod end 外横拉杆端
2. tie rod 横拉杆
3. boot 防尘罩
4. firewall flange 防火墙凸缘
5. steering gear input shaft 转向器输入轴
6. U-joint shield 万向节护罩
7. securing band 固定带
8. steering gear housing 转向器壳体
9. steering arm 转向臂
10. rubber bushing 橡胶衬套
11. rubber mounting pad 橡胶固定垫

· 149 ·

PART3 Chassis 底盘

13.3 Recirculating ball type steering system 循环球式转向系统

在蜗轮蜗杆结构间加入了钢球减小阻力,同时将圆周运动变化为水平运动,由于钢球在螺纹之间滚动,就像反复循环一样,所以得名循环球结构(图3-13-5)。

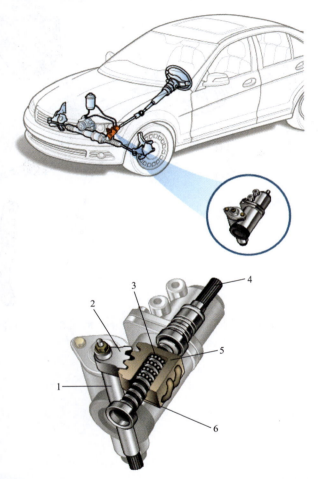

图3-13-5 Recirculating ball type steering system 循环球式转向系统

1. pitman shaft 转向垂臂轴
2. sector gear 扇形齿
3. recirculating ball bearings 循环球轴承
4. steering shaft 转向轴
5. ball nut rack 球螺母齿条
6. worm gear 蜗杆

循环球式转向系统分解如图3-13-6所示。

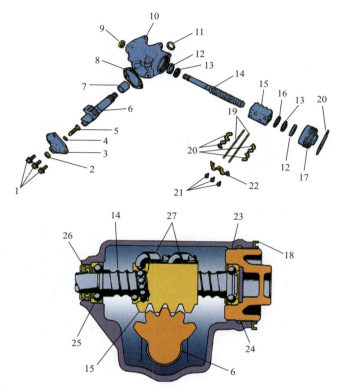

图3-13-6　A typical recirculating ball type steering system gear 循环球式转向系统分解

1. side cover bolts 侧盖螺栓
2. adjustment locknut 调整锁止螺母
3. side cover and bushing 侧盖和衬套
4. adjustment shim 调整垫片
5. adjustment bolts 调整螺栓
6. sector shaft 齿扇轴
7. sector shaft bushing 齿扇轴衬套
8. gasket 垫片
9. worm shaft seal 蜗杆油封
10. steering gear housing 转向器壳
11. sector shaft seal 齿扇轴油封
12. bearing cup 轴承盖
13. bearing 轴承
14. worm shaft 蜗杆
15. ball nut 球螺母
16. bearing retainer 轴承承托
17. worm bearing adjuster 蜗杆轴承调整器
18. locknut 锁止螺母
19. recirculating balls 循环球
20. ball guides 球导管
21. guide cover bolts 导管盖螺栓
22. ball guide clamp 球导管夹
23. adjuster plug 调节器塞
24. lower worm bearing 蜗杆下轴承
25. upper worm bearing 蜗杆上轴承
26. oil seal 油封
27. balls and guides 循环球和导管

PART3 Chassis 底盘

13.4 Steering system components 转向系统部件（图3-13-7）

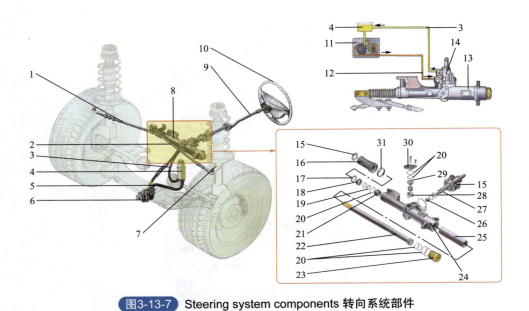

图3-13-7　Steering system components 转向系统部件

1. right tie rod 右横拉杆
2. left tie rod 左横拉杆
3. lower pressure pipe 低压油管
4. reservoir 储油罐
5. suction pipe 吸油管
6. vane pump 叶片泵
7. steering arm 转向臂
8. power steering gear 动力转向器
9. steering shaft 转向轴
10. steering wheel 转向盘
11. pump 油泵
12. high pressure pipe 高压油管
13. steering gear 转向器
14. rotary valve 转阀
15. dust boot clip 防尘罩挡圈
16. crimping dust boot 波纹防尘罩
17. retaining ring 挡环
18. rack seal seat 齿条油封座
19. ring 环
20. O-ring seal O形密封圈
21. bearing bush 支撑衬套
22. rack 齿条
23. seal block 密封挡盖
24. steering gear case 转向器壳
25. cylinder sleeve 缸筒
26. roll bearing 滚轴承
27. pinion 小齿轮
28. block 压块
29. seal seat 密封座
30. cover plate 盖板
31. clamp 夹箍

13.5 Hydraulic power assisted steering（PAS）system 液压助力转向系统

所谓助力转向，是指借助外力，使驾驶者用更少的力就能完成转向。助力转向按动力的来源可分为液压助力和电动助力两种。

机械式液压助力系统主要包括齿轮齿条转向结构和液压系统（液压助力泵、液压缸、活塞等）两部分（图3-13-8）。

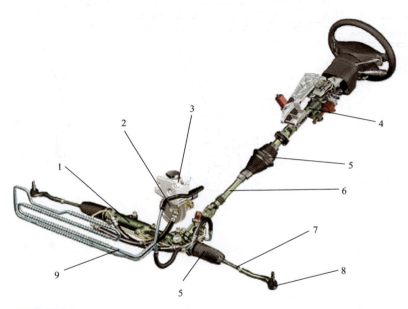

图3-13-8 Hydraulic power assisted steering system 液压助力转向系统

1. power cylinder 动力缸
2. steering pump 转向助力泵
3. fluid reservoir 储油罐
4. steering column 转向柱
5. boot 护罩
6. steering drive shaft 转向传动轴
7. tie rod 横拉杆
8. ball joint 球头
9. return line 回油管

PART3 Chassis 底盘

液压助力转向系统的工作原理是通过液压泵（由发动机皮带带动）提供油压推动活塞，进而产生辅助力推动转向拉杆，辅助车轮转向（图3-13-9）。

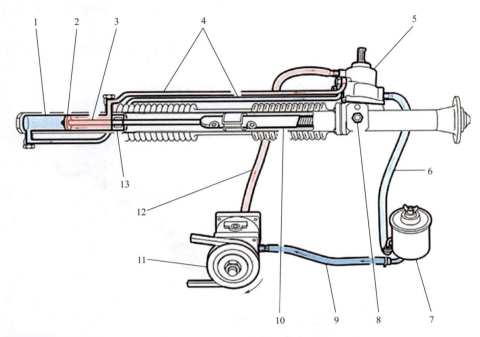

图3-13-9 Hydraulic power assisted steering system operation 液压助力转向系统工作原理

1. ram cylinder 柱塞缸
2. piston 活塞
3. piston rod 活塞杆
4. pressure lines 压力管
5. steering gear 转向器
6. return line 回油管
7. reservoir 储油罐
8. pressure pad adjusting screw 压力垫调节螺钉
9. suction line 进油管
10. rack 齿条
11. high-pressure pump 高压泵
12. high-pressure expansion hose 高压受控膨胀软管
13. seal 密封

13.6 Electric power steering（EPS）system 电动助力转向系统

电动助力转向系统由电机直接提供转向助力，主要由传感器、控制单元和助力电机构成，没有了液压助力系统的液压泵、液压管路、转向柱阀体等结构，结构非常简单（图3-13-10）。

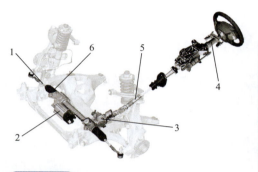

1. steering tie rod 转向拉杆
2. power-assisted motor 助力电机
3. steering gear 转向机（器）
4. steering column 转向柱
5. steering drive shaft 转向传动轴
6. boot 护罩

图3-13-10 Electric power steering system 电动助力转向系统

电动助力转向原理：驾驶员在操纵方向盘进行转向时，转矩传感器检测到转向盘的转向以及转矩的大小，将电压信号输送到电子控制单元，电子控制单元根据转矩传感器检测到的转矩电压信号、转动方向和车速信号等，向电动机控制器发出指令，使电动机输出相应大小和方向的转向助力转矩，从而产生辅助动力。

丰田SUV电动助力转向采用无刷直流电机驱动，电压为42V（图3-13-11）。

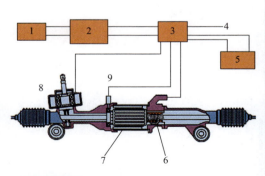

1. 288V battery 288V电池
2. DC-DC converter 288-43.5V 288-43.5V DC-DC 转换器
3. EPS ECU 电动助力转向ECU
4. CAN BUS Controller Area Network 控制器局域网的总线
5. 12V battery 12V电池
6. ball screw reduction gear 滚珠螺杆减速齿轮
7. electric motor 电机
8. torque sensor 转矩传感器
9. motor rotation sensor 电机转速传感器

图3-13-11 The electric power steering in Toyota SUV 丰田SUV电动助力转向

PART3 Chassis 底盘

Chapter 14
Brake system 制动系统

14.1 Overview 概述

制动系统的作用是使行驶中的汽车按照驾驶员的要求进行强制减速甚至停车，使已停驶的汽车在各种道路条件下（包括在坡道上）稳定驻车，使下坡行驶的汽车速度保持稳定。

工作原理就是将汽车的动能通过摩擦转换成热能。汽车制动系统主要由供能装置、控制装置、传动装置和制动器等部分组成，常见的制动器主要有鼓式制动器和盘式制动器。按制动系统的作用，制动系统可分为行车制动系统、驻车制动系统等（图3-14-1）。

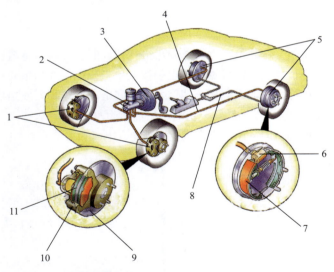

图3-14-1 Brake system 汽车制动系统

1. disc brake 盘式制动器
2. master cylinder 制动总泵
3. vacuum booster 真空助力器
4. brake line 制动油管
5. drum brake 鼓式制动器
6. wheel cylinder 制动分泵
7. brake shoe 制动蹄片
8. hand brake cable 手刹线
9. brake disc 制动盘
10. wheel cylinder 制动分泵
11. brake pad 制动片

14.2 Brake system configuration 制动系统的结构

制动系统部件如图3-14-2所示。

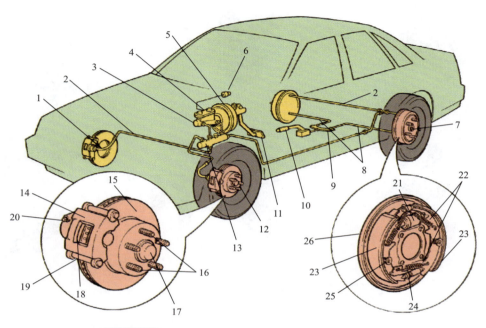

图3-14-2 Brake system components 制动系统部件

1. brake hose 制动软管
2. brake line 制动管线
3. master cylinder 主缸
4. brake fluid reservoir 制动储液罐
5. vacuum power booster 真空动力增压器
6. brake warning light 制动警告灯
7. brake drum 制动鼓
8. parking brake cables 驻车制动钢索
9. parking brake adjuster 驻车制动调节器
10. parking brake handle 驻车制动手柄
11. brake pedal 制动踏板
12. wheel hub 轮毂
13. combination valve 组合阀
14. caliper 制动钳
15. rotor or disc 转子或制动盘
16. wheel studs 车轮螺栓
17. dust cap 防尘盖
18. brake pad 制动片（闸片）
19. slide pin 滑动销
20. bleed valve 放气阀
21. wheel cylinder 轮缸
22. return springs 回位弹簧
23. brake shoe 制动蹄
24. brake adjuster 制动调节器
25. anchor point 支撑点
26. backing plate 制动底板

PART3 Chassis 底盘

制动系统的结构如图3-14-3所示。

图3-14-3　Brake system configuration 制动系统结构

1. rear wheel spindle 后轮轴
2. pull spring 拉力弹簧
3. brake shoe with wedge seat 带楔形支座的制动蹄
4. down spring 下拉弹簧
5. brake drum 制动鼓
6. rear slave cylinder 后制动轮缸
7. brake back plate 制动底板
8. vertical alignment pin 垂直定位销
9. master cylinder body 主缸缸体
10. second piston 第二活塞
11. central valve 中央阀
12. diaphragm return spring 皮膜回位弹簧
13. wedge rod plug 楔杆塞
14. active rod 顶杆
15. control valve plunger 控制阀柱塞
16. control valve assembly 控制阀组件
17. pushrod 推杆
18. valve seat 阀座

19. control valve body 控制阀体
20. first piston 第一活塞
21. horizontal alignment pin 水平定位销
22. diaphragm support 皮膜托板
23. diaphragm 皮膜
24. rear case assembly 后壳体组件
25. front case assembly 前壳体组件
26. seal ring 密封圈
27. brake fluid 压力油
28. vacuum 真空
29. mid state 中间状态
30. atmosphere 大气
31. force by pressing brake pedal 踩制动踏板产生的力
32. fully working 充分工作时
33. mid working 中间工作阶段时
34. no working 未工作时
35. vacuum interface 真空接口
36. to ABS hydraulic control unit 至ABS液压单元
37. brake master cylinder 制动主缸
38. bolt 螺栓
39. rubber bushing 橡胶衬套
40. plastic sleeve 塑料套
41. holding spring 保持弹簧
42. brake caliper support 制动钳支架
43. piston dust 活塞防尘罩
44. friction pad 摩擦块
45. bleeding screw boot 排气螺钉防尘帽
46. brake caliper case 制动钳壳体
47. bleeding seat 排气孔座
48. seal 油封
49. piston 活塞
50. brake plate 制动盘
51. friction 摩擦块
52. piston boot 活塞防尘罩
53. piston 活塞
54. no working 未作用时
55. working 起作用时
56. vacuum booster integrated with the master cylinder 带制动主缸真空助力器

14.3 Hydraulic braking system 液压制动系统

在踩下制动踏板时,推动制动总泵的活塞运动,进而在油路中产生压力,制动液将压力传递到车轮的制动分泵推动活塞,活塞推动制动蹄向外运动,进而使得摩擦片与制动鼓发生摩擦,从而产生制动力(图3-14-4)。

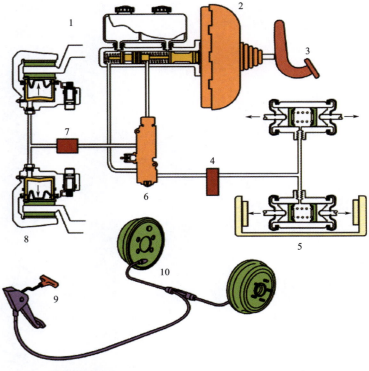

图3-14-4 Hydraulic braking system 液压制动系统

1. master cylinder 主缸
2. power booster 助力器
3. brake pedal 制动踏板
4. proportioning valve 比例阀
5. drum brake(rear)鼓式制动器(后)
6. brake warning light switch 制动警告灯开关
7. metering valve 计量阀
8. disc brake(front)盘式制动器(前)
9. parking brake 驻车制动
10. parking brake cables 驻车制动钢索

14.4 Drum brake 鼓式制动器

鼓式制动器主要包括制动轮缸、制动蹄、制动鼓、摩擦片、回位弹簧等部分。通过液压装置使摩擦片与车轮转动的制动鼓内侧面发生摩擦，从而起到制动的效果（图3-14-5）。

1. friction disc 摩擦片
2. wheel cylinder 制动轮缸
3. brake drum 制动鼓
4. return spring 回位弹簧

图3-14-5 Drum brake configuration 鼓式制动器结构

鼓式制动器分解如图3-14-6所示。

图3-14-6 Drum brake exploded view 鼓式制动器分解图

1. return springs 回位弹簧
2. adjusting lever link 调节杆连杆
3. brake shoe 制动蹄
4. wheel cylinder 轮缸
5. anchor 铰轴
6. holddown pins 固定销
7. backing plate 底板
8. parking brake strut 驻车制动支杆
9. parking brake lever 驻车制动杠杆
10. adjuster lever 调节杠杆
11. lever return spring 调节杠杆回位弹簧
12. adjusting link 调整连杆
13. lever pivot 调节杆支撑
14. holddown springs 固定弹簧

PART3 Chassis 底盘

鼓式制动器原理：在踩下制动踏板时，推动制动总泵的活塞运动，进而在油路中产生压力，制动液将压力传递到车轮的制动轮缸推动活塞，活塞推动制动蹄向外运动，进而使得摩擦衬片与制动鼓发生摩擦，从而产生制动力（图3-14-7）。

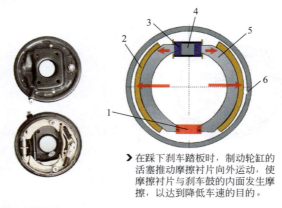

▶ 在踩下刹车踏板时，制动轮缸的活塞推动摩擦衬片向外运动，使摩擦衬片与刹车鼓的内面发生摩擦，以达到降低车速的目的。

图3-14-7 Drum brake operation 鼓式制动器工作原理

1. carrier rod 顶杆
2. friction lining 摩擦衬片
3. piston 活塞
4. wheel cylinder 制动轮缸
5. brake shoe 制动蹄
6. brake drum 制动鼓

14.5 Disc brake 盘式制动器

盘式制动器也叫碟式制动器，主要由制动盘、制动钳、摩擦片、分泵、油管等部分构成。盘式制动器通过液压系统把压力施加到制动钳上，使制动摩擦片与随车轮转动的制动盘发生摩擦，从而达到制动的目的（图3-14-8）。

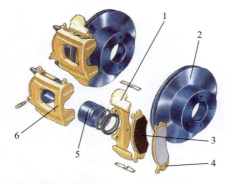

1. brake caliper mounting bracket 制动钳安装支架
2. brake disc 制动盘
3. friction plate 摩擦片
4. brake pad 制动衬块
5. brake caliper piston 制动钳活塞
6. brake caliper 制动钳

图3-14-8 Disc brake 盘式制动器

盘式制动器原理：盘式制动器主要通过施加在制动钳上的压力，使得摩擦片夹住旋转的制动盘（图3-14-9）。

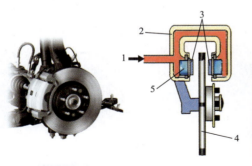

1. brake fluid 制动液
2. brake caliper 制动钳
3. brake friction plate 制动摩擦片
4. brake disc 制动盘
5. piston 活塞

图3-14-9　Disc brake operation
盘式制动器工作原理

盘式制动器分解如图3-14-10所示。

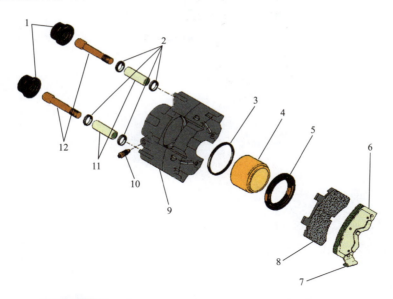

图3-14-10　Disc brake exploded view 盘式制动器分解图

1. bolt boots 螺栓护罩
2. bushings 衬套
3. piston seal 活塞密封
4. piston 活塞
5. dust boot 防尘罩
6. outboard brake pad 外侧制动衬块
7. wear sensor 磨损传感器
8. inboard brake pad 内侧制动衬块
9. caliper body 钳体
10. bleeder screw 放气螺钉
11. sleeves 套筒
12. mounting bolts 安装螺栓

14.6 Brake booster 制动助力器

　　制动助力器，是在人力液压制动传动装置的基础上，为了减轻驾驶员的踏板力的制动加力装置。它通常利用发动机进气管的真空为动力源，对液压制动装置进行加力。它在制动踏板和制动主缸之间，装有一个膜片式的助力器。膜片的一侧与大气连通，在制动时，使另一侧与发动机进气管连通，从而产生一个比踏板力大几倍的附加力，此时，主缸的活塞除了受踏板力外，还受到真空助力器产生的力，因此可以提高液压，从而减轻踏板力（图3-14-11）。

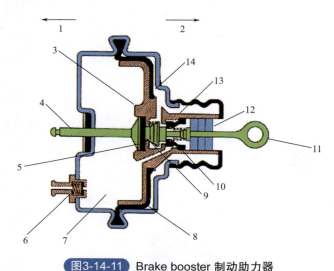

图3-14-11　Brake booster 制动助力器

1. forward 向前
2. rearward 向后
3. diaphragm hub 膜片毂
4. master cylinder push rod 主缸推杆
5. reaction disc 反作用盘
6. check valve 单向阀
7. vacuum chamber 真空室
8. diaphragm 膜片
9. valve plunger 阀塞
10. poppet assembly 锥阀总成
11. operating rod 操纵杆
12. filter 滤清器
13. valve housing 阀壳体
14. atmospheric chamber 大气室

典型真空制动助力总成：真空管与发动机进气歧管相连，制动踏板行程传感器是防抱死制动系统输入信号传感器（图3-14-12）。

1. brake pedal travel sensor 制动踏板行程传感器
2. brake pedal pivot 制动踏板支轴
3. pushrod 推杆
4. brake pedal 制动踏板
5. vacuum booster 真空助力器
6. check valve 单向阀
7. vacuum hose 真空软管

图3-14-12 Typical vacuum brake booster assembly 典型真空制动助力总成

14.7 Anti-locked braking system（ABS）防抱死制动系统

防抱死制动系统是一种具有防滑、防锁死等优点的汽车安全控制系统。ABS主要由ECU控制单元、车轮转速传感器、制动压力调节装置和制动控制电路等部分组成（图3-14-13）。

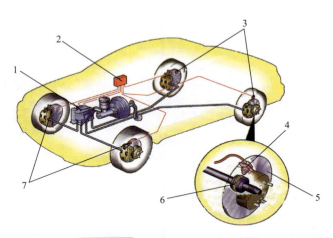

图3-14-13 ABS system ABS系统

1. ABS control unit ABS 控制单元
2. ABS controller ABS 控制器
3. rear wheel speed sensor 后轮车速传感器
4. inducer 感应器
5. brake disc 制动盘
6. pulse generator 脉冲发生器
7. front wheel speed sensor 前轮车速传感器

防抱死制动系统的布置如图3-14-14所示。

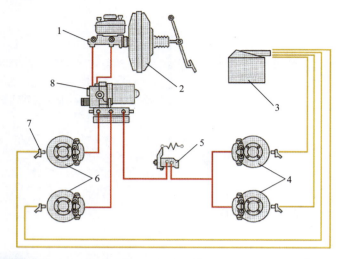

图3-14-14 Anti-locked braking system（ABS）layout 防抱死制动系统的布置

1. master cylinder 主缸
2. brake servo or booster 制动伺服或助力器
3. electronic control unit 电控单元
4. rear disc brakes 后盘式制动器
5. load apportioning valve（if used）负载比例阀（若使用）
6. front disc brakes 前盘式制动器
7. wheel speed sensor 轮速传感器
8. hydraulic modulator 液压调节器

ABS工作原理：制动过程中，ECU通过轮速传感器判断车轮是否被抱死，如车轮即将抱死，ECU发出命令，通过制动调节装置，减少制动动力，防止车轮抱死（图3-14-15）。

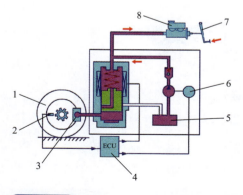

1. wheel 车轮
2. wheel speed sensor 轮速传感器
3. brake wheel cylinder 制动分泵
4. ABS ECU ABS 控制单元
5. reservoir 储液罐
6. motor 电动机
7. brake pedal 制动踏板
8. brake master cylinder 制动总泵

图3-14-15 ABS operation ABS工作原理

14.8 Electronic stability control system 电子稳定性控制系统

电子稳定性控制（ESC），主要由控制总成及转向传感器（监测方向盘的转向角度）、车轮传感器（监测各个车轮的速度转动）、侧滑传感器（监测车体绕纵轴线转动的状态）、横向加速度传感器（监测汽车转弯时的离心力）等组成。控制单元通过这些传感器的信号对车辆的运行状态进行判断，进而发出控制指令（图3-14-16）。

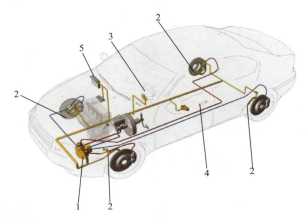

图3-14-16 Electronic stability control system 电子稳定性控制系统

1. hydraulic modulator with attached ECU 液压调节器及相连的ECU
2. wheel speed sensors 轮速传感器
3. steering angle sensor 转向角传感器
4. yaw rate and lateral acceleration sensor 横摆角速度和侧向加速度传感器
5. communication with engine management 与发动机管理系统的通信

稳定性控制系统部件如图3-14-17所示。

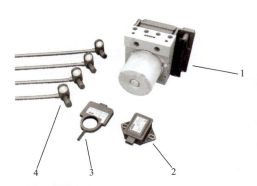

1. hydraulic modulator with ECU 液压调节器及ECU
2. position sensor 位置传感器
3. steering sensor 转向传感器
4. wheel speed sensors 轮速传感器

图3-14-17 Components of an electronic stability control system 稳定性控制系统部件

14.9 Traction control system 牵引力控制系统

牵引力控制系统的机械结构具有能防止车辆在雪地等湿滑路面上行驶时驱动轮空转，使车辆能平稳地起步、加速，支持车辆行驶的基本功能。牵引力控制系统利用轮速传感器信息对驱动轮施加制动，同时减小发动机的驱动力（图3-14-18）。

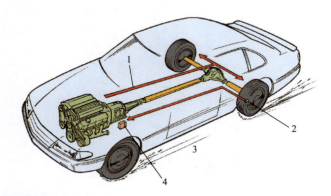

图3-14-18　Typical traction control system 典型牵引力控制系统

1. power reducer 驱动力减弱装置
2. wheel speed sensor 轮速传感器
3. speed information 速度信息
4. engine traction and braking control unit 发动机牵引力和制动控制单元

PART 4

Automotive body 车身

- Chapter 1 Overview 概述
- Chapter 2 Frame 车架
- Chapter 3 Automotive safety system 汽车安全系统

PART 4 Automotive body 车身

Chapter 1

Overview 概述

车身安装在底盘的车架上,用以驾驶员、旅客乘坐或装载货物。轿车、客车的车身一般是整体结构,货车车身一般是由驾驶室和货厢两部分组成。典型乘用车车身的结构如图4-1-1所示。

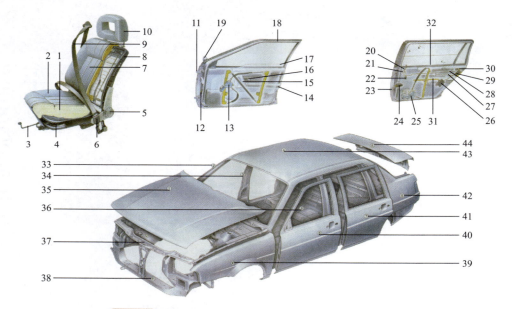

图4-1-1 A typical passenger car body 典型乘用车车身

1. cushion seat 坐垫支座
2. cushion 坐垫
3. seat position front and rear adjustment knob 座椅前后位置调节手柄
4. seat position front and rear adjustment mechanism 座椅前后位置调节机构
5. back angle adjustment knob 背靠角度调节旋钮
6. safe belt buckle 安全带锁扣
7. seat back 座椅靠背
8. back skeleton 背靠骨架
9. safe belt 安全带
10. headrest 头枕

11. front door hinge 前车门铰链
12. door opening limiter 车门开度限位器
13. front door electric window mechanism 前车门电动摇窗机
14. inner locks lever 内锁内扳手
15. inner handle 内拉手
16. inner armrest 内扶手
17. door lock button 门锁锁定按钮
18. front door welded assembly 前车门焊接总成
19. rear mirror 后视镜
20. short lock lever 短锁杆
21. angle lever 角度杠杆
22. electric window mechanism switch 电动摇窗机开关
23. rear door hinge 后车门铰链
24. rear door opening limiter 后车门开度限位器
25. rear door electric window mechanism 后车门电动摇窗机
26. rear central locking motor 后集控门锁电机
27. door lock open lever 门锁开启拉杆
28. long lock lever 长锁杆
29. door lock 门锁
30. outer handle open pin 外拉手开启销
31. window glass bracket 窗玻璃托槽
32. window outer seal 车窗外侧密封条
33. front pillar 前柱
34. middle pillar 中柱
35. engine hood 发动机罩
36. floor pan 地板
37. mud board and front longitudinal member 挡泥板和前纵梁
38. cowl 前围
39. front fender 前翼
40. front door 前车门
41. rear door 后车门
42. rear fender 后翼子板
43. roof 顶盖
44. trunk 行李厢

PART 4 Automotive body 车身

Chapter 2

Frame 车架

2.1 Overview 概述

车架是支撑全车的基础，承受着在其上所安装的各个总成的各种载荷（图4-2-1）。

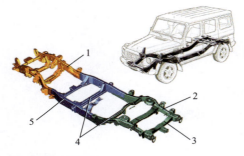

1. front side member 前边梁
2. rear side member 后边梁
3. rear cross member 后横梁
4. middle cross member 中横梁
5. longitudinal member 纵梁

图4-2-1 Trapezoid frame 梯形车架

2.2 Types of automotive body 车身分类

车身按受力分类一般分为非承载式车身和承载式车身两类。

2.2.1 Non-unitized body 非承载式车身

非承载式车身是指车架承载着整个车体，发动机、悬挂和车身都安装在车架上，车架上有用于固定车身的螺孔以及固定弹簧的基座的一种底盘形式（图4-2-2）。

1. suspensions mounted on the frame 悬挂固定在车架上
2. power assembly mounted on the frame 动力总成固定在车架上
3. brackets connected with the body 与车身连接处

图4-2-2 Non-unitized body 非承载式车身

2.2.2 Unitized body 承载式车身

承载式车身的特点是汽车没有车架，车身就作为发动机和底盘各总成的安装基体，车身兼有车架的作用并承受全部载荷（图4-2-3）。

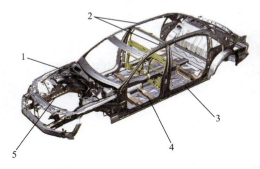

1. engine shroud 发动机挡板
2. roof rails 车顶纵梁
3. rocker panel 门槛板
4. floor panel enforcement beam 底板加强梁
5. engine mounting bracket 发动机固定架

图4-2-3 Unitized body 承载式车身

承载式车身的分解如图4-2-4所示。

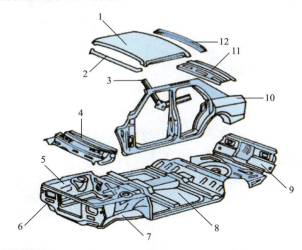

图4-2-4 Unitized body exploded view 承载式车身分解图

1. roof 顶盖
2. front window frame upper sash 前风窗框上部
3. reinforcement support 加强撑
4. outer cowl 前围外板
5. reinforcement splash guard 强挡泥板
6. radiator frame 散热器框架
7. floor front longitudinal member 底板前纵梁
8. floor panel parts 底板部件
9. trunk back panel 行李厢后板
10. quarter panel parts 侧门框部件
11. back panel 后围板
12. rear window frame upper sash 后风窗框上部

PART 4 Automotive body 车身

Chapter 3
Automotive safety system 汽车安全系统

汽车安全系统主要分为两个方面,一方面是主动安全系统,另外一方面是被动安全系统。主动安全的作用就是避免事故的发生;而被动安全则是在发生事故时汽车对车内成员的保护或对被撞车辆或行人的保护,如安全带、安全气囊、车身的前后吸能区、车门防撞钢梁都属被动安全设计(图4-3-1)。

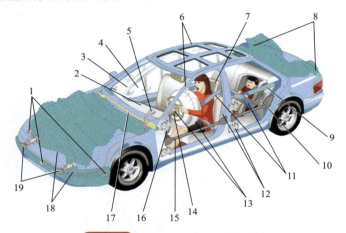

图4-3-1 Safety system 安全系统

1. front impact sensors 前撞击传感器
2. padded instrument panel 带衬垫的仪表盘
3. laminated windshield 夹层挡风玻璃
4. side airbag 侧气囊
5. diagnostic module 诊断模块
6. high-strength steel safety cage surrounding passengers 乘客周围的高强度钢制安全框架
7. head restrains 头枕
8. rear crumple zones 后挤压区
9. child safety seat compatible safety belts 儿童安全座椅相适应的安全带
10. child seat accommodations 儿童座椅设施
11. front and rear lap/shoulder safety belts 前和后膝/肩安全带
12. reinforced door hinges and latches 增强门铰链和锁
13. airbag and igniter (shown deployed) 气囊和点火器(显示展开情况)
14. energy-absorbing steering column 吸能转向柱
15. side-guard door beams 侧护卫门梁
16. padded knee bolster 棉服膝垫
17. cross-car beams for side impact 防侧面碰撞的横车梁
18. front crumple zones 前挤压区
19. energy-absorbing bumper mounts 吸能保险杠支撑

PART 5

Automobile electrical system
汽车电器

- Chapter 1　Electrical system introduction　汽车电器概述
- Chapter 2　Starting system　启动系统
- Chapter 3　Charging system　充电系统
- Chapter 4　Ignition system　点火系统
- Chapter 5　Instruments　仪表
- Chapter 6　Air conditioning system　空调系统
- Chapter 7　Air bag　安全气囊
- Chapter 8　Intelligent vehicle　智能汽车

PART5 Automobile electrical system
汽车电器

Chapter 1
Electrical system introduction 汽车电器概述

汽车电器由电源和用电设备两大部分组成。电源包括蓄电池和发电机。用电设备包括发动机的启动系统、汽油机的点火系统和其他用电装置（图5-1-1）。

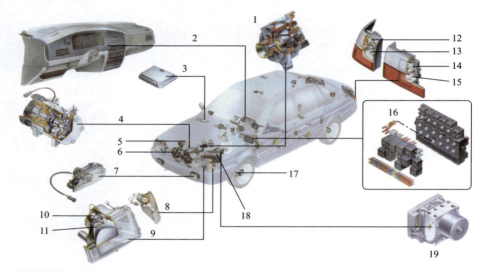

图5-1-1 Automobile electric equipment distribution and constitute 汽车电器分布与组成

1. alternator 交流发电机
2. instrument panel bracket 汽车仪表架
3. automobile engine ECU 汽车发动机电控单元
4. automobile air conditioner compressor 汽车空调压缩机
5. dual tone horn 双音喇叭
6. engine radiator fan 发动机散热风扇
7. front fog light 前雾灯
8. automobile steering light 汽车转向灯
9. automobile headlight 汽车前照灯
10. headlight 前照灯
11. parking light 驻车灯
12. rear steering light 后转向灯
13. brake light 制动灯
14. reverse light 倒车灯
15. rear fog light 后雾灯
16. automobilr fuse and relay box 汽车熔丝和继电器盒
17. wheel speed sensor for ABS control system 车轮转速传感器，用于ABS控制
18. storage battery 蓄电池
19. ABS ECU ABS 电控单元

Starting system 启动系统

2.1 Overview 概述

启动系统由蓄电池、点火开关、启动继电器、起动机等组成。启动系统的功用是通过起动机将蓄电池的电能转换成机械能，启动发动机运转（图5-2-1）。

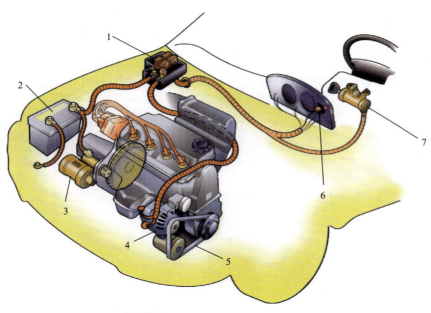

图5-2-1 Starting system 启动系统

1. main fuse 主保险丝
2. battery 电池
3. starter 起动机
4. alternator 交流发电机
5. alternator belt 交流发电机皮带
6. charging system light 充电系统指示灯
7. ignition switch 点火开关

PART5 Automobile electrical system 汽车电器

2.2 Starter components and operation 起动机部件与工作原理

起动机用三个部件来实现整个启动过程。直流电动机引入来自蓄电池的电流并且使起动机的驱动齿轮产生机械运动;传动机构将驱动齿轮啮合入飞轮齿圈,同时能够在发动机启动后自动脱开;起动机电路的通断则由一个电磁开关来控制(图5-2-2)。

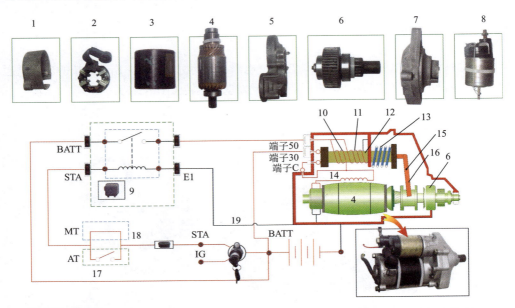

图5-2-2 Starting system structure and operating principle 启动系统结构与工作原理

1. starter rear cover 起动机后盖壳
2. electric bush bracket 电刷架
3. starter cover 起动机外壳
4. armature 电枢
5. gear cap 齿轮盖
6. one-way clutch 单向离合器
7. driving end cover 驱动端外壳
8. magnetic switch 电磁开关
9. starter relay 起动机继电器
10. suction coil 吸引线圈
11. holding coil 保持线圈
12. core 铁芯
13. return spring 回位弹簧
14. magnetic winding 磁场绕组
15. pivot 支轴
16. fork 拨叉
17. neutral start switch 空挡启动开关
18. 7.5A fuse 7.5A保险丝
19. ignition switch 点火开关
BATT 电池端子
STA 启动机端子
E1 接地端子
MT 手动变速器端子
AT 自动变速器端子
IG 点火开关端子

2.3 Starter construction 起动机结构（图5-2-3）

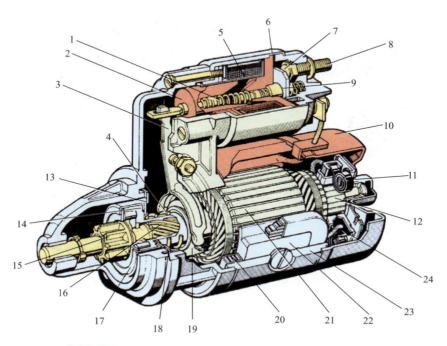

图5-2-3　A cutaway of a typical starter motor 起动机剖面图

1. solenoid plunger return spring 电磁阀柱塞回位弹簧
2. solenoid plunger 电磁阀柱塞
3. shift lever 换位杆
4. meshing spring 啮合弹簧
5. solenoid windings 电磁线圈绕组
6. solenoid 电磁线圈
7. contact point 触点
8. terminal 接线柱
9. moving contact point 移动触点
10. starter end frame 起动机端盖
11. brush spring 电刷弹簧
12. commutator 换向器
13. brake disc 制动盘
14. driver 驱动板
15. pinion gear 小齿轮
16. armature shaft 电枢轴
17. overrunning clutch 超越离合器
18. stop 止块
19. guide ring 导向环
20. field winding 磁场绕组
21. armature pole 电枢极
22. pole piece 极靴
23. starter housing 起动机壳体
24. brush 电刷

PART5 Automobile electrical system
汽车电器

分解的起动机如图5-2-4所示。

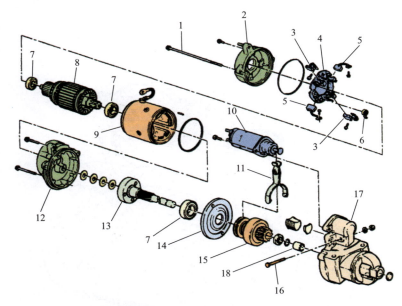

图5-2-4　Starter exploded view 起动机分解图

1. through bolt 贯通式螺栓
2. commutator end frame 换向器端盖
3. ground brush 地线电刷
4. brush holder 电刷保持架
5. insulated brush 绝缘的电刷
6. brush spring 电刷弹簧
7. bearing 轴承
8. armature 电枢
9. field frame 磁极框架
10. solenoid 电磁线圈
11. shift lever 换位杆
12. armature support 电枢支撑
13. drive shaft 驱动轴
14. shaft support 轴支撑
15. clutch drive 离合器传动装置
16. pivot pin 枢轴销
17. drive end frame 驱动端盖
18. bushing 衬套

2.3.1 Starter gear-reduction mechanism 起动机齿轮减速机构

在电动机的电枢轴与驱动齿轮之间安装齿轮减速器，可以在降低电动机转速的同时提高其转矩（图5-2-5）。

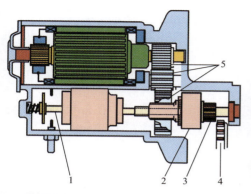

1. plunger 柱塞
2. overrunning clutch 超越离合器
3. pinion gear 小齿轮
4. flex plate 柔性盘
5. reduction gears 减速齿轮

图5-2-5　A typical gear-reduction starter
典型减速起动机

2.3.2 Starter one-way clutch 起动机单向离合器

当启动时，起动机通过单向离合器带动曲轴旋转，当发动机启动后，由于它的转速高于启动电机的转速，单向离合器就把启动电机与发动机的转动脱开，以保护启动电机避免损坏（图5-2-6）。

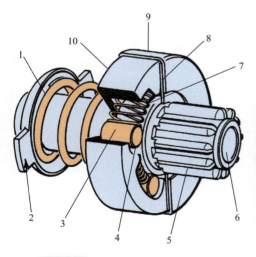

1. mesh spring 啮合弹簧
2. drive flange 驱动凸缘
3. roller 滚子
4. collar 卡环
5. pinion 小齿轮
6. bushing 衬套
7. roller spring 滚柱弹簧
8. roller retainer 滚柱保持架
9. shell 壳体
10. clutch housing 离合器壳

图5-2-6　Starter one-way clutch
起动机单向离合器

PART5 Automobile electrical system 汽车电器

Chapter 3

Charging system 充电系统

3.1 Overview 概述

汽车充电系统由蓄电池、交流发电机及工作状态指示装置组成。在充电系统中，一般还包括调压器、点火开关、充电指示灯、电流表和保险装置等（图5-3-1）。

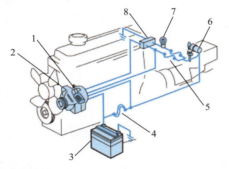

1. regulator 调节器
2. alternator 交流发电机
3. battery 电池
4. fusible link 可熔性连接
5. fuse 保险丝
6. ignition switch 点火开关
7. indicator 指示灯
8. relay 继电器

图5-3-1 The charging system 充电系统

3.2 Generator 发电机

汽车发电机是汽车的主要电源，其功用是在发动机正常运转时（怠速以上），向所有用电设备（起动机除外）供电，同时向蓄电池充电。汽车用发电机可分为直流发电机和交流发电机，以及有电刷和无电刷发电机（图5-3-2）。

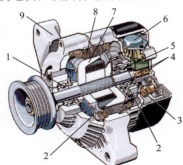

1. bearing 轴承
2. fan 风扇
3. rectifier 整流器
4. slip rings 滑动环
5. bearing 轴承
6. voltage regulator and brush holders 电压调节器和电刷保持架
7. rotor 转子
8. stator 定子
9. housing 壳体

图5-3-2 Cutaway alternator 剖开的交流发电机

典型交流发电机分解如图5-3-3所示。

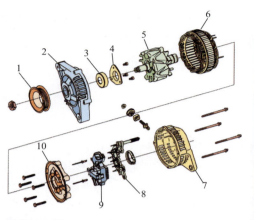

1. drive pulley 驱动带轮
2. drive end frame 驱动端盖
3. bearing 轴承
4. retainer 挡板
5. rotor 转子
6. stator 定子
7. rear end frame 后端盖
8. diode assembly 二极管总成
9. regulator 调节器
10. fan guide 导风板

图5-3-3 An exploded view of a typical alternator 典型交流发电机分解图

3.2.1 Alternator construction 交流发电机结构

发电机通常由定子、转子、端盖及轴承等部件构成。定子由定子铁芯、线包绕组、机座以及固定这些部分的其他结构件组成。定子的功用是产生交流电。转子由转子铁芯（或磁极、磁扼）绕组、护环、中心环、滑环、风扇及转轴等部件组成。转子的功用是产生磁场，安装在定子里边（图5-3-4）。

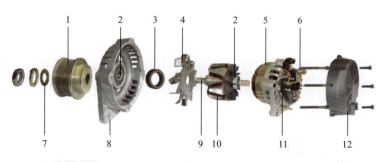

图5-3-4 Alternator disassembled 分解的交流发电机

1. pulley 带轮
2. bearing 轴承
3. thrust pad 止推垫片
4. fan 风扇
5. stator 定子
6. bush 电刷
7. washer 平垫
8. front cover 前端盖
9. shaft 轴
10. rotor 转子
11. regulator set 调节器组件
12. rear cover 后端盖

3.2.2 Principles of alternator operation 交流发电机的工作原理

当外电路通过电刷使励磁绕组通电时，便产生磁场，使爪极被磁化为N极和S极。当转子旋转时，磁通交替地在定子绕组中变化，根据电磁感应原理可知，定子的三相绕组中便产生交变的感应电动势（图5-3-5）。

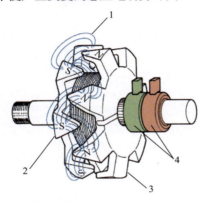

1. magnetic lines of force 磁力线
2. rotor assembly 转子总成
3. rotor windings（alternator field）转子绕组（交流发电机磁场）
4. slip rings 滑动环

图5-3-5 An alternator operation
交流发电机的工作原理

3.3 Storage battery 蓄电池

蓄电池主要负责启动汽车发动机和为车内电控系统供电，保证车辆的正常运行。在不供电时通过安装在发动机上发电机的为其充电，在发动机不工作时为电控系统供电。

3.3.1 Storage battery construction 蓄电池结构

蓄电池由正负极板、隔板、壳体、电解液和接线桩头等组成，放电的化学反应是依靠正极板活性物质和负极板活性物质在电解液的作用下进行的（图5-3-6）。

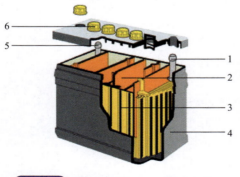

1. negative terminal 负极接线柱
2. separator 隔板
3. plates and separator 极板与隔板
4. battery case 电池壳体
5. positive terminal 正极接线柱
6. vent caps 通风盖

图5-3-6 Storage battery construction
蓄电池结构

蓄电池极板如图5-3-7所示。

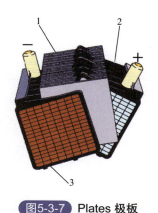

1. separator 隔板
2. set of positive plates 正极板组
3. set of negative plates 负极板组

图5-3-7　Plates 极板

3.3.2　Lead-acid battery principle 铅酸蓄电池原理

铅酸蓄电池的基本原理就是放电时将化学能转化为电能，在充电时将电能转化为化学能（图5-3-8）。铅酸蓄电池放电时，在蓄电池的电位差作用下，负极板上的电子经负载进入正极板形成电流，同时在电池内部进行化学反应。负极板上每个铅原子放出两个电子后，生成的铅离子（Pb^{2+}）与电解液中的硫酸根离子反应，在极板上生成难溶的硫酸铅（$PbSO_4$）。

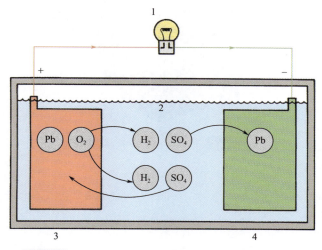

图5-3-8　Lead-acid battery principle 铅酸蓄电池原理

1. load 负荷
2. electrolyte 电解液
3. positive plate（PbO_2）正极板（二氧化铅）
4. negative plate（Pb）负极板（铅）

PART5 Automobile electrical system 汽车电器

Chapter 4

Ignition system 点火系统

4.1 Overview 概述

能够在火花塞两电极间产生电火花的全部设备称为发动机点火系统，通常由蓄电池、发电机、分电器、点火线圈和火花塞等组成（图5-4-1）。

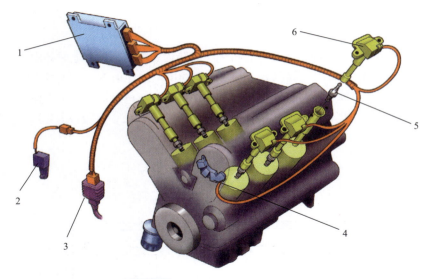

图5-4-1 Ignition system 点火系统

1. engine control module/powertrain control module（ECM/PCM）发动机控制模块/传动系控制模块
2. radio noise condenser 无线电防干扰电容器
3. ignition control module（ICM）点火控制模块
4. crankshaft position/cylinder position（CKP/CYP）sensor 曲轴位置/气缸位置传感器
5. spark plug 火花塞
6. ignition coil 点火线圈

4.2 Conventional mechanical contact type ignition system operation 传统机械触点式点火系统工作原理

传统机械式点火系统由机械装置完成点火能量的形成、点火顺序控制和点火时刻的控制的整个点火过程（图5-4-2）。

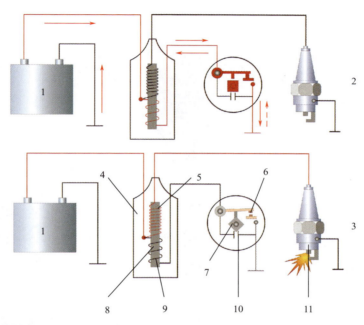

图5-4-2 Conventional mechanical contact type ignition system operation
传统机械触点式点火系统工作原理

1. storage battery 蓄电池
2. low voltage circuit 低压电路
3. high voltage circuit 高压电路
4. ignition coil 点火线圈
5. secondary winding 次级绕组
6. breaker 断点
7. cam 凸轮
8. iron coil 铁芯
9. primary winding 初级绕组
10. capacitor 电容器
11. spark plug 火花塞

PART5 Automobile electrical system
汽车电器

4.3 Electronic ignition system 电子点火系统

电子点火系统有一个点火用电子控制装置，内部有发动机在各种工况下所需的点火控制曲线图（MAP图）。通过一系列传感器如发动机转速传感器、进气管真空度传感器（发动机负荷传感器）、节气门位置传感器、曲轴位置传感器等来判断发动机的工作状态，在MAP图上找出发动机在此工作状态下所需的点火提前角，按此要求进行点火。然后根据爆震传感器信号对上述点火要求进行修正，使发动机工作在最佳点火时刻（图5-4-3）。

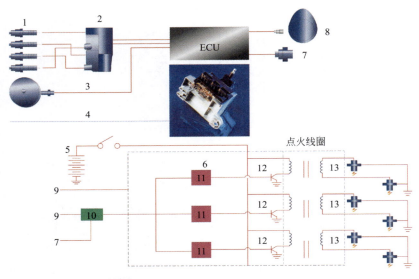

图5-4-3 Electronic ignition system 电子点火系统

1. spark plug 火花塞
2. ignition coil and ignition module 点火线圈和点火模块
3. crankshaft position sensor 曲轴位置传感器
4. signal generation wheel 信号发生轮
5. ignition switch 点火开关
6. ignition module 点火模块
7. detonation sensor 爆震传感器
8. camshaft position sensor 凸轮轴位置传感器
9. crankshaft position sensor 曲轴位置传感器
10. PCM（power control module）功率控制模块
11. control circuit 控制电路
12. primary 初级
13. secondary 次级

4.4 Spark plug 火花塞

火花塞的作用是把高压导线送来的脉冲高压电放电，击穿火花塞两电极间空气，产生电火花以此引燃气缸内的混合气体（图5-4-4）。

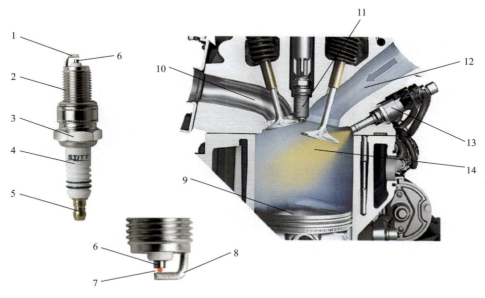

图5-4-4　Spark plug structure 火花塞结构

1. side electrode 侧电极
2. fixing thread 固定螺纹
3. hex bolt 六角螺栓
4. insulator 绝缘体
5. ground nut 接地螺母
6. center electrode 中心电极
7. spark plug clearance 火花塞间隙
8. side electrode 侧电极
9. piston 活塞
10. exhaust gas passage 排气道
11. spark plug 火花塞
12. intake passage 进气道
13. injector 喷油器
14. combustion chamber 燃烧室

PART5 Automobile electrical system 汽车电器

Chapter 5

Instruments 仪表

汽车仪表由各种仪表、指示器，特别是驾驶员用警示灯报警器等组成，为驾驶员提供所需的汽车运行参数信息（图5-5-1）。

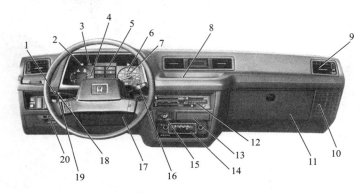

图5-5-1 Instruments 仪表

1. turn signal lever 转向信号手柄
2. turn signal 转向信号
3. bright light signal 大灯信号
4. fuel gauge 燃油表
5. warning lights 警告灯
6. speedometer 车速表
7. odometer 里程表
8. tray 托架
9. vent 通风口
10. radio speaker 收音机扬声器
11. glove compartment 储物箱
12. ventilation controls 通风控制开关
13. ashtray 烟灰缸
14. radio and controls 收音机和控制开关
15. lighter 点烟器
16. windshield wiper and washer controls 挡风雨刷和清洗器控制开关
17. ignition switch 点火开关
18. lights switch 灯光开关
19. hazard light switch 紧急灯开关
20. fuse box 保险丝盒

Chapter 6
Air conditioning system 空调系统

6.1 Overview 概述

汽车空调系统是实现对车厢内空气进行制冷、加热、换气和空气净化的装置（图5-6-1）。

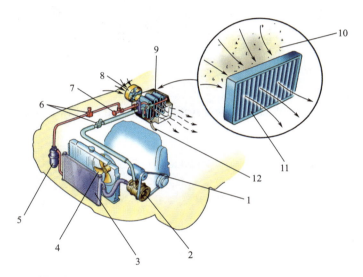

图5-6-1　Air conditioning system schematic 空调系统示意图

1. compressor belt 压缩机皮带
2. compressor 压缩机
3. condenser 冷凝器
4. condenser fan 冷凝器风扇
5. receiver/dryer 接收器/干燥器
6. service valves 维修阀
7. expansion valve 蒸发阀
8. blower 鼓风机
9. evaporator and heater core（under dash）蒸发器和暖风芯（仪表板下）
10. pollen and dust 粉尘
11. micron filter 微米级滤波器
12. condensation drain tube 冷凝排水管

·191·

PART5 Automobile electrical system 汽车电器

6.2 Air conditioning system components 空调系统组成

空调系统由制冷系统、供暖系统、通风和空气净化装置及控制系统组成（图5-6-2）。

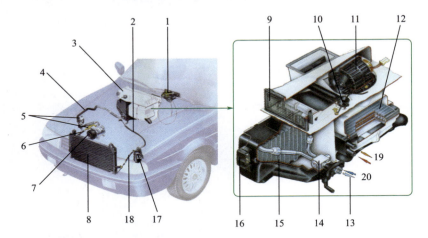

图5-6-2 Air conditioning system components 空调系统组成

1. heating and air conditioning control device 暖风与空调控制装置
2. "L" pipe "L" 形管
3. heating system exchanger 暖风系统热交换器
4. "S" pipe "S" 形管
5. silencer 消声器
6. "D" pipe "D" 形管
7. A/C compressor 空调压缩机
8. condenser 冷凝器
9. heating air filter cover 热风罩滤网
10. vacuum valve 真空阀
11. blower 鼓风机
12. heater core 加热器芯
13. refrigerant 制冷剂
14. expansion valve 膨胀阀
15. evaporator core 蒸发器芯
16. thermostat 温控器
17. drier receiver 储液干燥器
18. "C" pipe "C" 形管
19. to engine 通往发动机
20. hot water（from engine water passage）热水（来自发动机水道）

6.3 Air conditioning system operation 空调系统原理

首先，压缩机吸收来自蒸发器的气体制冷剂并进行加温加压，再送到冷凝器进行降温处理，但是压强还是很高，之后到达储液干燥器进行干燥处理，再到达膨胀阀，在这进行降温降压处理，最后是送到蒸发器，吸收热量（图5-6-3）。

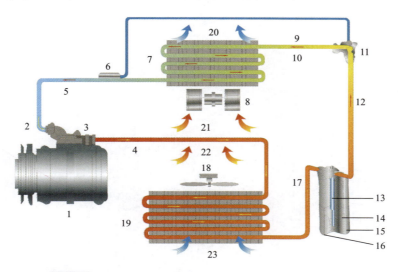

图5-6-3　Air conditioning system operation 空调系统原理

1. compressor 压缩机
2. lower pressure service valve 低压侧服务阀
3. high pressure service valve 高压侧服务阀
4. high-temperature high-pressure gas 高温高压气体
5. low-temperature low-pressure gas 低压低温气体
6. thermal cylinder 热感缸
7. evaporator 蒸发器
8. blower motor 风机电动机
9. low-temperature low-pressure liquid 低压低温液体
10. low-temperature low-pressure refrigerant mist 低压低温雾状制冷剂
11. expansion valve 膨胀阀
12. liquid refrigerant 液态制冷剂
13. liquid storage cylinder pipe 储液筒管
14. dryer 干燥剂
15. filter 滤网
16. reservoir 储液罐
17. medium-temperature high-pressure liquid 中温高压液体
18. engine cooling fan 发动机冷却风扇
19. condenser 冷凝器
20. cold wind 冷风
21. air in car 车厢内空气
22. hot wind 热风
23. cold air in the front of the car 前方冷空气

PART5 Automobile electrical system 汽车电器

6.4 Compressor 压缩机

压缩机从吸气管吸入低温低压的制冷剂气体，通过电机运转带动活塞对其进行压缩后，向排气管排出高温高压的制冷剂气体，为制冷循环提供动力，从而实现压缩→冷凝（放热）→膨胀→蒸发（吸热）的制冷循环（图5-6-4）。

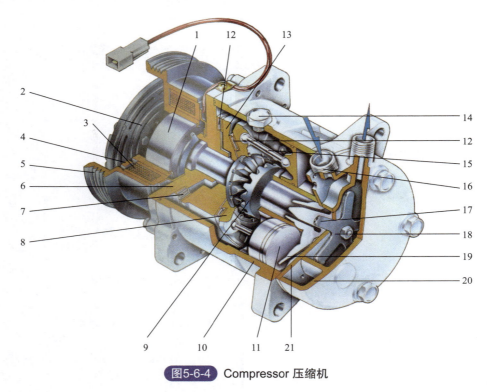

图5-6-4 Compressor 压缩机

1. bearing 轴承
2. suction plate 吸盘
3. coil 线圈
4. magnetic clutch 电磁离合器
5. ribbed belt pulley 多楔带带轮
6. front cover 前盖
7. seal ring 密封圈
8. planetary disk with bevel gear 带锥齿轮的行星盘
9. fixed bevel gear 固定锥齿轮
10. cylinder 缸体
11. piston 活塞
12. thrust bearing 推力轴承
13. swash plate 斜盘
14. fill plug 注油塞
15. link 连杆
16. in and out port 进出接口
17. exhaust valve 排气阀片
18. valve limit plate 阀片限位板
19. suction valve 吸气阀门
20. end cover 头盖
21. valve plate 阀板

Chapter 7
Air bag 安全气囊

安全气囊，简称SRS（supplementary restraint system，辅助约束系统），指安装在汽车上的充气软囊，在车辆发生撞击事故的瞬间弹出，以达到缓冲的作用，保护驾驶和乘客的安全（图5-7-1）。

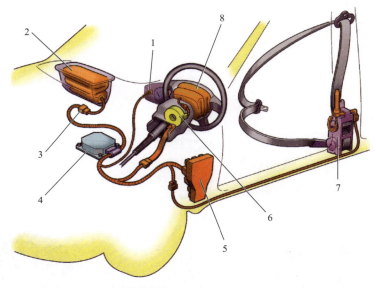

图5-7-1 Air bag 安全气囊

1. SRS indicator light　SRS 指示灯
2. front passenger's airbag 前乘客气囊
3. gold-plated electrical connectors 镀金电接头
4. SRS unit（including "G" sensors）SRS 单元（包括G 传感器）
5. under-dash fuse/relay box 仪表盘下的保险丝/继电器盒
6. cable reel 电缆卷筒
7. front seat belt tensioner 前座椅安全带束紧器
8. driver's airbag 驾驶员侧气囊

PART5 Automobile electrical system 汽车电器

Chapter 8

Intelligent vehicle 智能汽车

8.1 Intelligent vehicle 智能汽车

智能汽车是指通过搭载先进传感器、控制器、执行器等装置，运用信息通信、互联网、大数据、云计算、人工智能等新技术，具有部分或完全自动驾驶功能，由单纯交通运输工具逐步向智能移动空间转变的新一代汽车。智能汽车通常也被称为智能网联汽车、自动驾驶汽车、无人驾驶汽车等。优步自动驾驶汽车如图5-8-1所示。

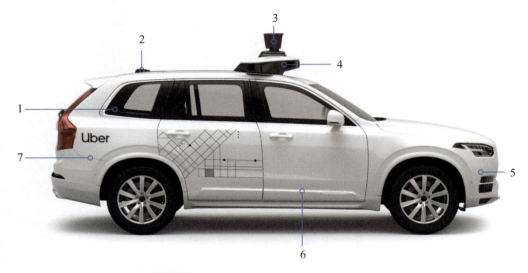

图5-8-1 Uber self-driving car优步自动驾驶汽车

1. telematics, cellular data communication 远程通信，蜂窝数据通信
2. Global Position System(GPS), localization and data collection 全球定位系统，定位与数据采集
3. Light Detection And Ranging (LIDAR), three dimensional canning 激光雷达，三维扫描
4. cameras, high resolution imagery 摄像机，高分辨率图像
5. radar, object detection and velocity 雷达，目标检测与测速
6. Vehicle Interface Module (VIM) 车辆接口模块
7. self-driving computer, main system computer 自动驾驶计算机，主系统计算机

8.2 Advanced driver assistance system 先进驾驶辅助系统

先进驾驶辅助系统（advanced driver assistance system，ADAS）是智能汽车的初级阶段。利用安装在车辆上的传感、通信、决策及执行等装置，监测驾驶员、车辆及其行驶环境并通过影像、灯光、声音、触觉提示/警告或控制等方式辅助驾驶员执行驾驶任务或主动避免/减轻碰撞危害的各类系统的总称。先进驾驶辅助系统应用如图5-8-2所示。

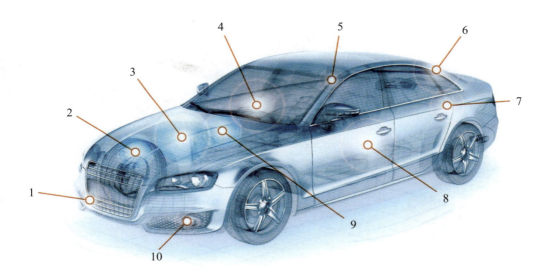

图5-8-2　Advanced driver assistance system applications 先进驾驶辅助系统应用

1. cross traffic assist 车侧交通辅助
2. emergency brake system and adaptive cruise control 紧急制动系统和自适应巡航控制
3. night vision/surround view camera 夜视/全景摄像头
4. front view camera system 前视摄像系统
5. interior camera/driver monitoring 内部摄像机/驾驶员监视
6. smart camera rear-remote park assist, park assist/self-parking 智能后摄像头－遥控驻车辅助或驻车辅助/自动驻车
7. side impact assist 侧面防撞辅助
8. blind spot detection/surround view 盲区检测/环绕视图
9. radar fusion center 雷达融合中心
10. high beam control（自适应）远光灯控制

PART5 Automobile electrical system
汽车电器

在ADAS中，通常融合多个传感器信息实时感知周边环境，为车辆计算系统提供精准的路况数据、障碍物和道路标线等相关信息。软件系统根据传感器的输入实时构建汽车周围环境的空间模型或计算行驶的危险级别。接着，将输出提供给驾驶人或指定系统应如何预警或主动干预车辆控制。奥迪A8汽车在ADAS中所用的周边环境观测传感器如图5-8-3所示。

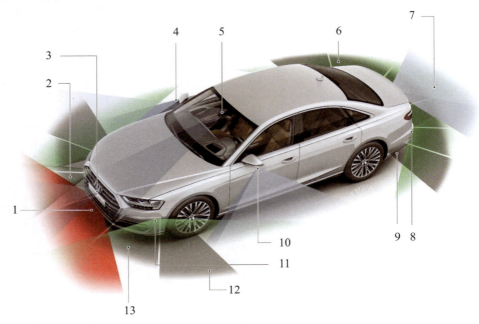

图5-8-3 Audi A8 sensors for environment observation 奥迪A8环境观测传感器

1. laserscanner 激光扫描仪
2. long range radar 远程雷达
3,4,7,10. 360° environment camera 360° 周边摄像头
5. front camera 前摄像头
6,13. ultra-sonic sensor 超声波传感器
8. mid-range radar 中程雷达
9,12. side ultra-sonic sensor 侧面超声波传感器
11. mid range radar 中程雷达

8.3 Adaptive cruise control 自适应巡航控制

自适应巡航控制（adaptive cruise control，ACC）属于先进驾驶辅助系统，可实时监测车辆前方行驶环境，在设定的速度范围内自动调整行驶速度，以适应前方车辆和/或道路条件等引起的驾驶环境变化。奥迪A8自适应巡航控制主要部件如图5-8-4所示。

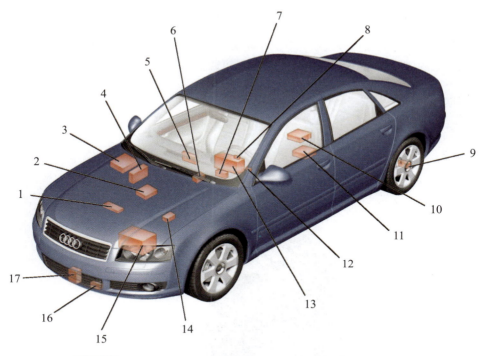

图5-8-4　Audi A8 adaptive cruise control奥迪A8自适应巡航控制

1. start control module 启动控制模块
2. data bus on board diagnostic interface (gateway) 车载诊断接口数据总线（网关）
3. Motronic Engine Control Module (ECM) 多点喷射发动机控制模块
4. transmission control module 自动变速器控制模块
5. front information display and control head 前部信息显示和操纵板
6. multimedia control head 多媒体操纵板
7. vehicle electrical system control module 汽车电气系统控制模块
8. steering angle sensor 转向角传感器
9. ABS wheel speed sensors ABS 车轮转速传感器
10. central control module for comfort system 舒适系统中央控制模块
11. control module for towing sensor 挂车识别传感器控制模块
12. steering column electronic systems control module 转向柱电子系统控制模块
13. control module with indicator unit in instrument panel insert 组合仪表的显示屏控制模块
14. sender for rotation rate 摆动速度传感器
15. ABS control module ABS 控制模块
16. outside air temperature sensor 车外温度传感器
17. distance regulation sensor, control module for distance regulation 车距调节传感器，车距调节控制模块

8.3.1 Distance regulation sensor 车距调节传感器

奥迪将雷达作为自适应巡航控制的车距调节传感器。雷达发射出调频信号，通过接收反射回来的信号测量车距。支架上的转接板可调整传感器位置（图5-8-5）。

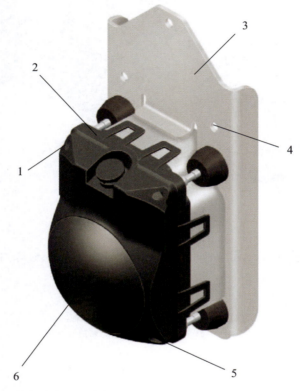

图5-8-5　Distance regulation sensor 车距调节传感器

1. horizontal adjusting screw 水平调节螺栓
2. adapter plate 转接板
3. holder 支架
4. mounting hole 固定螺栓孔
5. vertical adjusting screw 垂直调节螺栓
6. distance regulation sensor, control module for distance regulation 车距调节传感器，车距调节控制单元

8.3.2 Operation of adaptive cruise control 自适应巡航控制系统的操作

自适应巡航控制操纵杆有两个位置，推至ON位置可接通自适应巡航控制。将操纵杆推至OFF位置可关闭巡航控制（图5-8-6）。

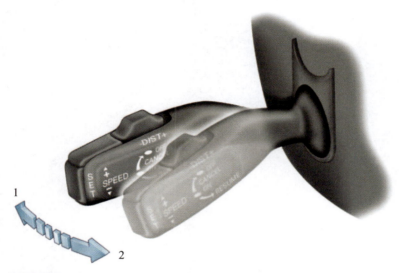

图5-8-6　Operation of adaptive cruise control 自适应巡航控制系统的操作

1. adaptive cruise control OFF 自适应巡航关闭
2. adaptive cruise control ON 自适应巡航接通

PART 6

New energy vehicle 新能源汽车

- Chapter 1　New energy vehicle classification　新能源汽车分类
- Chapter 2　New energy vehicle motor　新能源汽车电机
- Chapter 3　New energy vehicle battery　新能源汽车电池
- Chapter 4　Battery electric vehicle　纯电动汽车
- Chapter 5　Hybrid electric vehicle　混合动力电动汽车
- Chapter 6　Fuel cell electric vehicle　燃料电池汽车
- Chapter 7　Natural gas vehicle　天然气汽车
- Chapter 8　LPG vehicle　液化石油气汽车

Chapter 1
New energy vehicle classification 新能源汽车分类

新能源汽车是指采用非常规的车用燃料作为动力来源（或使用常规的车用燃料、采用新型车载动力装置），综合车辆的动力控制和驱动方面的先进技术，形成的技术原理先进、具有新技术、新结构的汽车。新能源汽车从燃料方面，可以分为电动汽车、燃气汽车、醇类汽车和生物柴油汽车等。

1.1 Electric vehicle 电动汽车

电动汽车大致分为纯电动汽车、混合动力电动汽车和燃料电池电动汽车等。电动汽车的一个共同特点是汽车完全或部分由电机驱动。

1.1.1 Battery electric vehicle 纯电动汽车

纯电动汽车（Battery Electric Vehicle, BEV）是全部采用电力驱动的汽车，利用驱动电机来驱动车辆（图6-1-1）。

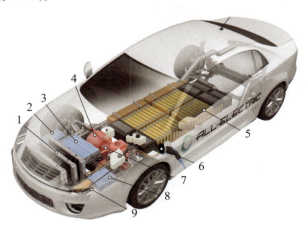

图6-1-1 Battery electric vehicle 纯电动汽车

1. thermal system (cooling) 热管理系统（冷却）
2. DC/DC converter DC/DC 转换器
3. power electronics controller 功率电子控制器
4. electric traction motor 驱动电机
5. traction battery pack 动力电池包
6. charge port 充电口
7. transmission 变速器
8. onboard charger 车载充电器
9. battery (auxiliary) 辅助电池

PART 6 New energy vehicle 新能源汽车

1.1.2 Hybrid electric vehicle 混合动力电动汽车

混合动力电动汽车（Hybrid Electric Vehicle, HEV）一般为油电混合，就是利用燃油发动机和电机共同为汽车提供动力（图6-1-2）。混合动力车上的装置可以在车辆减速、制动、下坡时回收能量，并通过电机为汽车提供动力。

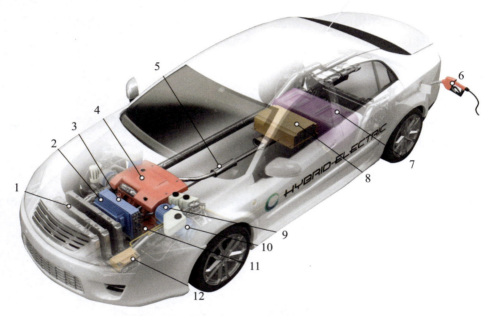

图6-1-2 Hybrid electric vehicle 混合动力电动汽车

1. thermal system (cooling) 热管理系统（冷却）
2. DC/DC converter DC/DC 转换器
3. power electronics controller 功率电子控制器
4. internal combustion engine (spark-ignited) 内燃机（火花点燃式）
5. exhaust system 排气系统
6. fuel filler 加油口
7. fuel tank (gasoline) 油箱（汽油）
8. traction battery pack 动力电池包
9. electric traction motor 驱动电机
10. electric generator 发电机
11. transmission 变速器
12. battery (auxiliary) 辅助电池

插电式混合动力电动汽车（Plug-in Hybrid Electric Vehicle, PHEV）是可以实现外部充电的混合动力电动汽车，电池比较大，可选择纯电动模式行驶，续航里程较长（图6-1-3）。

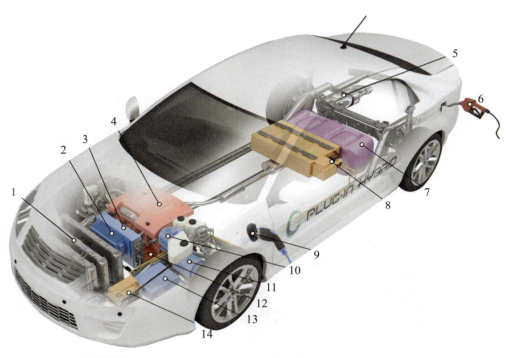

图6-1-3　Plug-in hybrid electric vehicle 插电式混合动力电动汽车

1. thermal system (cooling) 热管理系统（冷却）
2. DC/DC converter DC/DC 转换器
3. power electronics controller 功率电子控制器
4. internal combustion engine (spark-ignited) 内燃机（火花点燃式）
5. exhaust system 排气系统
6. fuel filler 加油口
7. fuel tank (gasoline) 油箱（汽油）
8. traction battery pack 动力电池包
9. charge port 充电口
10. electric traction motor 驱动电机
11. electric generator 发电机
12. transmission 变速器
13. onboard charger 车载充电器
14. battery (auxiliary) 辅助电池

PART 6 New energy vehicle
新能源汽车

1.1.3 Fuel cell electric vehicle 燃料电池电动汽车

燃料电池电动汽车（Fuel Cell Electric Vehicle, FCEV），又称燃料电池汽车（Fuel Cell Vehicle, FCV），是通过氢气和氧气的化学作用直接变成电能的，而不是经过燃烧。燃料电池的化学反应过程不会产生有害产物，因此燃料电池汽车是无污染汽车（图6-1-4）。

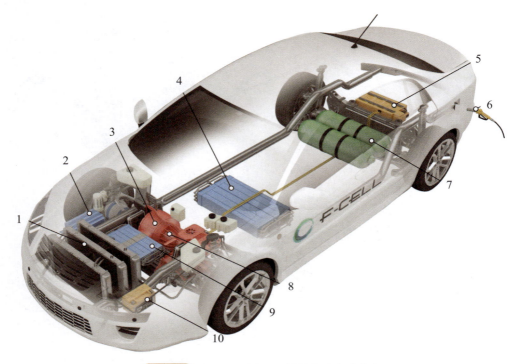

图6-1-4 Fuel cell vehicle 燃料电池电动汽车

1. thermal system (cooling) 热管理系统（冷却）
2. DC/DC converter DC/DC 转换器
3. electric traction motor 驱动电机
4. fuel cell stack 燃料电池堆
5. battery pack 电池包
6. fuel filler 加氢口
7. fuel tank (hydrogen) 储氢瓶
8. transmission 变速器
9. power electronics controller 功率电子控制器
10. battery (auxiliary) 辅助电池

1.2 Gas vehicle 燃气汽车

燃气汽车主要分为液化石油气汽车和压缩天然气汽车两种。天然气汽车主要以压缩天然气（CNG）、液化天然气（LNG）、液化石油气（LPG）为燃料。

1.2.1 Compressed natural gas vehicle 压缩天然气汽车

压缩天然气汽车（Compressed Natural Gas Vehicle, CNGV）是以压缩天然气（CNG）作为汽车燃料的车辆。对在用车来讲，可在保留原车供油系统的情况下，增加一套专用压缩天然气装置，形成压缩天然气汽车，燃料的转换仅需拨动开关（图6-1-5）。

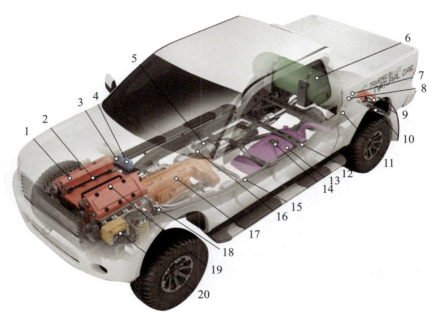

图6-1-5 Compressed natural gas vehicle 压缩天然气汽车

1. internal combustion engine (spark-ignited) 内燃机（火花点燃式）
2. fuel injection system (natural gas) 燃油喷射系统（天然气）
3. Electronic Control Module (ECM) (gasoline) 电控模块（汽油）
4. Electronic Control Module (ECM) (natural gas) 电控模块（天然气）
5. exhaust system 排气系统
6. fuel tank (compressed natural gas) 气瓶（压缩天然气）
7. manual shut off 手动关闭阀
8. high pressure regulator 高压调节器
9. fuel filler (gasoline) 加油口（汽油）
10. fuel filler (natural gas) 加气口（天然气）
11. natural gas fuel filter 天然气滤清器
12. fuel line (natural gas) 燃料管路（天然气）
13. fuel tank (gasoline) 油箱（汽油）
14. fuel pump 燃油泵
15. fuel line (gasoline) 燃油管路（汽油）
16. fuel selector switch 燃料选择开关
17. transmission 变速器
18. natural gas sensors 天然气传感器
19. fuel injection system (gasoline) 燃油喷射系统
20. battery 电池

PART 6 New energy vehicle 新能源汽车

1.2.2 Liquefied natural gas vehicle 液化天然气汽车

液化天然气（Liquefied Natural Gas，LNG）是天然气经净化处理，在常压下深冷至-162℃，由气态变成液态。液化天然气汽车（Liquefied Natural Gas Vehicle，LNGV）是以低温液态天然气为燃料的天然气汽车。LNG能量密度大（约为CNG的3倍），一般适用于大型货运汽车（图6-1-6）。

图6-1-6 Liquefied natural gas truck 液化天然气货车

1. fuel injection system 燃油喷射系统
2. internal combustion engine (spark-ignited) 内燃机（火花点燃式）
3. Electronic Control Module (ECM) 电子控制模块
4. battery 电池
5. exhaust system 排气系统
6. fuel filler 加气口
7. fuel tank (liquefied natural gas) 气瓶（液化天然气）
8. transmission 变速器
9. fuel line 燃料管路

1.2.3 Liquefied petroleum gas vehicle 液化石油气汽车

液化石油气汽车（Liquefied Petroleum Gas Vehicle, LPGV）是以液化石油气（LPG）为燃料的汽车（图6-1-7）。液化石油气是丙烷和丁烷的混合物，通常伴有少量的丙烯和丁烯。液化石油气是在提炼原油时生产出来的，或从石油或天然气开采过程挥发出的气体。

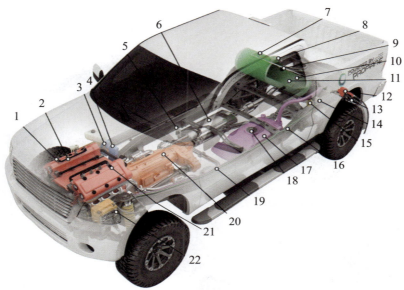

图6-1-7　Liquefied petroleum gas vehicle （LPGV）液化石油气汽车

1. fuel injection system (liquefied petroleum gas) 燃油喷射系统（液化石油气）
2. internal combustion engine (spark-ignited) 内燃机（火花点燃式）
3. Electronic Control Module (ECM) (gasoline) 电控模块（汽油）
4. Electronic Control Module (ECM) (liquefied petroleum gas) 电控模块（液化石油气）
5. fuel selector switch 燃料选择开关
6. exhaust system 排气系统
7. overfill protection device 过充防护装置
8. pressure gauge 压力表
9. pressure relief valve 卸压阀
10. float assembly 浮子总成
11. fuel tank (liquefied petroleum gas) 气瓶（液化石油气）
12. fuel filler (gasoline) 燃料加注口（液化石油气）
13. fuel filler (gasoline) 加油口（汽油）
14. fuel filter 燃油滤清器
15. tank valve 油箱阀
16. fuel line (liquefied petroleum gas) 燃料管路（液化石油气）
17. fuel tank (gasoline) 燃油箱（汽油）
18. fuel pump 油泵
19. fuel line (gasoline) 燃油管路（汽油）
20. transmission 变速器
21. fuel injection system (gasoline) 燃油喷射系统
22. battery 电池

PART 6 New energy vehicle 新能源汽车

1.3 Methanol and alcohol-powered vehicle 醇类汽车

醇类汽车是利用醇类燃料做能源驱动的汽车。醇类燃料主要指甲醇和乙醇,都属于含氧燃料。以甲醇为燃料的汽车称为甲醇汽车;以乙醇为燃料的汽车称为乙醇汽车(图6-1-8)。

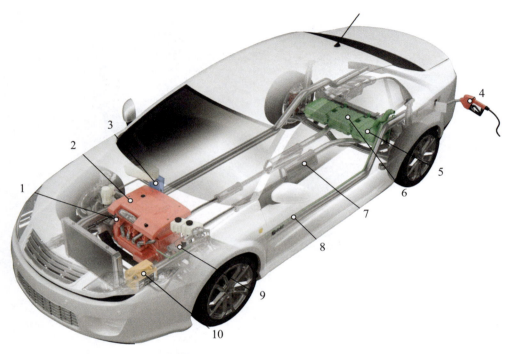

图6-1-8 Ethanol fuel vehicle 乙醇燃料汽车

1. fuel injection system 燃油喷射系统
2. internal combustion engine (spark-ignited) 内燃机(火花点燃式)
3. Electronic Control Module (ECM) 电子控制模块
4. fuel filler 加注口
5. fuel tank (ethanol/gasoline blend) 油箱(乙醇与汽油混合物)
6. fuel pump 燃料泵
7. exhaust system 排气系统
8. fuel line 燃料管路
9. transmission 变速器
10. battery 电池

1.4 Biodiesel vehicle 生物柴油汽车

生物柴油（Biodiesel）是指以油料作物、野生油料植物和工程微藻等水生植物油脂以及动物油脂、餐饮垃圾油等为原料油通过酯交换工艺制成的可代替石化柴油的再生性柴油燃料。生物柴油汽车就是指使用全部或部分的生物柴油作为燃料的汽车（图6-1-9）。

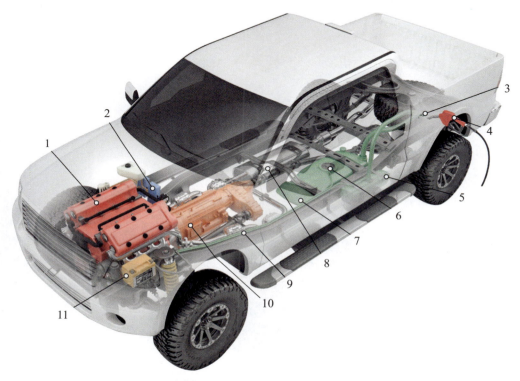

图6-1-9　Biodiesel vehicle 生物柴油汽车

1. internal combustion engine (compression-ignited) 内燃机（火花点燃式）
2. Electronic Control Module (ECM) 电控模块
3. diesel exhaust filler 柴油排放（处理液）加注口
4. fuel filler 加油口
5. Diesel Exhaust Fluid (DEF) tank 柴油排放处理液罐
6. fuel pump 燃油泵
7. fuel tank (biodiesel) 油箱（生物柴油）
8. aftertreatment system 后处理系统
9. fuel line 燃油管路
10. transmission 变速器
11. battery 电池

PART 6 New energy vehicle 新能源汽车

Chapter 2
New energy vehicle motor 新能源汽车电机

新能源汽车常用电机有直流电机、交流异步电机、永磁同步电机和开关磁阻电机等。

2.1 DC motor 直流电机

2.1.1 直流电机结构

直流电机可以将直流电流形式的电能转化为动能。它由一个固定部件——定子和一个转动支撑部件——转子（电枢）组成，主要部件如图6-2-1所示。

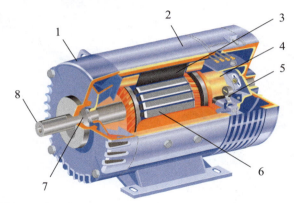

图6-2-1 Major components of a DC motor 直流电机主要部件

1. end bracket 端盖
2. frame 机架
3. stator 定子
4. commutator 换向器
5. brush assembly 电刷总成
6. armature 电枢
7. bearings 轴承
8. shaft 轴

2.1.2 直流电机工作原理

直流电机的定子有一对N、S极，电枢绕组的末端分别接到两个换向片上，电刷与两个换向片接触。如果给两个电刷加上直流电源，则有直流电流从电刷流入，经过线圈从电刷流出。根据电磁力定律，载流导体受到电磁力的作用，形成了一个转矩，使得转子逆时针转动，如图6-2-2（a）所示。转子转到图6-2-2（b）所示的位置，无电流流过。转子转到图6-2-2(c)所示的位置，直流电流换向，载流导体产生的转矩使得转子继续转动。

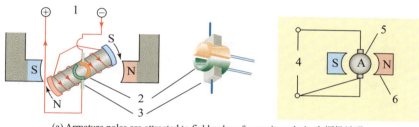

(a) Armature poles are attracted to field poles of opposite polarity 电枢极被吸引到极性相反的励磁上。电枢磁极与相反极性的磁场磁极相吸

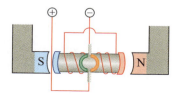
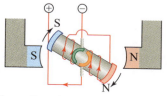

(b) At the gap in the commutator and no current flows 在换向片空隙位置时，无电流流动

(c) Current flows through the armature coil in the reverse direction 电流以反方向流经电枢线圈

图6-2-2　Permanent-magnet DC motor operation 永磁直流电机工作原理

1. DC supply 直流电源
2. commutator 换向片
3. brush 电刷

4. DC supply 直流电源
5. armature 电枢
6. permanent magnet 永磁铁

2.2 AC asynchronous motor 交流异步电机

2.2.1 交流异步电机结构

交流异步电机的特点是不为转子直接提供电流，而是通过与定子旋转磁场的磁场感应产生转子磁场。因为转子使用了定子旋转磁场产生的感应电流，所以通常异步电机也被称为感应式电机（Induction motor）。转子绕组不是由绝缘导线绕制而成，而是铝条或铜条与端环焊接而成或铸造而成，形状与鼠笼相似（图6-2-3）。

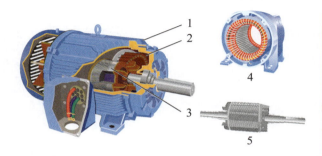

1. enclosure 电机壳
2. stator 定子
3. rotor 转子
4. three phase stator winding 三相定子绕组
5. squirrel cage rotor 笼型转子

图6-2-3　Squirrel cage induction motor 笼式感应电机

2.2.2 交流异步电机工作原理

当异步电机的三相定子绕组通入三相交流电后，将产生一个旋转磁场（图6-2-4）。该旋转磁场切割转子绕组，从而在转子绕组中产生感应电动势，电动势的方向由右手定则来确定。由于转子绕组是闭合通路，转子中便有电流产出，电流方向与电动势方向相同，而载流的转子导体在定子旋转磁场作用下将产生电磁力，电磁力的方向可用左手定则确定。由电磁力进而产生电磁转矩，驱动电机旋转，并且电机旋转方向与旋转磁场方向相同。

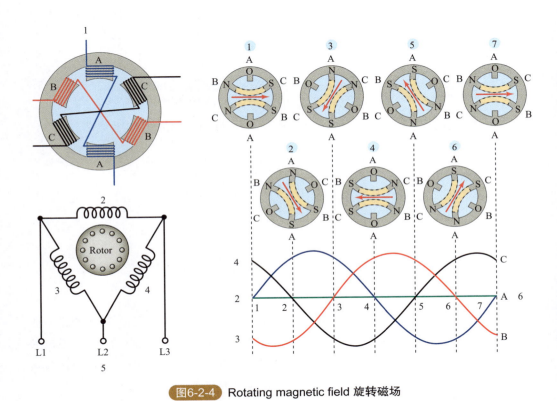

图6-2-4　Rotating magnetic field 旋转磁场

1. two poles wound in each single phase winding 每一单相绕组的两极绕线
2. phase A　A相
3. phase B　B相
4. phase C　C相
5. stator connection to three phase supply 接三相电源的定子接头
6. three phase input 三相输入

O 表示线圈电流为零
①~⑦表示旋转磁场转动的位置

2.3 Permanent magnet synchronous motor 永磁同步电机

2.3.1 永磁同步电机结构

永磁同步电机（Permanent Magnet Synchronous Motor, PMSM）结构如图6-2-5所示。转子采用径向永久磁铁做成的磁极，转子上安装铷铁硼磁钢。转子与旋转磁场同步旋转，旋转磁场的速度取决于电源频率。

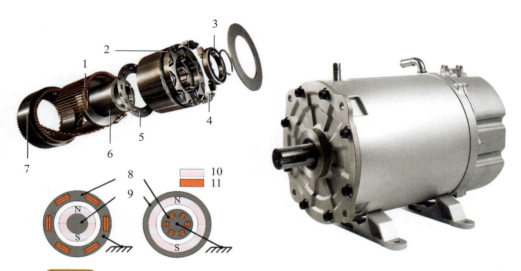

图6-2-5 Permanent magnet synchronous motor construction 永磁同步电机结构

1. bar wound wire 条形绕线
2. rotor core sections 转子芯断面
3. bearing support assembly 轴承支撑总成
4. magnets 磁铁
5. steel plate 钢片
6. rotor hub 转子毂
7. stator core 定子芯
8. stator 定子
9. rotor 转子
10. permanent magnets 永磁铁
11. windings 绕组

2.3.2 永磁同步电机工作原理

如果在定子的绕组上施加一个三相电流，就会产生相应的旋转磁场。转子的磁极随着该旋转磁场的方向进行相应的转动（图6-2-6）。转子转动的速度与旋转磁场的转速相同，该转速也被称为同步转速，同步电机也因此得名。通过三相电流的频率和极点数量可精确地确定同步电机的转速。

PART6 New energy vehicle
新能源汽车

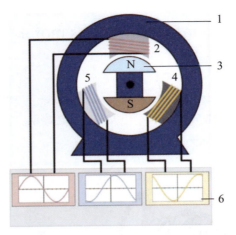

图6-2-6 The operation of a permanent magnet synchronous motor 永磁同步电机工作原理

1. stator 定子
2. winding U 绕组U
3. rotor 转子
4. winding V 绕组V
5. winding W 绕组W
6. phase of three-phase current 三相电流的相位

2.4 Switched reluctance motor 开关磁阻电机

2.4.1 开关磁阻电机结构

开关磁阻电机（Switched Reluctance Motor, SRM）结构如图6-2-7所示。定子和转子均为凸极结构，定子和转子的齿数不等，定子齿上套有线圈，两个空间位置相对的定子齿线圈相串联，形成一相绕组。转子由铁芯叠片而成，其上无绕组。

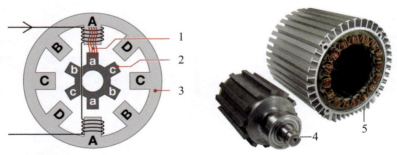

图6-2-7 Switched reluctance motor construction 开关磁阻电机结构

1. flux 磁通
2. rotor 转子
3. stator 定子
4. rotor 转子
5. stator 定子

2.4.2 开关磁阻电机工作原理

开关磁阻电机的工作原理遵循"磁阻最小原理"——磁通总是沿着磁阻最小的路径闭合,随磁场扭曲会产生磁性引力,促使电机转动。当给其中一相绕组励磁时,所产生的磁场力使离该定子极最近的一对转子极旋转到其轴线与励磁定子极轴线重合的位置上,并使该相励磁绕组的电感最大。按照定子绕组的分布,以一个方向依次给各相绕组通电,转子齿会和所通电的定子齿依次吸合而连续旋转(图6-2-8)。

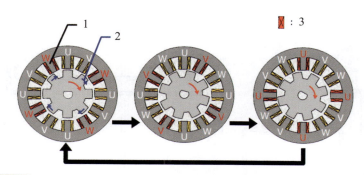

图6-2-8 The operation of switched reluctance motor 开关磁阻电机工作原理

1. electromagnet 电磁铁
2. magnetic attraction 磁性引力
3. current direction 电流流向

2.5 Hub motor 轮毂电机

轮毂电机又称车轮内装电机(In-wheel motor),将动力装置、传动装置和制动装置都整合到轮毂内,使电动车辆的机械部分大为简化(图6-2-9)。多数轮毂电机采用永磁同步电动机结构,基本原理与永磁同步电机相同。

1. brake shoes 制动蹄
2. suspension 悬架
3. harness 线束
4. tire 轮胎
5. rim 轮辋
6. permanent magnets 永磁体
7. motor rotor 电机转子
8. bearing 轴承
9. motor controller 电机控制器
10. motor stator 电机定子
11. motor windings 电机绕组

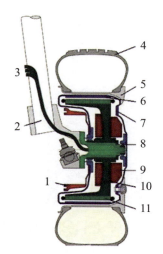

图6-2-9 Sectional view of a hub motor 轮毂电机剖面图

·217·

PART6 New energy vehicle 新能源汽车

2.6 Motor cooling system 电机冷却系统

电动汽车驱动电机与控制器的冷却系统主要有电动泵、散热器、冷却管道等。冷却液带走驱动电机、逆变器、DC/DC 转换器、充电器等产生的热量，冷却水泵带动冷却液在冷却管道中循环流动，通过散热器散热（图6-2-10）。为使散热器热量散发更充分，通常还在散热器后方设置风扇。

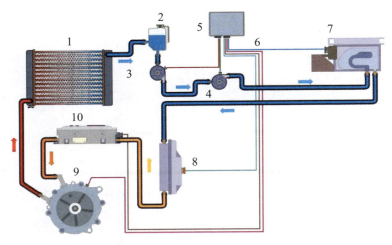

图6-2-10 Motor cooling system 电机冷却系统

1. radiator (cooling fans not shown) 散热器（冷却风扇没有展示出来）
2. reservoir 储液罐
3. electric pump #1 1号电动泵
4. electric pump #2 2号电动泵
5. electric vehicle control module 电动汽车控制模块
6. temperature signals 温度信号
7. on-board charger 车载充电器
8. DC/DC converter DC/DC 转换器
9. traction motor 驱动电机
10. inverter 逆变器

Chapter 3

New energy vehicle battery 新能源汽车电池

新能源汽车常用电池有锂离子电池、镍氢电池、超级电容器和飞轮电池等。

3.1 Lithium ion battery 锂离子电池

3.1.1 锂离子电池的结构

锂离子电池由正极、负极、隔板、电解液和安全阀等组成。圆柱形锂离子电池结构如图6-3-1所示。

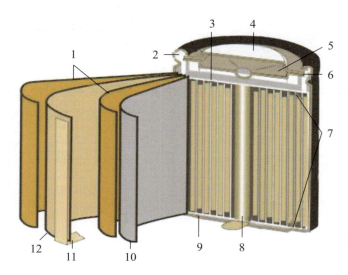

图6-3-1 Cylindrical lithium ion battery structure schematic diagram
圆柱形锂离子电池结构示意图

1. separator 隔板
2. (Positive Temperature Coefficient, PTC) 正温度系数热敏电阻（用于检测锂电池外表的温度）
3. cathode lead 负极引线
4. cathode cover 负极盖
5. safety vent 安全通风阀
6. gasket 垫片
7. insulator 绝缘板
8. center pin 中心轴
9. container 壳体
10. cathode 负极
11. anode lead 负极引线
12. anode 正极

3.1.2 锂离子电池的工作原理

电池充电时，锂离子从正极材料的晶格中脱出，通过电解质溶液和隔板嵌入到负极中（图6-3-2）。放电时，锂离子从负极中脱出，通过电解质溶液和隔板嵌入到正极材料晶格中。在整个充、放电过程中，锂离子往来于正、负极之间。

PART6 New energy vehicle
新能源汽车

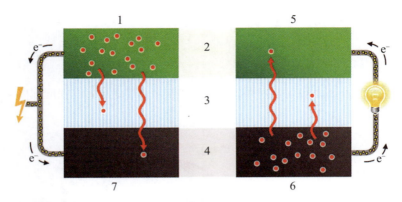

图6-3-2 The operation of a lithium ion battery 锂离子电池的工作原理

1. charge 充电
2. cathode 负极
3. separator, electrolyte 隔板，电解液
4. anode 正极
5. discharge 放电
6. electron 电子
7. lithium ion 锂离子

3.2 Ni-MH battery 镍氢电池

3.2.1 镍氢电池的结构

单体电池都由正极板、负极板和装在正极板和负极板之间的隔板组成（图6-3-3）。

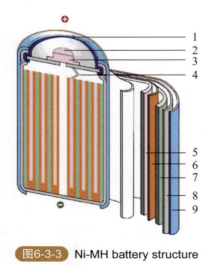

图6-3-3 Ni-MH battery structure 镍氢电池构造

1. gasket 密封圈
2. positive terminal 正极端
3. gas release vent 放气孔
4. positive tab 正极极耳
5. positive electrode (NiOOH) 正极（氢氧化氧镍）
6. separator 隔板
7. negative electrode (MH) 负极（金属氢化物）
8. case (negative terminal) 壳体（负极端）
9. jacket 外壳

3.2.2 镍氢电池的工作原理

镍氢电池正极的活性物质为氢氧化氧镍NiOOH（放电时）和氢氧化镍Ni(OH)$_2$（充电时），负极板的活性物质为氢H$_2$（放电时）和水H$_2$O（充电时），电解液为氢氧化钾溶液（图6-3-4）。充电时，水H$_2$O在电解质溶液中分解为氢离子H$^+$和氢氧离子OH$^-$，氢离子被负极吸收，负极从金属转化为金属氢化物。正极由氢氧化镍Ni(OH)$_2$变成氢氧化氧镍（NiOOH）和水H$_2$O；放电时，氢离子H$^+$离开负极，氢氧离子OH$^-$离开正极，氢离子和氢氧离子在电解质中结合成水H$_2$O并释放电能。正极由氢氧化氧镍（NiOOH）变成氢氧化镍Ni(OH)$_2$。

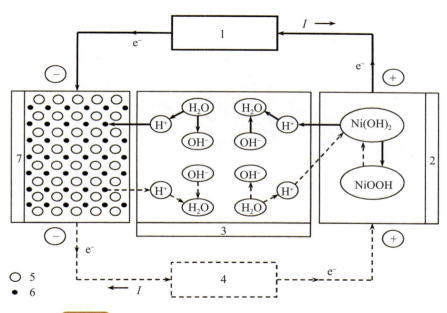

图6-3-4　The operation of a Ni-MH battery 镍氢电池工作原理

1. charger 充电器
2. positive electrode（Ni）正极（镍）
3. electrolyte 电解液
4. discharge 放电
5. metal hydride 金属氢化物
6. hydrogen 氢
7. negative electrode (MH) 负极（金属氢化物）

3.3 Fuel cells 燃料电池

3.3.1 燃料电池结构

氢气通过燃料电池的阳极催化剂分解成电子和氢离子（质子）。其中质子通过质子交换膜到达负极和氧气反应变成水和热量。对应的电子则从正极通过外电路流向负极产生电能（图6-3-5）。气体扩散层为参与反应的气体和生成的水提供传输通道、支撑催化剂。双极板又叫流场板，起到分隔氧化剂和还原剂等作用。

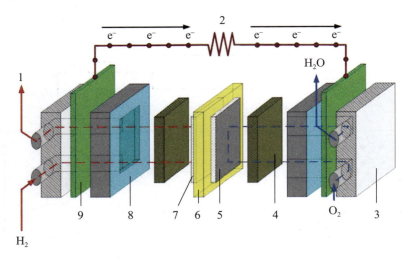

图6-3-5 Fuel cell structure 燃料电池结构

1. unused hydrogen 未使用的氢气	质子交换膜
2. electrons 电子	7. anode Pt/c 阴极催化剂
3. support block 支撑块	8. bipolar plate (carbon) 双极板（碳纤维纸）
4. gas diffusion layer (carbon) 气体扩散层（碳纤维纸）	9. terminal plate (Au-coated) 端子板（镀金）
5. cathode Pt/c 阳极催化剂	
6. Proton Exchange Membrane (PEM)	

3.3.2 燃料电池工作原理

在质子交换膜燃料电池中，电解质和质子能够在薄的聚合物膜之间渗透但不导电。氢流入燃料电池到达阳极，裂解成氢离子（质子）和电子。氢离子通过电解质渗透到阴极，而电子通过外部回路流动，提供电力。以空气形式存在的氧供应到阴极，与电子和氢离子结合形成水（图6-3-6）。

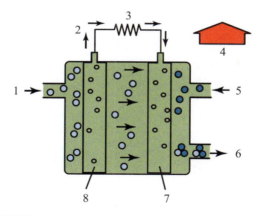

图6-3-6 The operation of a fuel cells 燃料电池工作原理

1. hydrogen（H）氢
2. electron flow 电子流动
3. load 负载
4. electricity 电力
5. air（O₂）空气
6. water（H₂O）水
7. positive electrode 正极
8. negative electrode 负极

3.4 Supercapacitor 超级电容器

3.4.1 超级电容器结构

超级电容器（Supercapacitor, Ultracapacitor）是指相对传统电容器而言具有更高容量的一种电容器。通过极化电解质来储存能量。超级电容器是介于电容器和电池之间的储能器件，它既具有电容器可以快速充放电的特点，又具有电池的储能特性（图6-3-7）。

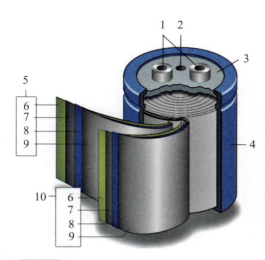

图6-3-7 Schematic construction of a wound supercapacitor 缠绕式超级电容器构造示意图

1. terminals 端子
2. safety vent 安全通风口
3. sealing disc 密封盘
4. aluminum can 铝壳
5. positive pole 正极
6. separator 隔板
7,9. carbon electrode 碳电极
8. collector 集流体
10. negative pole 负极

3.4.2 超级电容器工作原理

当电压加载到两电极上时,加在正极板上的电势吸引电解质中的负离子,负极板吸引正离子,从而在两电极的表面形成了一个双电层电容器。随着超级电容器的放电,正、负极板上的电荷被外电路释放,电解液界面上的电荷相应地减少(图6-3-8)。

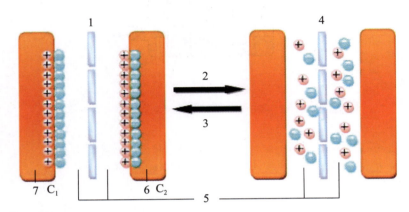

图6-3-8 The operation of a double layer supercapacitor 双电层超级电容器工作原理

1,4. separator 隔板
2. discharge 放电
3. charge 充电
5. electrolyte 电解液
6. negative electrode 负极
7. positive electrode 正极

3.5 Flywheel battery 飞轮电池

3.5.1 飞轮电池结构

飞轮电池实际是一种机电能量转换和储存装置,根据飞轮能够储存和释放能量的特性研制的一种机械式蓄电池,就是飞轮蓄电池。在飞轮的内部镶有永久性磁铁,外壳上装有感应线圈,这样飞轮就具有电机和发电机的双重功能(图6-3-9)。

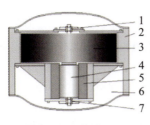
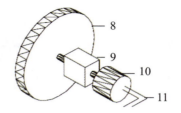

图6-3-9 Basic structure of flywheel battery 飞轮电池的基本结构

1,7. bearing 轴承
2. containment 外壳
3. flywheel rotor 飞轮转子
4. motor/generator rotor 电机/发电机转子
5. motor/generator stator 电机/发电机定子
6. vacuum or very low pressure 真空或低压
8. flywheel 飞轮
9. gearbox 变速器（与"transmission 含义等同，表示变速器"，余同）
10. motor/generator 电机/发电机
11. electric input or output 电力输入或输出

3.5.2 飞轮电池工作原理

充电时，电机作为电机运行，电机带动飞轮加速储能，能量以机械形式储存在高速旋转的飞轮中。放电时，电机作为发电机运行，高速旋转的飞轮利用其惯性作用带动电机减速运行，电机释放的电能通过电力电子转换器转换为负载所需的频率和电压，机械能转换为电能（图6-3-10）。

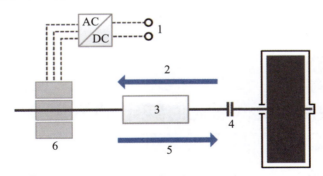

图6-3-10 The operation of a flywheel battery 飞轮电池工作原理

1. V_{DC} link V_{DC} 接线
2. kinetic energy from the flywheel used to drive the motor 飞轮的动能用于驱动电机
3. gearbox 变速器
4. clutch 离合器
5. electricity supplied to motor and accelerate the flywheel 向电机供电，加速飞轮
6. electric machine 电机

PART 6　New energy vehicle 新能源汽车

3.5.3　飞轮混合动力电动汽车

飞轮混合动力电动汽车包括飞轮储能系统和电机驱动系统（图6-3-11）。飞轮能够在汽车频繁加减速时回收能量。

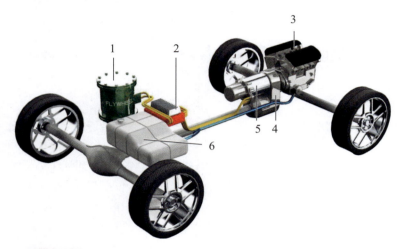

图6-3-11　Flywheel hybrid electric vehicle 飞轮混合动力电动汽车

1. flywheel storage system 飞轮储能系统
2. power electronics 功率电子元件
3. internal combustion engine 内燃机
4. transfer 分动器
5. electric traction motor/generator 驱动电机/发电机
6. fuel tank 油箱

Chapter 4

Battery electric vehicle 纯电动汽车

4.1　Overview 概述

纯电动汽车（battery electric vehicle, BEV）是指以车载电源为动力，用电机驱动车轮行驶的车辆。纯电动汽车将存储在电池中的电能高效地转化为车轮的动能，并能够在汽车减速制动时，将车轮的动能转化为电能充入电池。典型纯电动汽车主要部件如图6-4-1所示。

纯电动汽车除了电力驱动控制系统，其他部分的功能及其结构组成基本上与传统汽车类同（图6-4-2）。

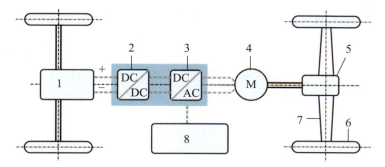

图6-4-1 Major components of battery electric vehicle 纯电动汽车主要部件

1. battery pack 电池组
2. inverter 逆变器
3. converter 转换器
4. electric motor 电机
5. mechanical transmission 机械变速器
6. drive wheel 驱动轮
7. drive shaft 半轴
8. ECU and battery management 电控单元和电池管理

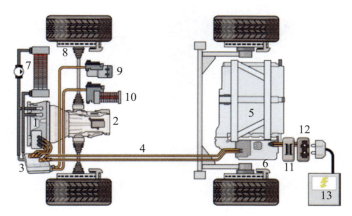

图6-4-2 The main components of a battery electric vehicle 纯电动汽车的主要组件

1. electric motor/generator 电机
2. transmission with differential 变速器和差速器
3. power electronics 功率电子装置
4. high voltage lines 高压导线
5. high voltage battery 高压电池
6. electronics box with control unit for battery regulation 电控箱和电池调节控制单元
7. cooling system 冷却系统
8. brake system 制动系统
9. high voltage air conditioner compressor 高压空调压缩机
10. high voltage heating 高压暖风装置
11. battery charger 充电器
12. charging contact for external charging 外部充电触点
13. external charging source 外接电源

PART 6 New energy vehicle 新能源汽车

4.2 Tesla Model S electric vehicle 特斯拉 Model S 电动汽车

特斯拉（Tesla）2008年发布第一款两门运动型跑车Roadster之后，陆续发布了Model S、Model X、Model Y 和 Model 3 等多款车型。下面介绍特斯拉Model S和Model 3纯电动汽车。Model S是特斯拉旗舰款高级电动轿车，拥有更长的续航里程、更快的加速性能以及更多的显示屏和更多的个性化配置。Model 3是一款面向大众、拥有门槛更低的纯电动车。

4.2.1 Tesla Model S powertrain 特斯拉 Model S 传动系

特斯拉Model S传动系组成如图6-4-3所示。

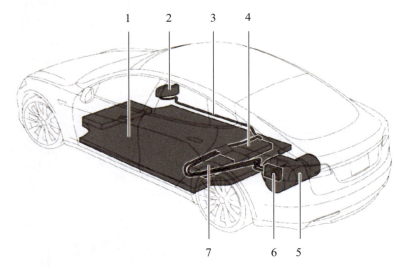

图6-4-3 Tesla Model S powertrain 特斯拉Model S传动系

1. battery 电池
2. DC/DC converter DC/DC 转换器
3. high voltage cabling 高压缆线
4. 10kW on-board master charger 10kW 车载主充电器
5. drive unit 驱动总成
6. charge port 充电口
7. optional: 10kW on-board slave charger 选装：10kW 车载辅助充电器

4.2.2 Tesla Model S high voltage system 特斯拉 Model S 高压系统

特斯拉Model S高压系统部件如图6-4-4所示。

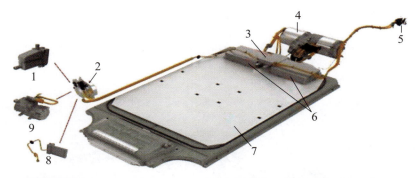

图6-4-4 Tesla Model S high voltage system 特斯拉Model S高压系统

1. PTC coolant heater PTC 冷却液加热器（采用PTC 热敏电阻元件为发热源）
2. DC to DC converter DC-DC 转换器
3. high voltage conjunction box 高压接线盒
4. drive unit 驱动总成
5. charge port 充电口
6. charger 充电器
7. high voltage battery 高压电池
8. PTC cabin heater PTC 座舱加热器
9. A/C Compressor A/C 压缩机

4.2.3　Tesla Model S drive unit 特斯拉Model S驱动总成

特斯拉Model S驱动总成由3部分组成，分别为三相交流感应电机、单级变速器、逆变器。这3个部分集成一体（图6-4-5）。

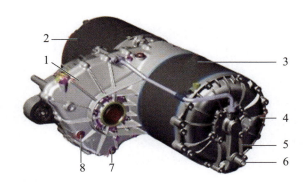

图6-4-5 Tesla Model S drive unit 特斯拉Model S驱动总成

1. transmission 变速器
2. inverter 逆变器
3. motor 电机
4. motor speed encoder 电机转速解码器
5. coolant manifold 冷却液歧管
6. coolant inlet 冷却液进口
7. transmission oil drain plug 变速器放油塞
8. transmission oil fill plug 变速器加油塞

4.2.4 Tesla Model S motor cooling system 特斯拉 Model S 电机冷却系统

特斯拉 Model S 电机采用液冷方式，定子周围布置冷却水套（图6-4-6）。

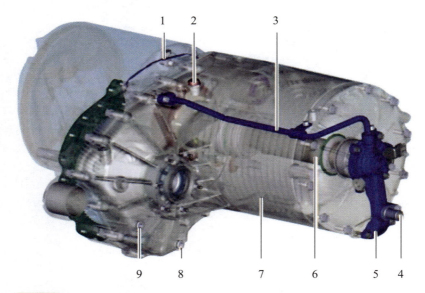

图6-4-6　Tesla Model S motor cooling system 特斯拉Model S电机冷却系统

1. air bleed pipe 放气管
2. transmission breathe 变速器通气口
3. coolant pipe 冷却液管
4. coolant inlet 冷却液入口
5. coolant manifold 冷却液歧管
6. rotor cooler 转子冷却装置
7. stator cooling jacket 定子冷却水套
8. transmission oil drain plug 变速器放油塞
9. transmission oil fill/level plug 变速器加油/油面塞

4.3　Tesla Model 3 electric vehicle 特斯拉 Model 3 电动汽车

特斯拉 Model 3 传动系组成如图6-4-7所示。高压电池安装于车身底部，负责能量的输出和储存。驱动总成包括三相交流感应电机、单级变速器、逆变器。

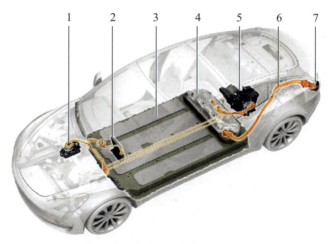

图6-4-7 Tesla Model 3 powertrain 特斯拉Model 3传动系

1. A/C Compressor 空调压缩机
2. cabin heater 座舱加热器
3. high voltage battery 高压电池
4. high voltage battery service panel

高压电池配电盒
5. rear drive unit 后驱动总成
6. high voltage cabling 高压电缆
7. charge port 充电口

4.3.1　Tesla Model 3 drive unit 特斯拉Model 3驱动总成

　　Model 3同样采用三合一电驱动系统，电机+逆变器+变速器（Motor+Inverter+Gearbox）。其中电机作为整车的动力来源，为车辆的行驶提供动力；变速器将电机的旋转传输到驱动轴；逆变器将直流电转换成交流电（图6-4-8）。

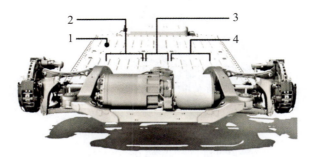

图6-4-8 Tesla Model 3 drive unit 特斯拉Model 3驱动总成

1. batte 电池
2. electric motor 电机
3. gearbox 变速器
4. inverter 逆变器

PART 6 New energy vehicle
新能源汽车

（1）电机　特斯拉的Roadster、Model S、Model X都采用感应电机，但Model 3首次采用嵌入式永磁同步电机（图6-4-9）。永磁同步电机在体积上更有优势，低中速领域效率更高，而感应电机则侧重于高速运转时的效率和大转矩。Model 3定位为量产型乘用车，更侧重于低中速效率，故采用嵌入式永磁同步电机。

图6-4-9　Tesla Model 3 motor 特斯拉Model 3电机

1. A, B and C field windings A、B 和 C 磁场绕组
2. rotor bearing 转子轴承
3. motor encoder 电机解码器
4. motor encoder sensor 电机解码传感器
5. rotor 转子
6. stator 定子

（2）单级变速器　特斯拉Model 3的电机转速范围很宽，故采用单级变速器，将电机的转速降低、转矩增大（图6-4-10）。

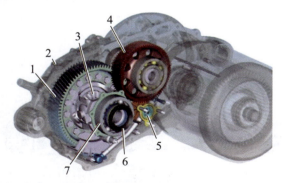

图6-4-10　Tesla Model 3 single speed gearbox 特斯拉Model 3单级变速器

1. ring gear 齿圈
2. gearbox casing 变速器壳体
3. differential gears 差速器齿轮
4. intermediate shaft gear 中间轴齿轮
5. oil pump 机油泵
6. driveshaft seal 半轴油封
7. differential bearing 差速器轴承

（3）逆变器　逆变器的作用是将电池的直流电转换为三相交流电，实现电机的驱动和制动能量回收控制。Model 3 逆变器通过采用 SiC（碳化硅）的新电源模块实现小型化（图6-4-11）。

图6-4-11　Tesla Model 3 inverter 特斯拉 Model 3 逆变器

1. drive inverter 驱动逆变器
2. high voltage cable inlet 高压线接口
3. high voltage cable connection cover 高压线接盖
4. 12V connector 12V 接口

4.3.2　Tesla Model 3 high voltage battery 特斯拉 Model 3 高压电池

特斯拉 Model 3 电池电压为350V，容量为230Ah，由四个模组构成（图6-4-12）。其中两个模组由25个电池模块构成，另外两个模组由23个电池模块构成。每个电池模块又由46个电芯组成，整个电池共有4416个电芯。

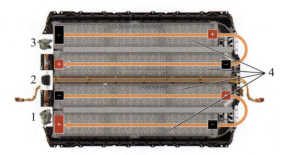

图6-4-12　Tesla Model 3 battery pack arrangement 特斯拉 Model 3 电池组排列

1. positive contactor 正极接触器
2. pyro fuse 高温保险丝
3. negative contactor 负极接触器
4. cell module 电芯模块

PART 6 New energy vehicle 新能源汽车

（1）电池冷却　冷却液沿着电池的4个模块组均匀分布，每个模块组有7个平行通道（1个通道又由28个微通道组成），从而确保电池均匀冷却（图6-4-13）。

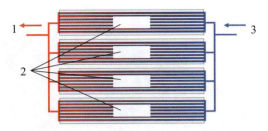

图6-4-13　Battery pack cooling system flow distribution 电池组冷却系统流量分布

1. coolant outlet 冷却液出口
2. module 模块
3. coolant inlet 冷却液入口

（2）高压电池配电盒　特斯拉Model 3电池配电盒内集成了电池管理系统（BMS）、充电系统、控制器、保险丝和DC转换器等高压部件（图6-4-14）。

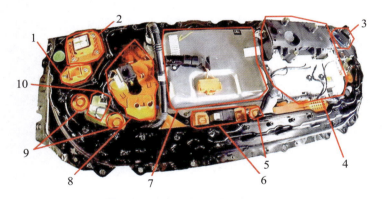

图6-4-14　Tesla Model 3 high voltage battery service panel 特斯拉Model 3高压电池配电盒

1. 3-phase charger port connector 三相充电器接口
2. charger port cable connector 充电口缆线接头
3. 12 Volt output 12V输出
4. high voltage controller circuit under this cover 高压控制器电路
5. regulator fuse 调节器保险丝
6. pyro-fuse 高温保险丝
7. power conversion unit (DC to DC converter) 功率转换单元（DC-DC 转换器）
8. current sensor and contactors for supercharging 超级充电的电流传感器和接触器
9. terminal 接线柱
10. negative contact 负极触点

4.4 Audi electric vehicle e-tron 奥迪电动汽车 e-tron

4.4.1 Overview 概述

奥迪 e-tron 纯电动 SUV 采用电池底部布局，配备容量 95kWh 的动力锂电池组。前后桥各配置了一台大功率驱动电机，组成双电机纯电动力总成（图 6-4-15）。

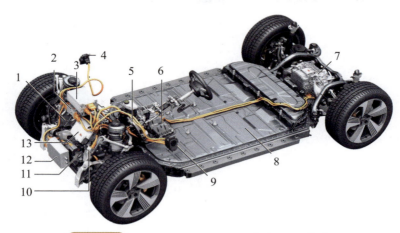

图 6-4-15 Audi e-tron powertrain 奥迪 e-tron 传动系

1. voltage converter 电压转换器
2. high voltage charge current distributor 高压充电分配器
3. high voltage battery charger 1 高压电池充电器 1
4. high voltage battery charging socket 2 高压电池充电插座 2
5. high voltage heater (PTC) 高压加热器（正温度系数加热元件）
6. switching unit for high voltage battery 高压电池切换单元
7. rear three-phase current drive 后三相电驱
8. high-voltage battery 1 高压电池 1
9. high-voltage battery charging socket 1 高压电池充电插座 1
10. highvoltage heater 2 (PTC) 高压加热器 2（正温度系数加热元件）
11. electrical air conditioner compressor 电动空调压缩机
12. highvoltage battery charger 2 高压电池充电器 2
13. front three-phase current drive 前三相电驱

4.4.2 Drive motor and transmission 驱动电机及变速器

奥迪 e-tron 电动 SUV 采用高集成度的电驱动桥（图 6-4-16）。e-tron 能够随行驶状况的变化连续调节前后桥分配的动力。在日常行驶中，车辆由后桥电机提供动力；当车辆在爬坡、全力加速或者传感器检测到后轮打滑时，车辆的 ECU 将在 0.03s 内让前桥电机完全介入，变成四驱系统。

PART 6 New energy vehicle 新能源汽车

图6-4-16　Drive motor and transmission 驱动电机及变速器

1. single speed transmission 单级变速器 2. engine ECU 发动机电控单元 3. selector lever, selector mechanism	选挡杆，换挡操纵机构 4. single speed transmission 单级变速器

（1）前桥驱动电机总成　前桥驱动电机总成包括电机、变速器和功率电子装置，这三个装置集成在一起（图6-4-17）。功率电子装置外部加装金属防护罩，防止碰撞后高压短路起火的风险。

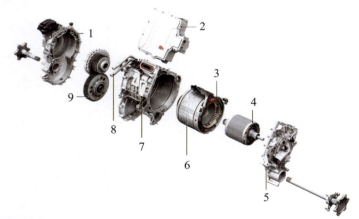

图6-4-17　Electric drive motor for front axle exploded diagram 前桥驱动电机分解图

1. gearbox housing 变速器壳体 2. power electronics 功率电子装置 3. stator 定子 4. rotor 转子 5. bearing plate 支撑板 6. stator carrier with cooling jacket 定子架及冷却套	7. housing 壳体 8. coolant connection 冷却液接口 9. gearbox with planet gear differential 变速器及行星齿轮差速器

· 236 ·

前驱动电机最大输出功率可达135kW，最大转矩为309Nm。电机与变速器连成一体（图6-4-18）。电机转子轴为空心轴，冷却液可进入电机轴，以便冷却。

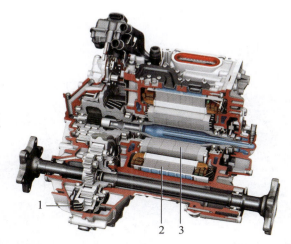

图6-4-18　Sectional view of electric drive motor and transmission for front axle 前桥驱动电机和变速器剖面图

1. single speed transmission 单级变速器 2. stator 定子	3. rotor 转子

（2）后桥驱动电机总成　与前桥电机总成一样，后桥驱动电机总成也将电机、变速器和功率电子装置集成在一起，简化了高压布线，结构更加紧凑。后驱传动采用同轴行星排布置和轻量化差速器结构，电机壳体与变速器前壳体整体压铸，共壳体设计（图6-4-19）。

图6-4-19　Electric drive motor for rear axle exploded diagram 后桥驱动电机分解图

1. coolant connection 冷却液接口 2. stator 定子 3. rotor 转子 4. transmission with planet gear dif-	ferential 变速器及行星齿轮差速器 5. stator carrier with cooling jacket 定子架及冷却套 6. power electronics 功率电子装置

· 237 ·

PART 6 New energy vehicle 新能源汽车

后桥电机通过同轴式结构来传递力矩,最大输出功率可达165kW,最大转矩为335Nm。电机定子采用三个呈120°布置的铜绕组,转子为铝制笼型(图6-4-20)。

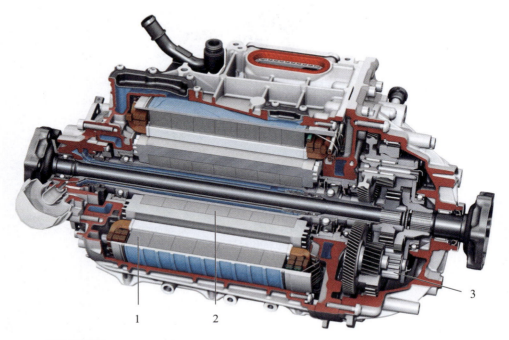

图6-4-20 Sectional view of electric drive motor and transmission for rear axle
后桥驱动电机和变速器剖面图

1. stator 定子
2. rotor 转子
3. single speed transmission 单级变速器

4.4.3 Electric drive cooling system 电驱动装置冷却

前桥和后桥上的电驱动装置是通过低温循环管路液冷的。定子和转子上都有冷却液流过。

(1)前桥电驱动装置冷却 前桥功率电子装置和电机彼此串联在冷却环路中,冷却液首先流经功率电子装置,然后对转子内部进行冷却。最后冷却液流经定子水套并返回到循环管路中(图6-4-21)。

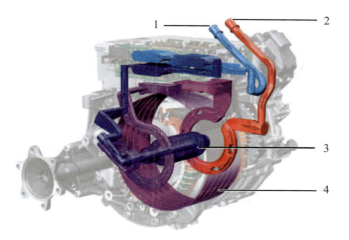

图6-4-21 Electric drive cooling system for front axle 前桥电驱动装置冷却系统

1. coolant inlet 冷却液入口
2. coolant outlet 冷却液出口
3. internal rotor cooling 内转子冷却
4. stator cooling jacket 定子冷却套

（2）后桥电驱动装置冷却 在后桥电驱动装置中，冷却液先流经功率电子装置，然后流经定子冷却水套、转子内水腔，最后再返回冷却液循环管路（图6-4-22）。

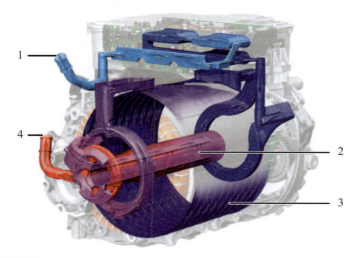

图6-4-22 Electric drive cooling system for rear axle 后桥电驱动装置冷却系统

1. coolant inlet 冷却液入口
2. internal rotor cooling 内转子冷却
3. stator cooling jacket 定子冷却套
4. coolant outlet 冷却液出口

· 239 ·

4.4.4 Power electronics 功率电子装置

功率电子装置（电驱动控制单元）的作用是为驱动电机提供所需的交流电流（DC-AC），还有就是在进行制动能量回收时将交流电转换为直流电进行存储（AC-DC）（图6-4-23）。每个电驱动装置上都安装有一个功率电子装置。功率电子装置通过螺栓直接与电机相连。

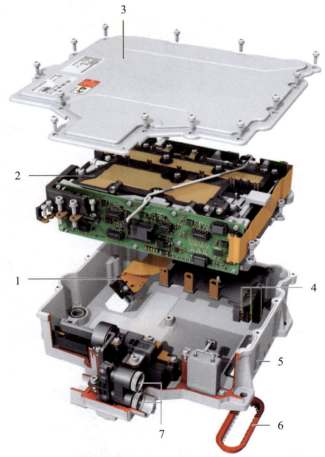

图6-4-23 Power electronics功率电子装置

1. 12 Volt connection 12V接口
2. control electronics 控制电子装置
3. cover 盖子
4. three-phase connection to stator windings 三相交流电接口，通向定子绕组
5. housing 壳体
6. seal 密封
7. DC connection from high voltage battery 高压电池直流电接口

4.4.5　High voltage battery 高压电池

奥迪e-tron电池的分解如图6-4-24所示。电池共有36个模块，每个模块由12个60Ah的电芯组成。电池功率为95kWh，满足400km续航里程。

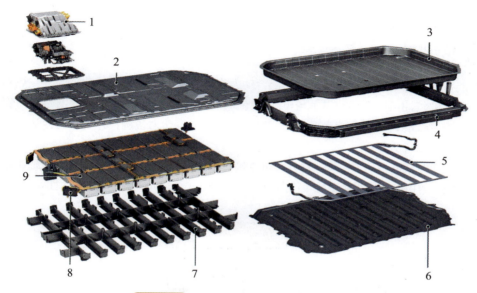

图6-4-24　High voltage battery 高压电池

1. BJB (Battery Junction Box) 电池接线盒
2. housing cover (aluminum sheet) 壳体盖（铝板）
3. housing tray 壳体盘
4. battery frame 电池架
5. cooling system 冷却系统
6. lower protection cover 下保护盖
7. aluminum crash structure 铝制防撞结构
8. BMC (Battery Management Contrcller) 电池管理控制器
9. cell module with twelve prismatic cells 12个方形电芯组成的模块

PART 6 New energy vehicle 新能源汽车

Chapter 5
Hybrid electric vehicle 混合动力电动汽车

5.1 Overview 概述

混合动力电动汽车，通常也称为混合动力汽车，指同时装备两种动力源——热动力源（传统的汽油机或者柴油机）与电动力源（电池与电机）的汽车。根据混合动力驱动的联结方式，混合动力系统主要分为三类：串联式混合动力系统、并联式混合动力系统和串并联式混合动力系统。

（1）串联式混合动力系统　由内燃机直接带动发电机发电，产生的电能通过控制单元传到电池，再由电池传输给电机转化为动能，最后通过变速机构来驱动汽车（图6-5-1）。

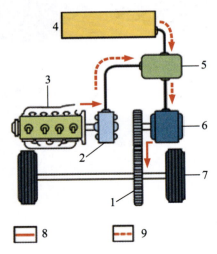

图6-5-1　A drawing of the power flow in a typical series hybrid electric vehicle
典型串联式混合动力电动汽车动力流程图

1. reduction gear 减速齿轮
2. generator 发电机
3. gasoline engine 汽油机
4. battery 电池
5. inverter 逆变器
6. motor 电机
7. drive wheels 驱动轮
8. drive power 驱动动力
9. electric power 电力

（2）并联式混合动力系统　并联式混合动力系统有两套驱动系统，传统的内燃机系统和电机驱动系统，两个系统既可以同时协调工作，也可以各自单独工作驱动汽车（图6-5-2）。

（3）串并联（混联）式混合动力系统　内燃机系统和电机驱动系统各有一套机械变速机构，两套机构或通过齿轮系，或采用行星轮式结构结合在一起，从而综合调节内燃机与电机之间的转速关系（图6-5-3）。

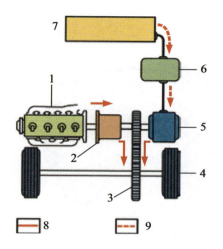

图6-5-2　A drawing of the power flow in a typical parallel hybrid electric vehicle
典型并联式混合动力电动汽车动力流程图

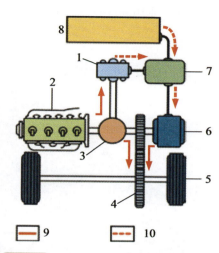

图6-5-3　A drawing of the power flow in a series parallel hybrid electric vehicle
串并联式混合动力电动汽车动力流程图

1. gasoline engine 汽油机
2. transmission 变速器
3. reduction gear 减速齿轮
4. drive wheels 驱动轮
5. motor/generator 电机/发电机
6. inverter 逆变器
7. battery 电池
8. drive power 驱动动力
9. electric power 电力

1. generator 发电机
2. gasoline engine 汽油机
3. power split device 功率分流装置
4. reduction gear 减速齿轮
5. drive wheels 驱动轮
6. motor 电机
7. inverter 逆变器
8. battery 电池
9. drive power 驱动动力
10. electric power 电力

PART 6 New energy vehicle 新能源汽车

5.2 Toyota hybrid system 丰田混合动力系统

下面以丰田普锐斯混合动力电动汽车为例介绍丰田混合动力系统（Toyota Hybrid System, THS）。

5.2.1 The main components of Prius hybrid system 普锐斯混合动力系统主要部件

普锐斯混合动力系统使用汽油机和电机两种动力，通过混联方式进行工作，达到低排放的效果。丰田混合动力系统的主要部件在车上的位置见图6-5-4。

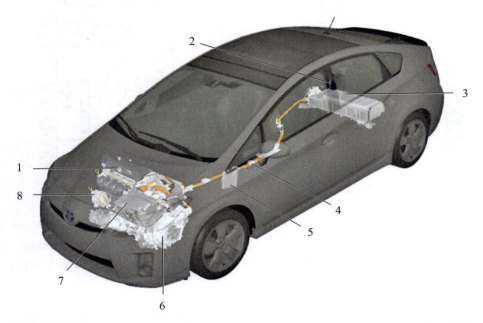

图6-5-4 The main components of Prius hybrid system 普锐斯混合动力系统主要部件

1. engine 发动机
2. auxiliary battery 辅助电池
3. high voltage battery 高压电池
4. high voltage harness 高电压线束
5. HV ECU 混合动力汽车电控单元
6. hybrid power transaxle 混合动力传动桥
7. inverter assembly 逆变器总成
8. compressor assembly 压缩机总成

5.2.2 Prius engine 普锐斯发动机

普锐斯采用阿特金森循环发动机，其热效率高，膨胀比大（图6-5-5）。

图6-5-5 Prius engine and motor 普锐斯发动机与电机

1. power split device 功率分流装置
2. electric motor 电机
3. generator/starter 发电机/起动机
4. 4 cylinder internal combustion engine 四缸内燃机

（1）阿特金森循环发动机工作原理　在传统发动机（奥托循环发动机）中，压缩比和膨胀比是一样的。阿特金森循环发动机与传统发动机相比，除了进气、压缩、做功和排气之外，还有一个"回流"行程，在压缩行程中，通过延迟关闭进气门，部分气缸内的空气燃油混合气被压"回流"到进气歧管中（图6-5-6）。其最大特点就是做功行程比压缩行程长，也就是我们常说的膨胀比大于压缩比，更长的做功行程可以更有效地利用燃烧后废气残存的高压，所以燃油效率比传统发动机更高一些。

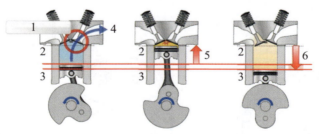

图6-5-6 Atkinson cycle engine working process 阿特金森循环发动机工作过程

1. delay intake valve closing time 延迟进气门关闭时间
2. TDC（Top Dead Center）上止点
3. BDC（Bottom Dead Center）下止点
4. backflow 回流
5. compression 压缩
6. power 做功

PART6 New energy vehicle
新能源汽车

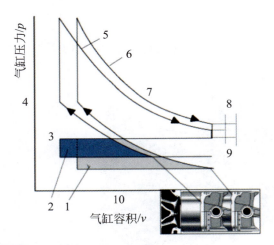

阿特金森发动机和传统发动机工作过程的比较如图6-5-7所示。两者的压缩起始点不同，阿特金森高膨胀比发动机压缩起始点较晚，因此泵气损失小。

图6-5-7　Engine indicator diagram 发动机的工作过程比较

1. conventional cycle pumping loss 传统循环泵气损失
2. high expansion ratio cycle pumping loss 高膨胀比循环泵气损失
3. Compression stroke 压缩冲程
4. cylinder pressure 气缸压力
5. high expansion ratio cycle 高膨胀比循环
6. conventional cycle 传统循环
7. expansion stroke 膨胀冲程
8. exhaust loss comparison 膨胀损失比较
9. compression starting point 压缩起始点
10. cylinder volume 气缸容积

实现阿特金森循环的关键是对发动机的配气机构进行合理的设计。利用可变气门定时系统VVT-i控制合适可变的进气门关闭时刻，进而控制不同工况下发动机的负荷（普锐斯混合动力发动机进气门关闭相位如图6-5-8所示，进气门关闭角度可在61°～102°范围内调整，气缸容积随着变化）。

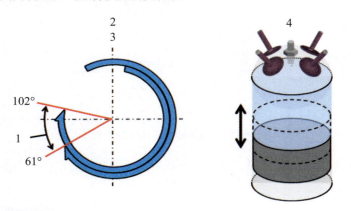

图6-5-8　Intake valve close phase change 进气门关闭相位变化

1. VVT-i (Variable Valve Timing intelligent) operation 智能可变气门正时工作情况
2. valve timing (intake valve) 气门正时（进气门）
3. TDC 上止点
4. cylinder volume 气缸容积

（2）冷却系统　普锐斯冷却系统增加了冷却液储热罐，当发动机冷启动时，冷却系统用辅助水泵将热冷却液送到发动机，发动机的"预热"可降低HC排放，如图6-5-9、图6-5-10所示。

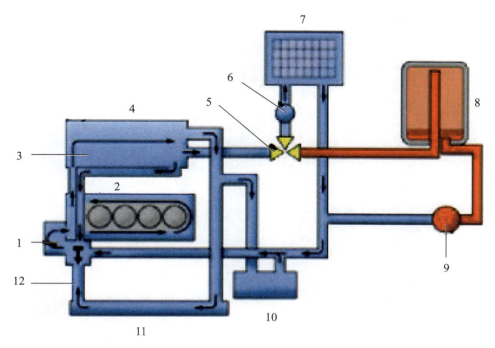

图6-5-9　Principle of Prius cooling system 普锐斯冷却系统原理

1. water pump 水泵
2. cylinder block 气缸体
3. bypass passage 旁通道
4. cylinder head 气缸盖
5. water valve 水阀
6. A/C water pump 空调水泵
7. heater core 加热器芯
8. coolant heat storage tank 冷却液储热罐
9. coolant heat storage water pump 冷却液储热水泵
10. throttle body 节气门体
11. radiator 散热器
12. thermostat 节温器

PART 6 New energy vehicle 新能源汽车

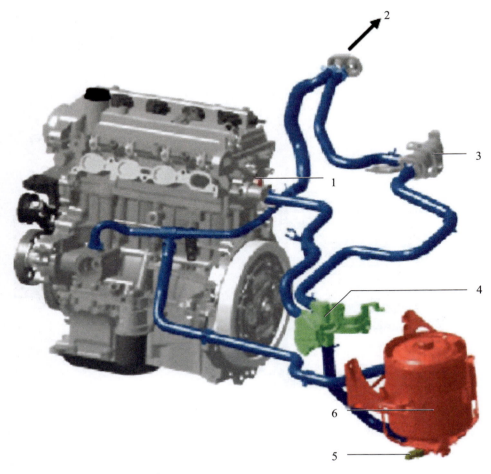

图6-5-10 Coolant heat storage tank冷却液储热罐

1. engine coolant temp.sensor (for engine control system) 发动机冷却液温度传感器（发动机控制系统）
2. to heater core 连到加热器芯
3. water pump (for heater) 加热器水泵
4. coolant flow control valve 冷却液流量控制阀
5. engine coolant temp.sensor (for coolant heat storage system) 发动机冷却液温度传感器（冷却液储热系统）
6. coolant heat storage tank 冷却液储热罐

5.2.3 Prius transaxle 普锐斯传动桥

普锐斯传动桥采用行星齿轮式无级变速机构，主要部件有MG1、MG2、组合齿轮单元、减速装置（包括主减速器驱动齿轮、主减速器从动齿轮、中间轴齿轮、差速器小齿轮）、减振器（也称阻尼器）等（图6-5-11）。

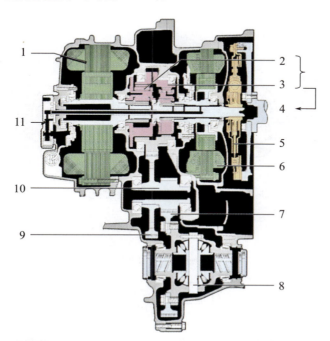

图6-5-11　Configuration of Prius transaxle 普锐斯传动桥结构

1. MG(Motor/Generator)2 电机/发电机2
2. motor reduction planetary gear 电机减速行星齿轮
3. power split planetary gear 功率分流行星齿轮
4. gears unit 组合齿轮单元
5. damper 减振器
6. MG(Motor/Generator)1 电机/发电机1
7. final reduction driven gear 主减速从动齿轮
8. differential pinion 差速器小齿轮
9. intermediate shaft gear 中间轴齿轮
10. final reduction driving gear 主减速驱动齿轮
11. oil pump 油泵

普锐斯传动桥通过组合齿轮单元传递动力（图6-5-12）。发动机、MG1、MG2、组合齿轮单元、减振器和油泵都安装在同心轴上。发动机输出的动力经过组合齿轮单元分为两部分：一部分驱动汽车；另一部分驱动MG1用来发电。

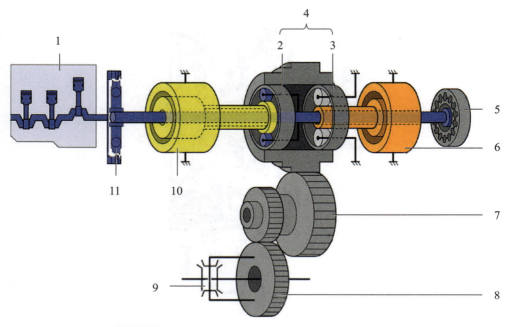

图6-5-12 Principle of Prius transaxle 普锐斯传动桥原理

1. engine 发动机
2. power split planetary gear 功率分流行星齿轮
3. motor reduction planetary gear 电机减速行星齿轮
4. gears unit 组合齿轮单元
5. oil pump 油泵
6. MG(Motor/Generator)2 电机/发电机2
7. intermediate shaft gear 中间轴齿轮
8. final reduction driven gear 主减速从动齿轮
9. differential pinion 差速器小齿轮
10. MG(Motor/Generator)1 电机/发电机1
11. damper 减振器

5.2.4 Prius motor/generator 普锐斯电机/发电机

普锐斯MG1（电机/发电机）和MG2（电机/发电机）为交流永磁同步电机，既可做电机，也可做发电机，二者可同时进行发电或动力输出（图6-5-13）。MG1主要用作发电机，其提供电能以驱动MG2并对高压电池充电。此外，启动发动机时，MG1用作起动机。MG2主要用作电机以驱动车辆，并利用MG1和高压电池提供的电能工作。此外，在减速过程中对HV蓄电池充电时，其用作发电机。

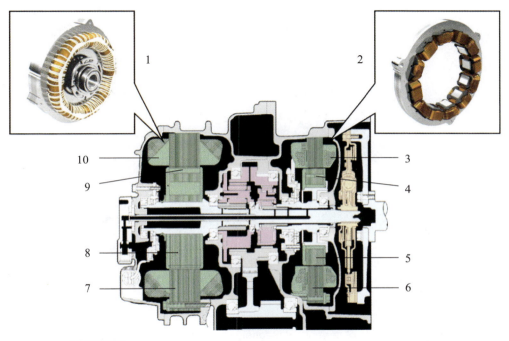

图6-5-13 Prius motor/generator configuration 普锐斯电机/发电机结构

1. MG(Motor/Generator)2 电机/发电机2
2. MG(Motor/Generator)1 电机/发电机1
3,10. stator coil 定子线圈
4,9. permanent magnet 永久磁铁
5,8. rotor 转子
6,7. stator 定子

PART 6 New energy vehicle
新能源汽车

电机的定子采用三相线圈结构（U相、V相和W相）（图6-5-14）。施加三相交流电时，在电机内部产生旋转磁场。根据转子方向和转速控制旋转磁场，通过旋转磁场吸引转子内的永久磁铁，从而产生转矩。发电时，转子（永久磁铁）旋转使磁场发生改变，同时由于电磁感应使电流流向定子线圈。

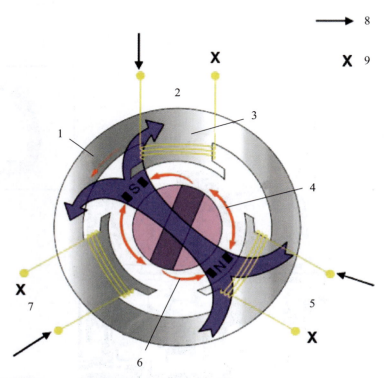

图6-5-14　Principle of permanent magnet synchronous motor 永磁同步电机原理

1. rotational magnetic field 旋转磁场
2. U phrase U 相
3. stator coil 定子线圈
4. repulsion 排斥
5. W phase W 相
6. attraction 吸引
7. V phase V 相
8. from inverter 从逆变器出来
9. connected internally in the motor 连到电机内部

解析器，又称转速传感器、旋转变压器等，安装在MG1和MG2内。主要由定子及定子绕组、转子及外壳等组成（图6-5-15）。旋转变压器与驱动电机同轴，安装在电机转子的轴端。在电机工作运行时，旋转变压器检测电机运转的转速及转角，并将信号传输给控制器。

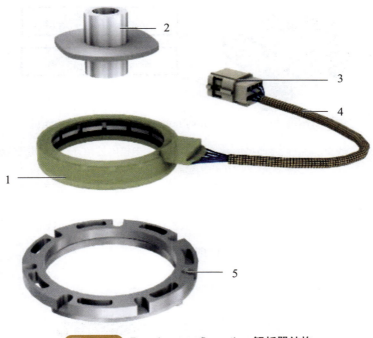

图6-5-15 Resolver configuration 解析器结构

1. stator 定子
2. rotor 转子
3. connector 接头
4. wire 线束
5. resolver casing 解析器壳体

5.2.5　Inverter assembly 逆变器总成

逆变器总成主要由以下四部分组成，如图6-5-16所示。MG ECU：用于控制逆变器和增压转换器；逆变器：产生用于驱动MG的三相交流电；增压转换器：将高压电池（直流电压201.6V）的电压最高升至直流电压650V；DC/DC转换器：将高压电池（直流电压201.6V）的电压降至直流电压14V（用于电气零部件）。

PART 6　New energy vehicle 新能源汽车

图6-5-16　Inverter assembly components 逆变器总成组成

1. MG ECU, controlling inverter assembly 电机/发电机电控单元，控制逆变器组件
2. inverter, AC⟵⟶DC 逆变器，交流⟵⟶直流
3. boost converter, DC 201.6V⟵⟶Max.DC 650V 增压转换器，直流201.6V⟵⟶Max 直流650V
4. DC/DC converter, DC 201.6V→DC 14V DC/DC 转换器，直流201.6V→直流14V

普锐斯逆变器总成的分解如图6-5-17所示。

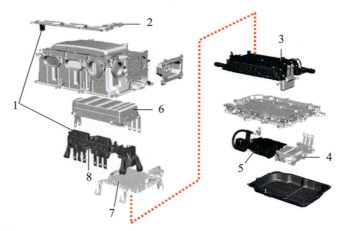

图6-5-17　Prius inverter assembly exploded diagram 普锐斯逆变器总成分解图

1. interlock switch 互锁开关
2. inverter cover 逆变器盖
3. IPMs(Intelligent Power Modules) 智能功率模块
4. reactor 电抗器
5. DC/DC converter DC/DC 转换器
6. capacitor 电容器
7. MG ECU 电机/发电机电控单元
8. inverter current sensor 逆变器电流传感器

逆变器将高压电池的高压直流电转换为三相交流电来驱动发电机MG1和电机MG2。增压转换器包括IPM、IGBT，将高压电池输出的额定电压DC 201.6V增压到DC 500V的最高电压（图6-5-18）。功率晶体管的启动由HV ECU控制。

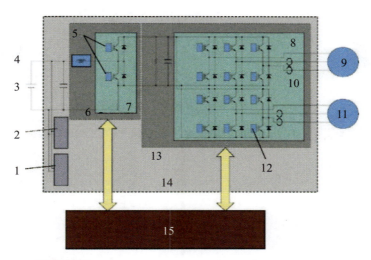

图6-5-18　Principle of inverter assembly逆变器总成原理

1. A/C inverter A/C 逆变器
2. DC/DC converter DC/DC 转换器
3. HV battery 高压电池
4. reactor 电抗
5. IGBT(Insulated Gate Bipolar Transistor) 绝缘栅双极型晶体管
6. boost converter 增压转换器
7,8.IPM(Intelligent Power Module) 智能功率模块
9. MG1 电机/发电机1
10. Current sensor 电流传感器
11. MG2 电机/发电机2
12. power transistor 功率晶体管
13. inverter 逆变器
14. inverter assembly 逆变器总成
15. HV ECU 混合动力汽车电控单元

5.2.6　DC/DC Converter DC/DC 转换器

　　DC/DC转换器将电池的电压从直流电压201.6V转换为直流电压14V，向汽车的电气零部件（如前照灯和音响系统）和HV ECU、A/C ECU提供直流电（图6-5-19）。

PART6 New energy vehicle 新能源汽车

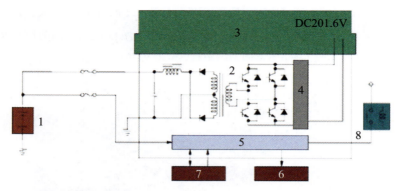

图6-5-19 Principle of DC/DC converter DC/DC转换器原理

1. auxiliary battery 辅助电池
2. DC/DC converter DC/DC 转换器
3. inverter 逆变器
4. input filter 输入滤波器
5. converter control circuit 转换器控制

电路
6. A/C ECU 空调电控单元
7. HV ECU 混合动力汽车电控单元
8. IG(IGNITION) 点火

5.2.7 Motor and inverter cooling system 电机和逆变器冷却系统

普锐斯采用配备有水泵的发电机（MG1）和电机（MG2）冷却系统，而且将其与发动机冷却系统分开（图6-5-20）。冷却系统的散热器集成在发动机的散热器中。这样散热器的结构得到简化，空间也得到有效利用。

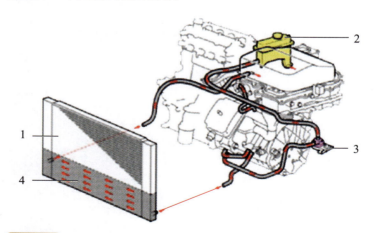

图6-5-20 Motor and inverter cooling system 电机和逆变器冷却系统

1. radiator (for engine) 发动机散热器
2. receiver tank 回收罐
3. water pump 水泵
4. radiator (for inverter) 逆变器散热器

5.2.8　Prius hybrid control system 普锐斯混合动力控制系统

普锐斯混合动力控制系统主要部件如图6-5-21所示。HV ECU根据加速踏板位置传感器发出的信号检测加速踏板上所施加力的大小。HV ECU收到发电机（MG1）和电机（MG2）转速度传感器发出的车速信号，并根据挡位传感器的信号检测挡位。HV ECU根据这些信息确定车辆的行驶状态，对发电机（MG1）、电机（MG2）和发动机的动力进行最优控制。

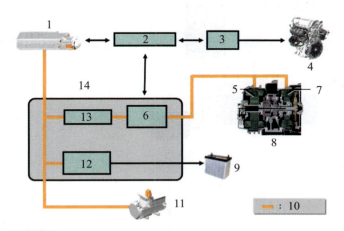

图6-5-21　Prius hybrid control system 普锐斯混合动力控制系统

1. high voltage battery 高压电池
2. HV (Hybrid Vehicle) ECU 混合动力汽车ECU
3. ECM(Electronic Control Module) 电控模块
4. engine 发动机
5. motor (MG2) 电机 (MG2)
6. inverter 逆变器
7. generator(MG1) 发电机(MG1)
8. hybrid power transaxle 混合动力传动桥
9. auxiliary battery 辅助电池
10. high voltage harness 高电压线束
11. compressor assembly 压缩机总成
12. DC/DC converter DC/DC 转换器
13. boost converter 增压转换器
14. inverter assembly 逆变器总成

普锐斯HV ECU接收每个传感器及各ECU（发动机ECM、蓄电池ECU和制动防滑控制ECU）的信息，根据这些信息计算所需的转矩和输出功率。HV ECU将计算结果发送给发动机ECM、变频器总成、蓄电池ECU和制动防滑控制ECU（图6-5-22）。

PART 6 New energy vehicle 新能源汽车

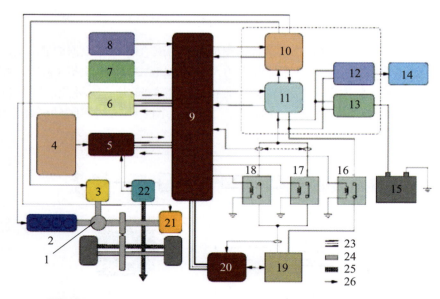

图6-5-22 Principle of hybrid control system 混合动力控制系统原理

1. planetary gear unit 行星齿轮单元
2. engine 发动机
3. MG1 电机/发动机1
4. speed sensor, yaw rate & deceleration, steering angle, brake pedal 转速传感器、横摆角速度和减速度、转向角、制动踏板
5. skid control ECU 防滑控制ECU
6. ECM 电控模块
7. accelerator pedal position sensor 油门踏板位置传感器
8. shift position sensor 换挡位置传感器
9. HV ECU 混合动力汽车ECU
10. inverter 逆变器
11. boost converter 增压转换器
12. A/C converter 空调转换器
13. DC/DC converter DC/DC 转换器
14. electric inverter, compressor 逆变器，压缩机
15. auxiliary battery 辅助电池
16 ~ 18. SMR 系统主继电器
19. HV battery 高压电池
20. battery ECU 电池ECU
21. MG2 电机/发动机2
22. brake ECU 制动ECU
23. CAN(Controller Area Network)控制器局域网络
24. mechanical power path 机械动力路线
25. hydraulic power path 液力路线
26. electrical signal 电信号

5.2.9 Prius battery 普锐斯电池

（1）普锐斯电池结构　普锐斯采用镍氢电池，六个1.2V的电芯串联组成一个7.2V的电池模块，28组模块串联构成蓄电池。总电压为201.6V。电池、电池ECU和SMR（系统主继电器）集中在一起，位于后排座后面的行李厢中，这样可更有效地使用车内空间（图6-5-23）。

· 258 ·

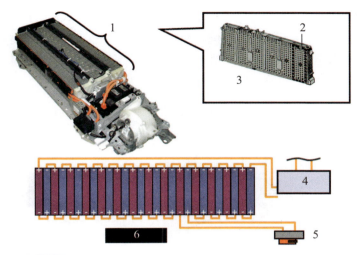

图6-5-23　Prius battery main components 普锐斯电池主要部件

1,6. 28 battery modules 28个电池模块
2. cell（1.2V）电芯（1.2V）
3. battery module (6 cell=7.2V) 电池模块（6个电芯=7.2V）
4. HV terminal box assembly 高压接线盒总成
5. service plug 维修插销

（2）系统主继电器　系统主继电器（System Main Relay, SMR）根据来自HV ECU的信号连接和断开高压电池和电源电缆。有3个SMR：SMRB、SMRG、SMRP。SMRB位于高压电池正极侧；SMRG位于高压电池负极侧；SMRP位于连接至预充电电阻器的蓄电池负极侧（图6-5-24）。

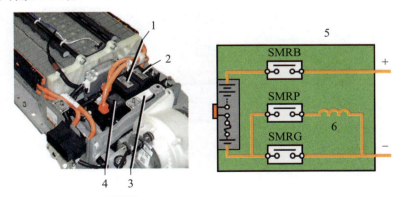

图6-5-24　System main relay 系统主继电器

1. SMRG 系统主继电器G
2. SMRB 系统主继电器B
3. precharge resistor 预充电电阻器
4. SMRP 系统主继电器P
5. HV battery 高压电池
6. precharge resistor 预充电电阻器

（3）电池冷却系统　重复充电/放电时，高压电池会产生热量，为确保其工作正常，车辆为高压电池配备了专用的冷却系统。行李厢右侧的冷却风扇可以通过后排座椅右侧的进气口吸出车内空气（图6-5-25）。此后，从电池顶部右侧进入的空气从上到下流经电池模块并将其加以冷却。然后，空气流经排气管和车内，最终排到车外。

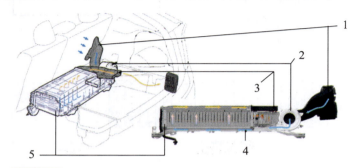

图6-5-25　High voltage battery cooling system 高压电池冷却系统

1. intake air duct 进气管
2. HV battery cooling fan 高压电池冷却风扇
3. exhaust vent duct 排风管
4. cooling air flow 冷却空气流
5. HV battery 高压电池

（4）荷电状态　SOC（State Of Charge）表示电池组剩余电量，为充电量与额定容量的百分比值。电池完全充电至其额定容量时，SOC为100%。电池电量完全耗尽时，SOC为0%。HV ECU根据接收的数据控制充电/放电，将SOC始终控制在稳定水平（图6-5-26）。

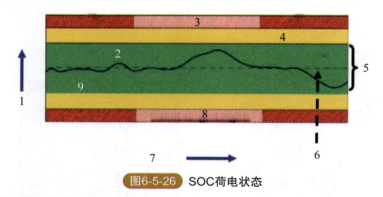

图6-5-26　SOC荷电状态

1. SOC 荷电状态
2. example of change in SOC　SOC变化实例
3. overcharged region 过充区
4. upper SOC control limit　SOC控制上限
5. control region 控制区
6. target SOC control 目标SOC控制
7. time 时间
8. undercharged region 过放区
9. lower SOC control limit　SOC控制下限

（5）电池ECU　电池ECU的功能主要有：估计充放电电流，向HV ECU发出充电和放电请求信息，以将SOC始终保持在中间水平；估计在充放电期间产生的热量，调整风扇，保持高压电池有适当的温度（图6-5-27）。

图6-5-27　Battery ECU 电池ECU

1. resistor 电阻
2. SMR2 系统主继电器2
3. SMR3 系统主继电器3
4. amperage sensor 电流传感器
5. modules 模块
6. battery ECU 电池ECU
7. SMR1 系统主继电器1
8. service plug connector 维修塞接头

Chapter 6

Fuel cell electric vehicle 燃料电池汽车

6.1 Overview 概述

　　燃料电池电动汽车（Fuel Cell Electric Vehicle, FCEV）是一种用车载燃料电池装置产生的电力作为动力的汽车。车载燃料电池装置所使用的燃料为高纯度氢气。奥迪h-tron quattro燃料电池汽车动力系统如图6-6-1所示，主要由燃料电池、电机、动力电池、功率电子装置等部件组成。

PART6 New energy vehicle
新能源汽车

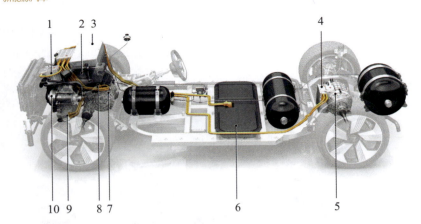

图6-6-1 Audi h-tron quattro drivetrain 奥迪h-tron quattro动力系统

1. hydrogen recirculation blower 氢循环鼓风机
2. fuel cell 燃料电池
3. DC/DC converter DC/DC 转换器
4. power electronics for rear motor 后电机功率电子装置
5. electric motor for rear axle 后桥电机
6. traction battery 动力电池
7. electric motor for front axle 前桥电机
8. power electronics for front electric motor 前电机功率电子装置
9. power electronics for air compressor 空气压缩机功率电子装置
10. air compressor 空气压缩机

6.2 Toyota Mirai fuel cell vehicle 丰田 Mirai 燃料电池汽车

丰田Mirai（未来）氢燃料汽车主要由燃料电池堆、氢气瓶、电池、升压器、电机等组成（图6-6-2）。

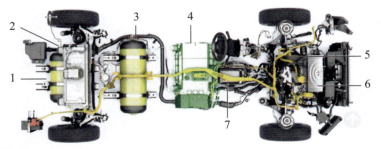

图6-6-2 The main components of Mirai fuel cell vehicle Mirai燃料电池汽车主要部件

1. hydrogen tank 氢气瓶
2. battery 电池
3. hydrogen tank 氢气瓶
4. fuel cell stack 燃料电池堆
5. electric motor and transaxle 电机和传动桥
6. power control unit 功率控制单元
7. fuel cell boost converter 燃料电池升压器

Mirai的动力电源包括燃料电池和高压电池（图6-6-3）。功率控制单元根据汽车的工作状态，精确地控制燃料电池输出功率和高压电池的充放电。燃料电池与功率控制单元、电机的连接方式为串联，以便在汽车运行的大部分时间具有较高效率。高压电池与燃料电池串联，用作燃料电池响应迟缓或汽车满负荷时提供辅助动力。

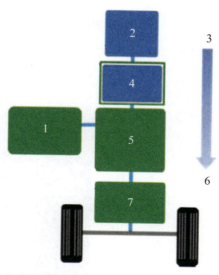

图6-6-3 Mirai principle Mirai工作原理

1. battery 电池
2. FC(Fuel Cell) stack 燃料电池堆
3. fuel cell 燃料电池
4. FC boost converter 燃料电池增压转换器
5. power control unit 功率控制单元
6. motor 650V 电机650V
7. motor 电机

6.2.1　Mirai fuel cell Mirai燃料电池

Mirai燃料电池是由370个电芯叠加组成，每个电芯发电的电压范围为0.6～0.8 V。Mirai燃料电池由燃料电池堆和燃料电池辅助系统组成（图6-6-4）。

图6-6-4 Mirai fuel cell Mirai燃料电池

1. FC stack 燃料电池堆
2. fuel cell boost converter 燃料电池升压器
3. auxiliary components 附属部件

6.2.2 fuel cell stack 燃料电池堆

燃料电池堆包括质子交换膜、催化剂层、气体扩散层等（图6-6-5）。燃料电池是利用氢气跟氧气化学反应过程中的电荷转移来形成电流，这一过程最关键的技术就是利用质子交换膜将氢气拆分。因为氢分子体积小，可以透过薄膜的微小孔洞游离到对面去，但是在穿越孔洞的过程中，电子被从分子上剥离，只留下带正电的氢质子通过。

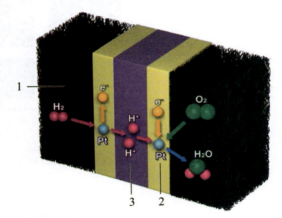

图6-6-5　Principle of fuel cell stack 燃料电池堆原理

1. gas diffusion layer 气体扩散层
2. catalyst layer 催化剂层
3. electrolyte membrane 电解质薄膜

6.2.3　Fuel cell auxiliary system 燃料电池辅助系统

燃料电池辅助系统包括氢气泵、空气滤清器、空气压缩机、排水管等。

（1）氢气泵　氢气泵经常与燃料电池壳体集成在一起，用于向燃料电池供给充足的氢气，因为进气压力较低，大约为1bar（1bar=10^5Pa）（图6-6-6）。

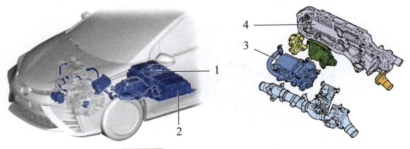

图6-6-6　Hydrogen pump 氢气泵

1,3. hydrogen pump 氢气泵
2. FC stack 燃料电池堆
4. stack manifold assembly 电池堆歧管总成

（2）空气滤清器　空气滤清器用于过滤进入燃料电池的杂质，如图6-6-7所示。电池内的化学反应需要活性的表面，任何污染物都会降低燃料电池的效率。

图6-6-7　Air cleaner空气滤清器

（3）空气压缩机　空气压缩机用于确保电流所需的空气流量（图6-6-8）。所需的电流越大，送入燃料电池的空气和氢气越多。

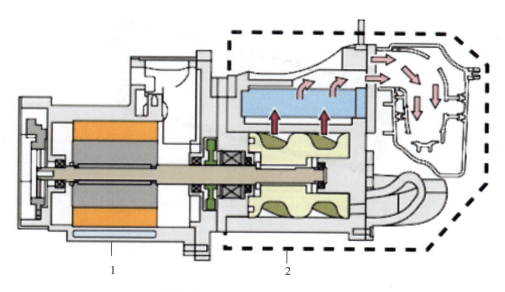

图6-6-8　Air compressor空气压缩机

1. motor 电机
2. impeller 泵轮

（4）排水管　燃料电池的排水管用于消除燃料电池产生的水（图6-6-9）。

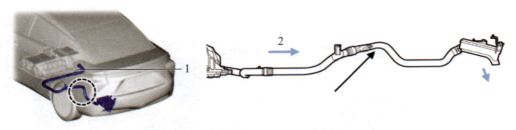

图6-6-9　Drainage pipe 排水管

1. drainage pipe 排水管
2. flow of air and water 空气和水流

6.2.4　High pressure hydrogen tank 高压储氢罐

储氢罐是气态氢的储存装置，用于给燃料电池提供氢气。图6-6-10为丰田Mirai氢燃料电动汽车的储气瓶结构，罐体采用碳纤维加凯夫拉复合材质，其强度可以抵挡轻型枪械的攻击。

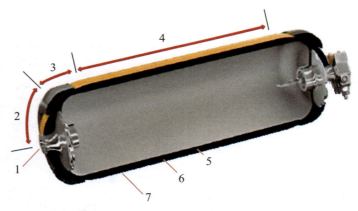

图6-6-10　High pressure hydrogen tank 高压储氢罐

1. boss 加注口
2. dome section 弧顶部分
3. boundary section 过渡部分
4. cylindrical section 直桶部分
5. plastic liner(seals in hydrogen) 塑料内衬（密封氢气）
6. carbon fiber reinforced plastic layer(ensures pressure resistance) 碳纤维强化塑料（增强抗压能力）
7. glass fiber reinforced plastic layer(protects surface) 玻璃纤维强化塑料（保护表面）

6.2.5 High voltage battery 高压电池

丰田 Mirai 采用镍氢电池作为辅助动力源，与丰田混合动力汽车所用的高压电池结构相同（图6-6-11）。

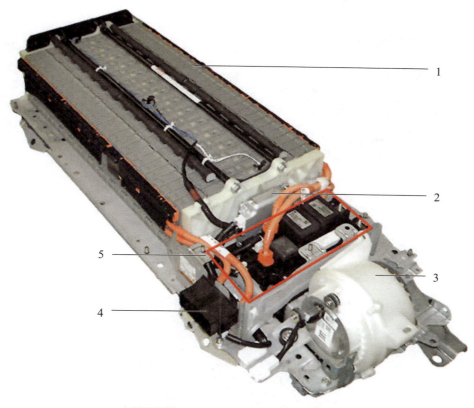

图6-6-11　High voltage battery 高压电池

1. battery module 电池模块
2. battery intelligent unit 电池智能单元
3. battery cooling fan 电池冷却风扇
4. service plug connector 维修插销连接器
5. junction box assembly 接线盒总成

6.2.6　Boost converter 升压器

升压器，也称燃料电池DC/DC转换器（FC DC-DC Converter, FDC），将燃料电池产生的222～296V之间的电压升压到650V，以便更好地驱动电机（图6-6-12）。

PART 6 New energy vehicle 新能源汽车

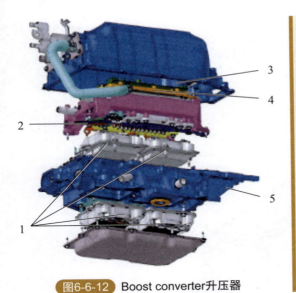

1. reactors 电抗器
2. capacitor 电容器
3. ECU(Electronic Control Unit) 电控单元
4. IPM(Intelligent Power Module) drive board 智能功率模块驱动板
5. cooling plate 冷却板

图6-6-12 Boost converter 升压器

6.2.7 Drive motor 驱动电机

丰田Mirai采用交流永磁同步驱动电机，如图6-6-13所示。

图6-6-13 Drive motor 驱动电机

1. stator 定子

2. rotor 转子

6.2.8　Mirai operation Mirai工作原理

空气（氧气）通过车辆前方的空气压缩机压入燃料电池堆中。在高压氢气瓶中储存的氢气也同时输送到燃料电池中。氢气和空气中的氧气在燃料电池堆中进行反应，产生电能和水。产生的电通过升压转换器后，提供给电机，驱动车辆行驶。唯一的产物——水，将通过水管排除车外（图6-6-14）。

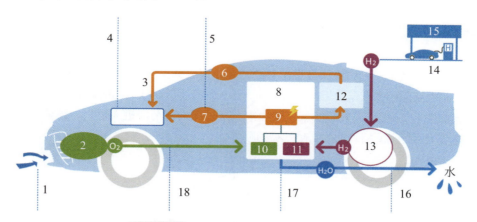

图6-6-14　Mirai operation Mirai工作原理

1. step 1　air(oxygen) taken in 第1步 吸入空气（氧气）
2. air(oxygen)　空气（氧气）
3. motor 电机
4. step 5　motor is activated and vehicle moves 第5步 驱动电机和发动车辆
5. step 4　electricity supplied to motor 第4步 将电能传输至电机
6,7. electricity 电能
8. fuel call stack 燃料电池堆
9. power generation 发电
10. oxygen 氧气
11. hydrogen 氢气
12. battery 电池
13. high pressure hydrogen tank 高压储氢罐
14. hydrogen refueling 补充氢气
15. hydrogen station 加氢站
16. step 6　water emitted outside vehicle 第6步 将水排出车外
17. step 3　electricity and water generated through chemical reaction 第3步 通过化学反应产生电能和水
18. step 2　oxygen and hydrogen supplied to fuel cell 第2步 将氧气和氢气传输至燃料电池

PART 6　New energy vehicle 新能源汽车

Chapter 7

Natural gas vehicle 天然气汽车

7.1 Overview 概述

　　天然气是从天然气田直接开采出来的，其主要成分是甲烷。目前大都将其压缩充入车用气瓶中储存和供汽车使用，即所谓的压缩天然气（CNG）。沃尔沃汽车压缩天然气供给系统如图6-7-1所示，天然气从气瓶出来，经过压力调节器进入燃气分配器，由ECM根据发动机运行工况精确地控制喷气嘴的喷气量。

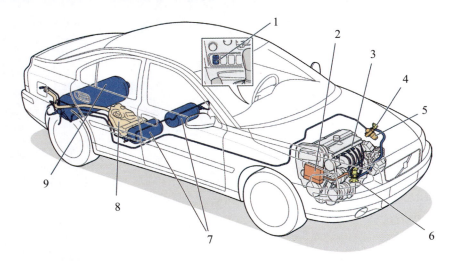

图6-7-1　Volvo CNG supply system 沃尔沃汽车压缩天然气供给系统

1. gas/petrol switch 燃气/汽油开关
2. ECM (Engine Control Module) 发动机控制模块
3. gas injectors 喷气嘴
4. pressure sensor 压力传感器
5. pressure regulator 压力调节器
6. gas distributor 燃气分配器
7. CNG tanks in steel 钢制CNG气瓶
8. petrol tank 汽油箱
9. CNG tank in carbon-lined aluminium 碳衬铝制CNG气瓶

7.2 Audi A4 Avant g-tron 奥迪 A4 Avant g-tron 天然气汽车

奥迪 A4 Avant g-tron 为天然气两用燃料汽车，搭载2.0 TFSI 发动机，具有较高燃烧效率（图6-7-2）。A4 Avant g-tron 每百公里仅消耗4kg 的天然气。当天然气气瓶压力下降到10bar时，发动机会无缝切换到汽油燃烧模式。

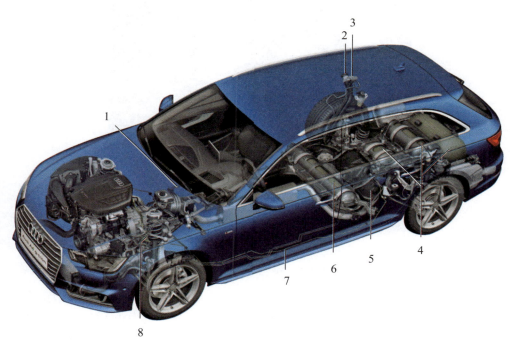

图6-7-2 Audi A4 Avant g-tron 奥迪 A4 Avant g-tron 天然气汽车

1. plastic lines(petrol) 塑料管路（汽油）
2. petrol filler neck 汽油加注管口
3. CNG filler neck CNG 加注管口
4,6. CNG tank CNG 气瓶
5. fuel tank (petrol) 燃油箱（汽油）
7. high pressure CNG line 高压CNG 管路
8. gas pressure regulator with sensor module and high pressure valve for gas operation 气体压力调节器、传感器模块和气体模式高压阀

7.2.1 CNG filler neck CNG加注管口

在车右侧的油箱盖下面，有CNG加注管口和汽油加注管口（图6-7-3）。

图6-7-3　CNG filler neck CNG加注管口

1. CNG filler neck CNG 加注管口
2. petrol filler neck 汽油加注管口

7.2.2　Non-return valve with filter 带有滤清器的止回阀

在CNG加注管口加入一个带滤清器的止回阀。加注的天然气会打开这个止回阀，天然气以最大260bar的压力进入CNG气瓶（图6-7-4）。天然气中较粗的杂质会被滤清器滤掉。

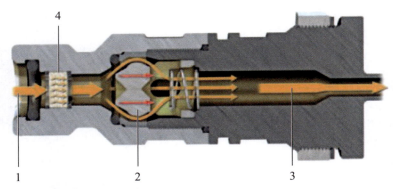

图6-7-4　Non-return valve with filter带有滤清器的止回阀

1. inflowing CNG 流入的CNG
2. non-return valve open 止回阀打开
3. to distributor 去往分配器
4. filter 滤清器

7.2.3　CNG tank and petrol tank CNG气瓶和汽油箱

4个圆筒形CNG气瓶布置在车辆的后部（图6-7-5）。每个气瓶的尺寸各不相同，这是为了适应其所处的空间位置要求。所有CNG气瓶（其中还包含一个25L的汽油燃油箱）都直接固定到车身上。

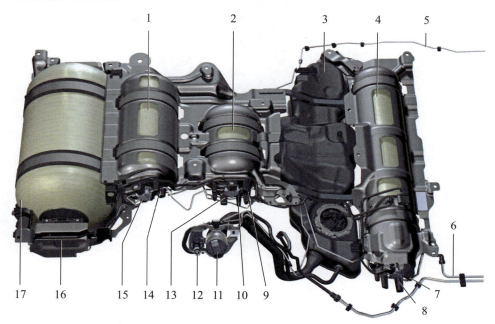

图6-7-5　CNG tank and petrol tank天然气气瓶和汽油箱

1. CNG tank 2 CNG 气瓶 2
2. CNG tank 3 CNG 气瓶 3
3. fuel tank (petrol) 燃油箱（汽油箱）
4. CNG tank 4 CNG 气瓶 4
5. high pressure CNG line 高压CNG 管路
6. plastic lines (petrol) 塑料管路（汽油）
7,10,14. protective cover for fuel tank valves 气瓶阀保护盖
8. tank shut-off valve 4 气瓶截止阀 4
9. distributor with non-return valve 带有止回阀的分配器
11. petrol filler neck 汽油加注管口
12. CNG filler neck 天然气加注管口
13. tank shut-off valve 3 气瓶截止阀 3
15. tank shut-off valve 2 气瓶截止阀 2
16. tank shut-off valve 1 气瓶截止阀 1
17. CNG tank 1 压缩天然气气瓶 1

7.2.4　CNG tank 压缩天然气气瓶

CNG气瓶采用复合材质制成（图6-7-6）。

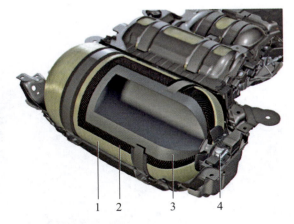

图6-7-6　CNG tank CNG气瓶

1. outer layer: glass fiber-reinforced polymer (GFRP) 外层：玻璃纤维增强塑料
2. middle layer: carbon fiber-reinforced polymer (CFRP) 中层：碳纤维增强塑料
3. inner layer: impermeable polyamid 内层：气密性聚酰胺
4. tank shut-off valve 气瓶截止阀

7.2.5　Tank shut-off valve assembly 气瓶截止阀总成

气瓶截止阀总成包括电动气瓶截止阀、手动气瓶截止装置、热熔保险装置、流量限制阀、天然气管接口等。截止阀总成被安装到气瓶上（图6-7-7）。

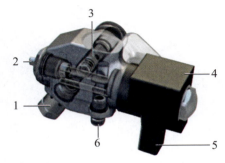

图6-7-7　Tank shut-off valve assembly 气瓶截止阀总成

1. thermal cut-out 热熔保险装置
2. manual tank shut-off device 手动气瓶截止装置
3. connection for CNG tank with flow limiter CNG 气瓶接口，带有流量限制阀
4. electrical tank shut-off valve 电动气瓶截止阀
5. electric connection 供电接头
6. connection for CNG line CNG 管接口

（1）电动气瓶截止阀 在未通电时，阀弹簧将阀压靠在阀座上，阀关闭。此时气瓶内向外流的天然气被切断（图6-7-8）。如果电磁线圈通电，阀将克服弹簧的压力开启，天然气又可以流出。电动气瓶截止阀由发动机ECU来控制。

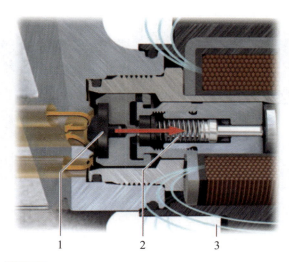

图6-7-8　Electrical tank shut-off valve电动气瓶截止阀

1. valve 阀
2. valve spring 阀弹簧
3. magnetic field 磁场

（2）手动气瓶截止装置 通过手动气瓶截止装置可以关闭气瓶截止阀（图6-7-9）。气瓶截止阀关闭时，天然气不能驱动汽车行驶。

图6-7-9　Manual tank shut-off device手动气瓶截止装置

1. manual tank shut-off device 手动气瓶截止装置
2. manual tank shut-off valve closed 手动气瓶截止阀已关闭
3. channel to electrical tank shut-off valve closed 通向电动气瓶截止阀的通道已关闭
4. channel to thermal cut-out 通向热熔保险装置的通道
5. thermal cut-out 热熔保险装置

（3）热熔保险装置 气瓶截止阀总成中有热熔保险装置（Thermal cut-out）。熔化材料封住通向大气的通道［图6-7-10（a）］。如果热熔保险装置在一定时间内持续受到高于110℃的加热，熔化材料就熔化，通道被打开，天然气将溢出气瓶而进入大气［图6-7-10（b）］。热熔保险装置可防止气瓶在受热温度过高时破裂。

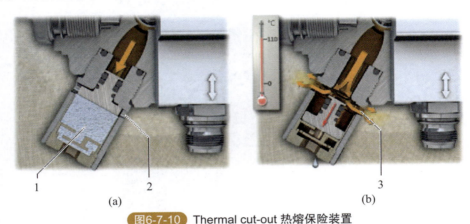

图6-7-10 Thermal cut-out 热熔保险装置

1. fusible link 熔化材料
2. channel leading to atmosphere closed 通向大气的通道被封闭
3. channel leading to atmosphere opened 通向大气的通道被打开

（4）流量限制阀 流量限制是气瓶截止阀的机械式安全功能。当高压一侧的压力突然降低时，流量限制功能可以防止天然气从气瓶不受控地流出（图6-7-11）。如果高压一侧的压力突然降低，比如在天然气管断裂时，压力差就会让阀关闭。

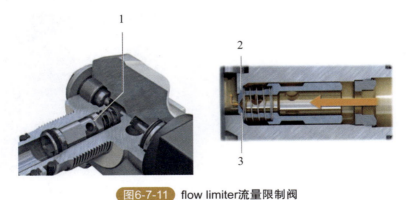

图6-7-11 flow limiter 流量限制阀

1. flow limiter 流量限制阀
2. sealing face 密封面
3. sealing cone with leakage port 密封锥，带有泄漏开口

7.2.6 Gas pressure regulator 气体压力调节器

气体压力调节器是二级式的，将天然气压力从约200bar减至5～10bar。气体压力调节器接口与剖面如图6-7-12、图6-7-13所示。传感器安装在气体压力调节器上，其功能是获取高压侧天然气压力值。高压天然气在减压过程中需要吸收大量的热量，为防止减压器结冰，将发动机冷却液引出到调节器对燃气进行加热。

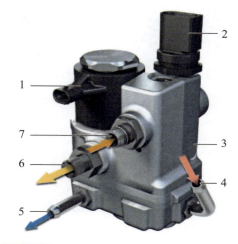

1. high pressure valve for gas operation 气体工作高压阀
2. sensor module 传感器模块
3. mechanical pressure relief valve 机械式卸压阀
4,5. coolant connection 冷却液接口
6. low pressure CNG connection 低压CNG接口
7. high pressure CNG connection 高压CNG接口

图6-7-12 Gas pressure regulator connection 气体压力调节器接口

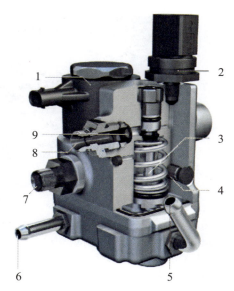

1. high pressure valve for gas operation 气体工作高压阀
2. sensor module 传感器模块
3. piston and spring 活塞和弹簧
4. mechanical pressure relief valve 机械式卸压阀
5,6. coolant connection 冷却液接口
7. low pressure CNG connection 低压CNG接口
8. high pressure CNG connection 高压CNG接口
9. filter 滤清器

图6-7-13 Gas pressure regulator sectional view 气体压力调节器剖面图

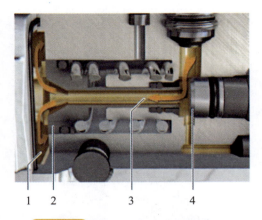

图6-7-14 Regulating piston 调节活塞

（1）第一级压力调节　第一级压力调节为机械式压力调节。调节活塞将天然气压力调节至约20bar。天然气从气瓶经过高压接口进入调压通道，发动机不工作时，弹簧将中间空心的活塞推离密封座，然后天然气从活塞空腔流到中间腔。发动机工作时，作用在活塞头部的压力若超过20bar，天然气的压力会克服弹簧力产生位移，直到活塞顶到密封座，将气道关闭，天然气不再流到中间腔（图6-7-14）。

1. central chamber 中间腔
2. regulating piston 调节活塞
3. inflowing CNG 流入的CNG
4. sealing seat 密封座

（2）第二级压力调节　在第二级压力调节中，气体工作高压阀以电子调节方式将天然气压力调节至5～10bar。已在第一级调节至约20bar的天然气压力作用到气体工作高压阀的针阀上。如果发动机ECU关闭气体工作高压阀，针阀关闭，通向低压接口的通道封闭［图6-7-15（a）］。若发动机ECU开启气体工作高压阀，衔铁连同阀针就被拉入电磁线圈内，针阀打开一条缝。天然气就以5～10bar的压力进入到低压区［图6-7-15（b）］。

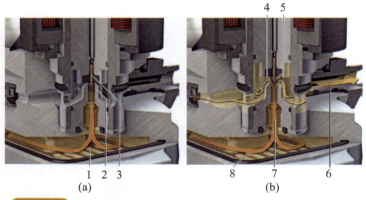

图6-7-15 High pressure valve for gas operation 气体工作高压阀

1. central chamber, approx.20bar 中间腔，（压力）约20bar
2. valve pintle seat 阀针座
3,5. valve pintle 阀针
4. low pressure zone 低压区
6. low pressure CNG connection 低压CNG接口
7. inflowing CNG 流入的CNG
8. central chamber 中间腔

7.2.7　Mechanical pressure relief valve 机械式卸压阀

天然气供给系统中，在低压侧的气体压力调节器内，还另有一个安全部件，就是这个机械式卸压阀。在出现故障时，如果低压侧的天然气压力超过了约14bar，卸压阀就会打开。这样就可防止天然气以很高的压力流入低压区（那可能会造成损坏的）（图6-7-16）。

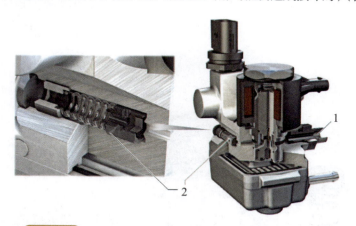

图6-7-16　Mechanical pressure relief valve 机械式卸压阀

1. low pressure CNG connection 低压CNG 接口
2. mechanical pressure relief valve 机械式卸压阀

7.2.8　Gas injection valve 喷气嘴

四个喷气嘴插在进气歧管上，将天然气喷入进气歧管内的进气门前端（图6-7-17）。

图6-7-17　Gas injection valve 喷气嘴

1. gas pressure regulator 气体压力调节器
2. gas injection 喷射气体
3. petrol injection 喷射汽油

PART 6　New energy vehicle 新能源汽车

喷气嘴在气体分配轨上的安装位置如图6-7-18所示。

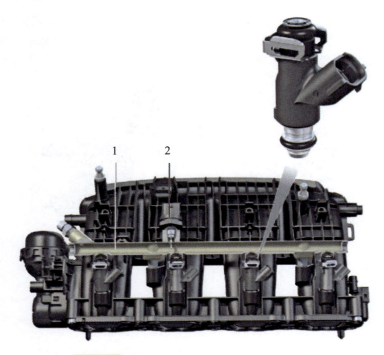

图6-7-18　Gas injection valve 喷气嘴安装位置

1. gas distributor rail 气体分配轨
2. gas distributor rail temperature and pressure sensor 气体分配轨温度和压力传感器

Chapter 8
LPG vehicle 液化石油气汽车

8.1　Overview 概述

液化石油气（Liquefied Petroleum Gas, LPG）是一种在常温常压下为气态的烃类混合物。液化石油气汽车具有两套燃料供应系统：一套供给液化石油气；另一套供给汽油或柴油。LPG供给系统主要部件如图6-8-1所示。

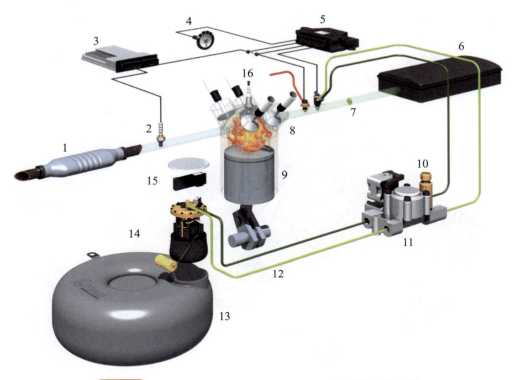

图6-8-1 LPG supply system components LPG供给系统部件

1. catalytic converter 催化转换器
2. oxygen sensor 氧传感器
3. petrol system ECU 汽油系统ECU
4. fuel switch 燃料开关
5. LPG system ECU LPG 系统ECU
6. air cleaner 空气滤清器
7. LPG injector LPG 喷嘴
8. petrol injector 汽油喷嘴
9. cylinder 气缸
10. LPG feed line LPG 供油管路
11. pressure regulator and sensor 压力调节器和传感器
12. LPG return line LPG 回油管路
13. LPG tank LPG 瓶
14. internal pump and valving 内泵和阀
15. pump control unit 泵控制单元
16. spark plug 火花塞

PART 6 New energy vehicle 新能源汽车

8.2 Volkswagen GOLF LPG vehicle 大众高尔夫液化石油气汽车

大众高尔夫液化石油气汽车有两套燃料供给系统，由储气瓶、加气管、燃料转换开关、蒸发器、滤清器、燃气轨和喷嘴等组成（图6-8-2）。

图6-8-2 The main components of Volkswagen GOLF LPG vehicle
大众高尔夫液化石油气汽车主要部件

1. gas filler neck 加气管口
2. gas mode control unit 气体模式控制单元
3. vaporiser with high pressure valve for gas mode 蒸发器及气体模式高压阀
4. gas filter 气体滤清器
5. gas fuel rail with gas injection valves and gas rail sensor 燃气轨、喷气嘴和燃气轨传感器
6. selection button with gas gauge and petrol or gas fuel selection switch 选择按钮、气量表、汽油或燃气选择开关
7. LPG tank with gas gauge sender, pressure relief valve, gas tank valve and automatic fill limiter LPG 气瓶、气量表、卸压阀、气瓶阀和自动限充阀

8.2.1 GOLF LPG supply system 高尔夫LPG供给系统

当燃料转换开关拨到LPG位置时，气瓶电磁阀通电。LPG液体从储气瓶出来，经过气瓶电磁阀到达蒸发器，经过降压、汽化变为接近大气压的气体。LPG气体流经滤清器到达燃气轨，燃气轨上的喷气嘴将适量的燃气喷入进气歧管（图6-8-3）。

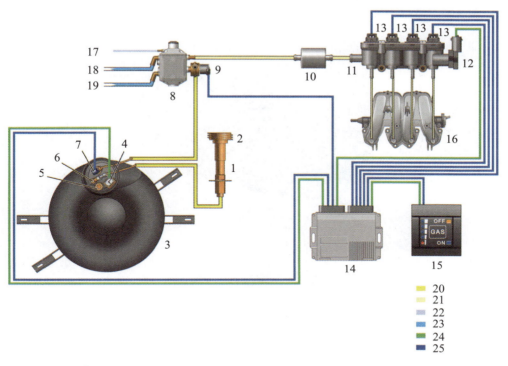

图6-8-3 GOLF LPG supply system schematics 高尔夫LPG供给系统示意图

1. gas filler neck 充气管口
2. adapter 适配器
3. tank 气瓶
4. gas gauge sender 气量表传感器
5. pressure relief valve 卸压阀
6. automatic fill limiter 自动限充阀
7. gas tank valve 气瓶阀
8. vaporiser 蒸发器
9. high pressure valve for gas mode 气体模式高压阀
10. gas filter 气体滤清器
11. gas fuel rail 燃气轨
12. gas rail sensor 燃气轨传感器
13. gas injection valves 喷气嘴
14. gas mode control unit 气体模式控制单元
15. selection button with gas gauge and petrol or gas fuel selection switch 气量表选择钮、汽油或燃气选择开关
16. intake manifold 进气歧管
17. vacuum hose to intake manifold 连到进气歧管的真空软管
18. coolant outlet 冷却液出口
19. coolant inlet 冷却液入口
20. LPG pipe approx.10bar LPG 管路（压力）约10bar
21. LPG pipe approx.1bar above intake manifold pressure LPG 管路（压力）大约1bar，高于进气歧管压力
22. vacuum hose 真空软管
23. coolant hose 冷却液软管
24. sensor signal cable 传感器信号缆线
25. actuator signal cable 执行器信号缆线

8.2.2 LPG tank 储气瓶

储气瓶安装在车尾部的行李厢内，其作用是储存LPG（图6-8-4）。

图6-8-4 LPG tank LPG储气瓶

8.2.3 LPG tank multivalve LPG气瓶集成阀

储气瓶上面安装了多个阀，用于保证储气瓶和燃料供给系统的安全使用，如图6-8-5所示。

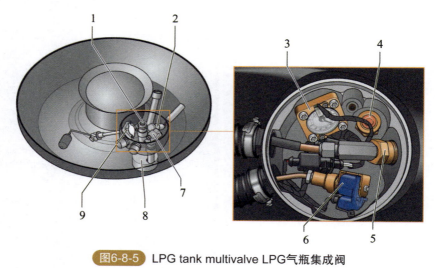

图6-8-5 LPG tank multivalve LPG气瓶集成阀

1. pressure relief valve 卸压阀
2. automatic fill limiter 自动限充阀
3,9. gas gauge sender 气体指示表传感器

4. pressure relief valve 卸压阀
5. automatic fill limiter 自动限充阀
6,7. gas tank valve 气瓶阀
8. swirl pot 旋流罐

（1）气瓶阀　气瓶阀（Gas tank valve）的作用是接通（或切断）气瓶到蒸发器的通道（图6-8-6）。

1. spring 弹簧
2. coil 线圈
3. plunger 柱塞
4. valve 阀
5. to vaporiser 连到蒸发器
6. from tank 来自气瓶

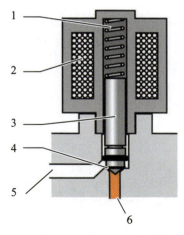

图6-8-6　Gas tank valve气瓶阀

（2）自动限充阀　充加LPG时，限充浮子随着LPG液面增加逐渐上浮［图6-8-7(a)］。当储气瓶内LPG达到设定的液面高度（75%～80%）时，自动限充阀（Automatic fill limiter）关闭，限制LPG继续充装，从而提供了由于温度升高所必需的LPG的膨胀空间［图6-8-7(b)］。

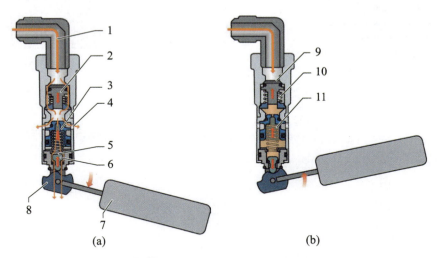

图6-8-7　Automatic fill limiter自动限充阀

1. filling pressure 充气压力
2. upper plunger 上柱塞
3. lower plunger 下柱塞
4. outlet openings 出口通道
5. lower valve chamber 下阀腔
6. shut-off valve 关闭阀
7. float 浮子
8. cam disk 凸轮圆盘
9. inlet channel 进气通道
10,11. spring 弹簧

（3）卸压阀　当储气瓶内压力低于设定的压力时，卸压阀（Pressure relief valve）保持关闭［图6-8-8（a）］；当压力超过设定的安全极限压力时，卸压阀自动打开释放LPG［图6-8-8（b）］，防止因压力过高而发生安全事故。

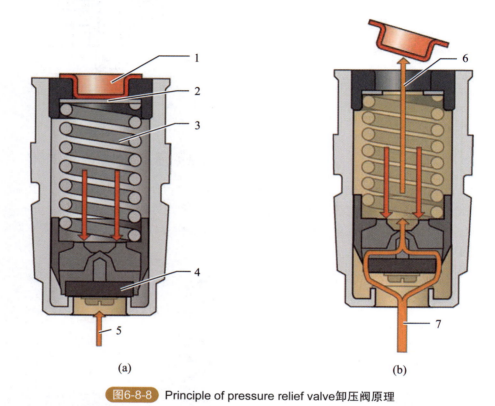

图6-8-8　Principle of pressure relief valve卸压阀原理

1. dust cap 防尘帽
2. outlet aperture 出气孔
3. valve spring 阀弹簧
4. valve disk 阀板
5. pressure in tank 气瓶压力
6. escaping LPG 泄出LPG
7. pressure in tank greater than 27.5bar 气瓶压力大于27.5bar

（4）气量表传感器　气量表传感器（Gas gauge sender）用于传感储气瓶内的液面高度，并将液面信号传到驾驶室内的气量表（图6-8-9）。

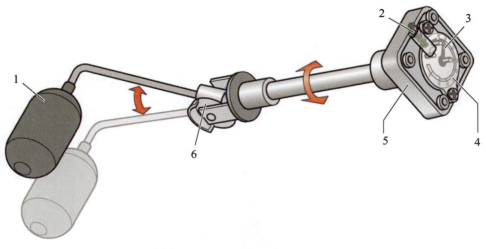

图6-8-9 Gas gauge sender气量表传感器

1. float 浮子
2. electrical connection to gas mode control unit 连到气体模式控制单元的电接头
3. needle 指针
4. gauge 指示表
5. top of housing 壳体顶部
6. gear mechanism 齿轮机构

气量表指示系统包括气量表、传感器和气体模式控制单元，如图6-8-10所示。

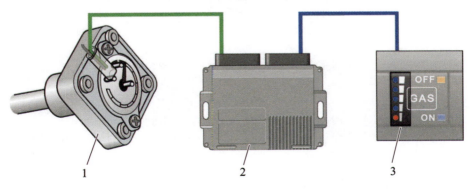

图6-8-10 Gas gauge components气量表部件

1. gas gauge sender 气量表传感器
2. gas mode control unit 气体模式控制单元
3. gas gauge 气量表

· 287 ·

8.2.4 Vaporiser 蒸发器

（1）蒸发器的接口　蒸发器（Vaporiser，又称调压器、汽化器）通过进气歧管真空接口与进气管连接，目的是根据工况控制调压器出口压力（图6-8-11）。通过两根水管与发动机的冷却水循环水管路连通。利用发动机循环热水，提供液态燃气进行气化所需的气化热。

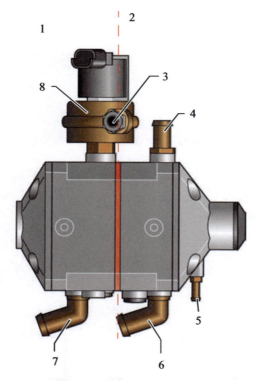

图6-8-11　Vaporiser connector 蒸发器接口

1. 1st stage, from 3 ~ 10bar to 1.6bar 第1级，从3 ~ 10bar 到1.6bar
2. 2nd stage, from 1.6bar to 1.0bar above intake manifold pressure 第2级，从1.6bar 到1.0bar，高于进气歧管压力
3. inlet from tank 来自气瓶的入口
4. outlet to gas filter 连到气体滤清器的出口
5. intake manifold vacuum connection 进气歧管真空接口
6. coolant outlet 冷却液出口
7. coolant inlet 冷却液入口
8. high-pressure valve for gas mode 气体模式高压阀

（2）蒸发器结构　蒸发器为两级减压器，主气路经过两级减压后出气。蒸发器的每级均由一个内腔，一个外腔和一个控制腔组成（图6-8-12）。LPG通过溢流通道从第一级流到第二级。每级都有一个阀门和柱塞。柱塞由螺栓固定到膜片上。每个弹簧腔中都有一个弹簧。第一级弹簧腔压力为大气压。第二级的弹簧腔压力为进气歧管压力。在第一级和第二级之间有一个橡胶密封垫，将LPG冷却管路隔开。

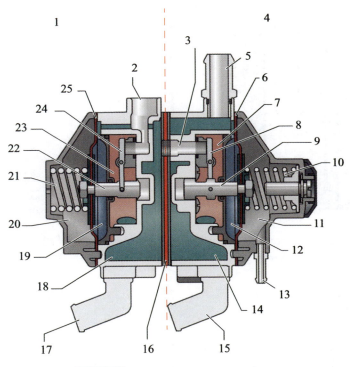

图6-8-12　Vaporiser section 蒸发器剖面

1. 1st stage 第1级
2. supply line from high pressure valve for gas mode 来自气体模式高压阀的供气管
3. overflow channel 溢流通道
4. 2nd stage 第2级
5. outlet to gas filter 气体滤清器出口
6,25. diaphragm 膜片
7,23. inner chamber 内腔
8,24. flap 阀瓣
9,22. plunger 柱塞
10,21. spring 弹簧
11,20. spring chamber 弹簧腔
12,19. control chamber 控制腔
13. intake manifold vacuum connection 进气歧管真空接口
14,18. outer chamber 外腔
15. coolant outlet 冷却液出口
16. rubber seal 橡胶密封
17. coolant inlet 冷却液入口

（3）蒸发器工作原理　蒸发器通过启闭阀门的节流，将进口压力减至某一需要的出口压力，并使出口压力保持稳定。天然气通过高压阀进入一级减压腔使一级膜片逐步左移，当一级减压腔气压达到一定值，膜片的推力完全克服一级弹簧的预紧力时，作用于杠杆的合力矩关闭阀瓣（图6-8-13）。燃气流量随发动机负荷变化而变化，在弹簧与膜片相互作用下，阀瓣随时调整开度，保证输出压力稳定，完成一级减压。

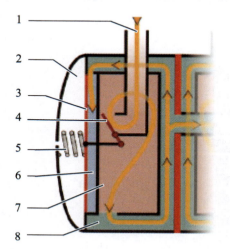

1. supply line from high pressure valve for gas mode 来自气体模式高压阀的供气管
2. spring chamber 弹簧腔
3. diaphragm 膜片
4. flap 阀瓣
5. spring 弹簧
6. control chamber 控制腔
7. inner chamber 内腔
8. outer chamber 外腔

图6-8-13　The 1st stage pressure reduction chamber一级减压腔

经过一级减压的气体进入二级减压腔，随发动机负荷的变化，膜片带动杠杆移动，调节阀瓣的开度（图6-8-14）。

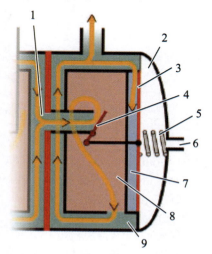

1. overflow channel 溢流通道
2. spring chamber 弹簧腔
3. diaphragm 膜片
4. flap 阀瓣
5. spring 弹簧
6. intake manifold vacuum connection 进气歧管真空接口
7. control chamber 控制腔
8. inner chamber 内腔
9. outer chamber 外腔

图6-8-14　The 2nd stage pressure reduction chamber二级减压腔

（4）蒸发器冷却管路　蒸发器冷却管路通过接头与发动机冷却系统连接（图6-8-15）。在蒸发器内部，橡胶密封将冷却管路分成一级和二级管路。通过两个溢流通道，LPG从一级管路流到二级管路。

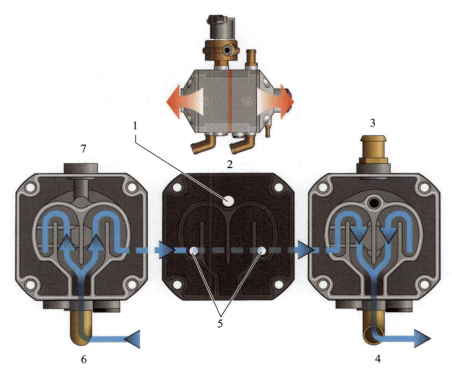

图6-8-15　Vaporiser coolant circuit蒸发器冷却管路

1. overflow channel LPG from the 1st to 2nd stage 从第1级到第2级的溢流通道
2. rubber seal 橡胶密封
3. 2nd stage 第2级
4. coolant, outlet 冷却液出口
5. coolant overflow channels 冷却液溢流通道
6. coolant, inlet 冷却液入口
7. 1st stage 第1级

8.2.5　High pressure valve for gas mode 气体模式高压阀

气体模式高压阀安装在蒸发器上，用于切断到蒸发器的供气，开闭由发动机ECU控制。当转换到汽油工作模式，关闭发动机，发生事故没有电时，高压阀自动关闭，不再向蒸发器供给LPG（图6-8-16）。

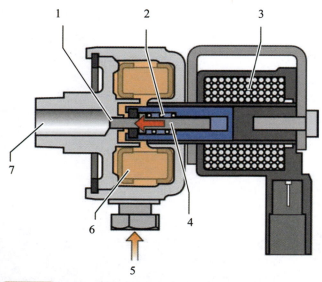

图6-8-16 High pressure valve for gas mode 气体模式高压阀

1. valve seat 阀座
2. spring 弹簧
3. coil 线圈
4. plunger 柱塞
5. from tank 来自气瓶
6. filter 滤清器
7. to vaporiser 连到蒸发器

8.2.6 Gas filter 燃气过滤器

安装在蒸发器和燃气轨之间，过滤掉杂质，保护喷气嘴（图6-8-17）。

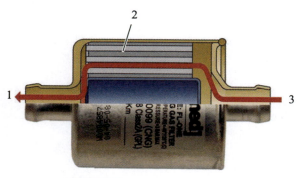

图6-8-17 gas filter 燃气过滤器

1. gas outlet, to gas fuel rail 气体出口，连到燃气轨
2. filter element 滤芯
3. gas inlet, from vaporiser 气体入口，来自蒸发器

8.2.7　Gas fuel rail 燃气轨

燃气轨安装在发动机进气歧管上，四个电控喷气嘴和燃气轨传感器集成在燃气轨上，传感器用于测量LPG的压力和温度（图6-8-18）。

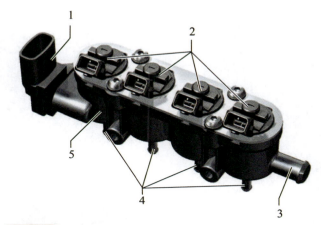

图6-8-18　Major components of gas fuel rail 燃气轨主要部件

1. gas rail sensor 燃气轨传感器
2. gas injection valves 喷气嘴
3. gas inlet 气体入口
4. gas outlet, hoses to intake manifold 气体出口，连到进气歧管的软管
5. gas fuel rail 燃气轨

来自滤清器的LPG流进燃气轨，喷气嘴将LPG喷入进气歧管（图6-8-19）。

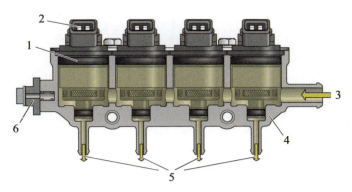

图6-8-19　Principle of gas fuel rail 燃气轨工作原理

1. gas injection valve 喷气嘴
2. electrical connection 电接头
3. gas inlet 气体入口
4. gas fuel rail 燃气轨
5. gas outlet, hoses to intake manifold 气体出口，连到进气歧管的软管
6. connection for pressure and temperature sensor 压力和温度传感器接口

8.2.8 Gas injection valve 喷气嘴

喷气嘴安装在燃气轨上,由发动机ECU控制喷气量(图6-8-20)。

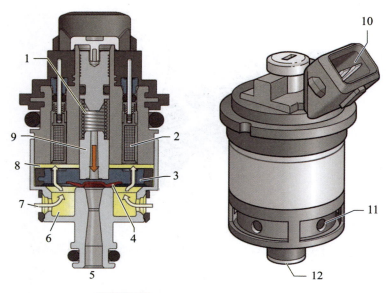

图6-8-20　Gas injection valve 喷气嘴

1. pressure spring 压力弹簧
2. solenoid 电磁线圈
3. armature 电枢
4. sealing lip 密封唇
5,12. gas outlet 气体出口
6. lower chamber 下腔
7,11. gas inlet 气体入口
8. upper chamber 上腔
9. plunger 柱塞
10. electrical connection 电接头

Reference 参考文献

[1] Denton T. Automobile Mechanical and Electrical Systems. Oxford: Butterworth Heinemann, 2018.

[2] Mehrdad Ehsani. Modern Electric, Hybrid Electric, and Fuel Cell Vehicles. 3rd ed. Boca Raton: CRC Press, 2018.

[3] [英]朱利安·哈皮安·史密斯.现代汽车设计概论.张金柱译.北京：化学工业出版社，2007.